Arsacids, Romans, and Local Elites

Arsacids, Romans, and Local Elites

Cross-Cultural Interactions of the Parthian Empire

edited by

Jason M. Schlude

and

Benjamin B. Rubin

OXBOW | books
Oxford & Philadelphia

Published in the United Kingdom in 2017 by
OXBOW BOOKS
The Old Music Hall, 106–108 Cowley Road, Oxford OX4 1JE

and in the United States by
OXBOW BOOKS
1950 Lawrence Road, Havertown, PA 19083

© Oxbow Books and the individual contributors 2017

Paperback Edition: ISBN 978-1-78570-592-2
Digital Edition: ISBN 978-1-78570-593-9

A CIP record for this book is available from the British Library

Library of Congress Cataloging-in-Publication Data

Names: Schlude, Jason M., editor, author. | Rubin, Benjamin B., editor,
  author.
Title: Arsacids, Romans, and local elites : cross-cultural interactions of
  the Parthian Empire / edited by Dr. Jason M. Schlude, College of Saint
  Benedict and Saint John's University and Dr. Benjamin B. Rubin, Williams
  College.
Description: Oxford ; Havertown, PA : Oxbow Books, 2017. | Includes
  bibliographical references.
Identifiers: LCCN 2017002720 (print) | LCCN 2017007928 (ebook) | ISBN
  9781785705922 (pbk.) | ISBN 9781785705939 (epub) | ISBN 9781785705946
  (mobi) | ISBN 9781785705953 (pdf)
Subjects: LCSH: Arsacid dynasty, 247 B.C.-224 A.D. | Parthians--History. |
  Iran--Social life and customs. | Iran--History--To 640.
Classification: LCC DS285 .A77 2017 (print) | LCC DS285 (ebook) | DDC
  939/.6--dc23
LC record available at https://lccn.loc.gov/2017002720

Printed in the United Kingdom by Hobbs the Printers Ltd

For a complete list of Oxbow titles, please contact:

UNITED KINGDOM
Oxbow Books
Telephone (01865) 241249, Fax (01865) 794449
Email: oxbow@oxbowbooks.com
www.oxbowbooks.com

UNITED STATES OF AMERICA
Oxbow Books
Telephone (800) 791-9354, Fax (610) 853-9146
Email: queries@casemateacademic.com
www.casemateacademic.com/oxbow

Oxbow Books is part of the Casemate Group

Front cover: Arch of Severus Septimus, Rome. Jean-Christophe Benoist. AR drachma. Mithradates I. Hecatompylos. Sellwood 1980: type 7.1. Sunrise Collection (U. S. A).
Back cover: Statue of Augustus of Prima Porta. Sailko.

Contents

List of Contributors

Dr. Björn Anderson
Assistant Professor
School of Art and Art History
University of Iowa
210 Art Building West
Iowa City, IA 52242
U. S. A.

Dr. Peter Edwell
Senior Lecturer
Department of Ancient History
Macquarie University
Building W6A 516
NSW, 2109
Australia

Dr. Kenneth R. Jones
Associate Professor of History and Classics
Department of History
Baylor University
One Bear Place #97306
Waco, TX 76798-7306
U. S. A.

Dr. Jeffrey D. Lerner
Professor
Department of History
Wake Forest University
Tribble Hall B-101
1834 Wake Forest Road
Winston-Salem, NC 27106
U. S. A.

Dr. Jake Nabel
Graduate Student in Classics
Department of Classics
Cornell University
120 Goldwin Smith Hall
Ithaca, NY 14853-3201
U. S. A.

Dr. J. Andrew Overman
Harry M. Drake Distinguished Professor
in the Humanities and Fine Arts
Department of Classics
Macalester College
Old Main 313
1600 Grand Ave.
St. Paul, MN 55105
U. S. A.

Dr. Benjamin B. Rubin
Assistant Professor of Classics
Department of Classics
Williams College
85 Mission Park Dr.
Williamstown, MA 01267
U. S. A.

Dr. Jason M. Schlude
Assistant Professor of Classics
Department of Languages and Cultures
College of Saint Benedict and Saint John's
University
Quad 255A
Collegeville, MN 56321
U. S. A.

Acknowledgments

The process of showing gratitude is always a joyful enterprise. So it is with happy appreciation that on behalf of the contributors to this volume we wish to recognize those who have supported the various stages of research, presentation, writing, and publication that have led to its realization. Firstly, we wish to thank the programming committee of the American Schools of Oriental Research (ASOR). The members of that committee approved a three-year panel on the Parthian empire between 2012 and 2014 that provided us with an opportunity to pursue the subject and present our findings at the annual meeting of ASOR. We are entirely grateful to Dr. Julie Gardiner of Oxbow Books who expressed interest early on in the publication of this research and has been entirely patient and supportive as the project has come together. We wish to acknowledge the organizations and individuals who gave permission for our publication of photographs from their collections, including the American Numismatic Society, Classical Numismatic Group, Ars Numismatica Classica, Sunrise Collection, Mediterranean Coins, Dr. G. R. Assar, and Francesco Bini. Finally, we thank our readers – those who would invest their time in studying the fascinating history of the ancient Near East in the time of the Parthian empire, a worthy subject indeed.

J. M. S.
B. B. R.

Introduction

Jason M. Schlude

This volume is the product of several years of research, presentation, discussion, and writing by a group of scholars on the subject of the Arsacid dynasty of Parthia and its interactions with neighboring states, both small and large. Each of the following chapters was originally delivered as a part of a panel devoted to Parthia at the annual meeting of the American Schools of Oriental Research in 2012, 2013, and 2014. Let us say from the outset how much we appreciate that the authors in this volume (and other scholars beyond them) accepted the invitation to contribute to those discussions. It proved a good opportunity to advance each of our understandings of the Parthian empire, as well as to engage other interested parties in the subject. And it is our hope now that those who have subjected themselves to the added toil of revising and expanding their pieces, or even of writing an entirely new piece, as was sometimes the case, for this volume will further the study of Parthia in a more formal, substantial, and effective way.

Scholars have invested a great deal of energy in reconstructing the narrative of Parthian history, especially its relationship with the Roman empire. This effort is understandable and necessary. Our information on Parthia is scattered and uneven, and our narrative is primarily based on the Graeco-Roman source tradition.[1] These synthetic studies started with that of Rawlinson, though Debevoise produced the classic study.[2] Others like Shippmann and Bivar have provided slightly more recent surveys that have proven useful,[3] but Debevoise remains valuable.

Such scholars have laid a foundation that has permitted others to investigate particular aspects of Parthian history, including the potential of the evidence to speak to more focused, thematic problems. For example, scholars have explored what could be called "intercultural communication." They have pursued how Arsacid kings and their subjects interacted with other peoples outside the Parthian empire. In this way, many have addressed squarely the confrontation of Rome and Parthia, and they have done so from various angles. Particularly superb among this latter class is Ziegler, who considers Roman-Parthian relations, and the conflicts that were a part of them, in the context of international law.[4] Also impressive and with a broader interest in Roman foreign policy (including relations with Parthia) more generally are Sherwin-White and Linz.[5] Campbell also provides a useful survey of the issue that explores the significance of diplomacy.[6] Still other scholars have produced studies that appreciate the Parthian perspective and imperial motivations in more depth, often considering the Parthians' knowledge and appropriation of earlier Hellenistic and Achaemenid traditions. These individuals include Wolski and Shayegan, who concern themselves especially with whether and to what extent the Arsacid dynasty modeled itself after the previous Achaemenid dynasty (i.e. the problem of the so-called "Achaemenid program" of the Parthians) and what implications this may have had for Parthian imperialism and military activity.[7] Colledge is another example, having provided a classic discussion of Parthian art that considers its Greek and Iranian cultural origins and debts.[8]

We intend for the present volume, *Arsacids, Romans, and Local Elites: Cross-Cultural Interactions of the Parthian Empire*, to contribute to this discussion of Parthian intercultural communication. The following papers are interested in the interactions of the Arsacids with their neighbors, especially Rome, and wish to explore them with an intentionally broad and flexible definition of intercultural communication that includes treatment of several manners of exchange, such as war, diplomacy, and art, as well as how local elites played an active part in the negotiation of Parthian-Roman relations. As for chronological period, by design the articles cover a large sweep in order to underscore the complexity and variety of these processes over time.

As the reader will see, three specific lines of inquiry are of interest, each of which engages with and has important implications for current scholarship. Firstly, the volume considers the nature and extent of Arsacid appropriation of Achaemenid and Greek cultural forms, which will illustrate how the Arsacid kings had at their disposal diverse cultural resources originating from the Achaemenids and Hellenistic dynasts and opportunistically selected and used them to entrench their power. Secondly, it explores how Arsacid kings and Roman statesmen engaged in meaningful diplomacy, purposely restricting military engagements in key moments, in order to achieve peace. This observation tempers the common emphasis on ruthless and boundless conflict between Rome and Parthia from the first century BCE through the third century CE. Thirdly, the volume looks at how local dynasts in border-states like Judaea, Osrhoene, and Hatra interacted with the Parthian and Roman empires, showing how Parthia and Rome did not hold a total monopoly on political and cultural agency in the Near East. As for how these lines of inquiry map onto individual chapters, consider the following.

In chapter one, Jeffrey Lerner analyzes the significance of the Parthian archer on the reverse of Parthian coinage from the time of Arsakes I in the mid-third century BCE through the reign of Mithradates I (c. 171–138 BCE). As he explains, on the coinage of Arsakes I the archer sits atop a *diphros* with an outstretched arm holding a bow, bowstring facing away from the archer's body, while under Mithradates the *diphros* has been replaced by an *omphalos*. Most scholars have understood this imagery as being borrowed from certain Seleucid coin types, in which Apollo sits upon an *omphalos* and also holds a bow. Even if the Parthians borrowed some elements from the Greeks, such as the *diphros*, Lerner finds it more likely that the Parthians minted these coins mainly based on Iranian models. In particular, he argues that the archer is rather in the guise of Ārash, who who was identified with ꓱrəxša and Miθra, concluding then that the Parthians were actually working from Achaemenid coins, such as the staters of the satrap of Cilicia, Tarkamuwa/Datames (386–362 BCE). As for the change to the *omphalos* on the coins of Mithradates, Lerner contends that readings likely differed among different groups. While the Greeks would have seen an Orientalized Apollo, Iranians and Parthians would have seen the *omphalos* as a symbol for the Greek-Bactrian lands that Mithradates conquered sometime between 163 and 150 BCE. Lerner argues the latter was the Parthian intention. In other words, this was no attempt to win over Greek subjects, but an imperial statement of victory over the Greeks for his Parthian and Iranian subjects. In this way, Lerner provides a careful and nuanced study of Parthian intercultural communication, in which early Arsacid kings borrowed pre-existing Achaemenid and Greek cultural forms to declare and project their success and power to an Iranian audience.

Chapter two explores the Roman and Arsacid experience of taking Seleucid hostages and captives in the Hellenistic period and how it later informed the practice in Roman-Parthian relations. Many scholars have explained the acquisition of Seleucid hostages and captives as motivated by imperialistic interests on the part of Romans or Arsacids; they attempted to use them as tools of foreign policy by acculturating them to Roman or Parthian interests in the hope that they would be sympathetic to those interests if they came to sit on the Seleucid throne. Jake Nabel points out how influential this Hellenistic cultural practice and experience was for the Romans and Parthians in their own interactions. In the earlier period, each side learned that these prisoners were of limited use in an aggressive foreign policy. The Romans released Antiochus IV to take up the Seleucid kingship in 178/177 BCE only to find him build up military resources in violation of the earlier treaty of Apamea and to pursue a foreign policy so aggressive in Egypt that it required Roman intervention on the "Day of Eleusis." Furthermore, Antiochus' potential acculturation to Roman interests may have alienated some of his constituents. As for the Parthians, they had a similar experience when they released Demetrius II *c.* 131 BCE. As a result, later on when the Arsacids sent hostages to Rome, both the Arsacids and Romans used these captives for increasingly domestic purposes. Arsacid kings, such as Phraates IV, sent select family members to Rome to deprive their domestic enemies of access to potential Arsacid rivals for the throne. And the Romans happily used these Arsacids not as part of a proactive policy of trying to install viable vassal kings in Parthia, but rather as domestic showpieces of power. This was most clearly shown in the public crowning of the Arsacid Tiridates as Armenian king by Nero in Rome. With that, Nabel makes clear that certain Hellenistic cultural practices were maintained in the negotiation of Parthian-Roman relations, but were put to fresh purposes.

In chapter three, Kenneth Jones investigates Mark Antony's campaign of 36 BCE in the Near East – a campaign traditionally understood as aggressively targeting the Parthians. From the start, Jones explicitly and rightly points out the obstacles for an investigation of the campaign by detailing the source problems. The most significant is the ultimate victory of Octavian over Antony at Actium in 31 BCE and Octavian's subsequent influence on the source tradition. As a result of this influence, ancient authors largely present Antony's campaign as directed against the Arsacid king Phraates IV and as a failure. Jones, however, argues that Antony's efforts in 36 BCE were directed against Media Atropatene, not Parthia, and resulted in notable victories that were celebrated in Rome and ultimately inspired king Artavasdes of Media to support the Roman cause as well. What is more, Antony and the Median king reinforced the concord with a planned marriage alliance between one of Antony's sons by Cleopatra VII of Egypt and a daughter of Artavasdes. As for Parthia, Jones offers the intriguing suggestion that the main interest of Antony was a peace with Parthia through a diplomatic settlement. In the end, while Jones' piece is an important revision of the historical narrative of this period, he utilizes it to highlight the continuing vitality of Hellenistic cultural forms in cross-cultural interactions of the Near East at this time. Antony, he contends, is best understood not as a single-minded, traditional Roman imperialist, but rather a Hellenistic dynast who appreciated the complexity of the Near East, was willing to negotiate peace with Parthia, and came to embrace dynastic political strategies.

Chapter four then investigates Roman-Parthian diplomacy in greater depth, focusing on the significance of the embassy in the Julio-Claudian period. Embassies between Parthia and Rome were a relatively frequent occurrence during the first centuries BCE and CE. As Jason Schlude and Benjamin Rubin show, scholars have traditionally characterized these embassies as elaborate political set pieces, which did little to foster genuine cultural understanding, and in some cases, even produced hostility and violence. They propose a different understanding. While such may be an apt description of diplomatic engagement during Sulla's time in the Near East in the 90s BCE and especially Crassus' time there in 54–53 BCE, this was the exception, not the rule. They argue that embassies were, in fact, important mechanisms of cross-cultural exchange serving to consistently stabilize Roman-Parthian relations in the first centuries BCE and CE, as shown by the role of Roman-Parthian embassies in the Julio-Claudian period (31/30 BCE-68 CE), especially in the time of Augustus (31/30 BCE–14 CE). Beginning in the reign of Augustus, embassies between Rome and Parthia resulted in the residence of high-level elites from one empire within the confines of the other, gift exchange, and the generation of material culture programs designed to define and advertise the relationship of Rome and Parthia for a domestic audience. These were tangible, accessible, and lasting agents of cross-cultural exchange. And the fact that they were subsequently enshrined in a variety of literary productions only reinforces the point. These diplomatic events led Romans and Parthians to an evolved understanding of one another and the creation of a symbolic world that was intensely competitive at times, but nevertheless produced collaboration and lengthy periods of limited conflict. They conclude that embassies encouraged mutual learning and enabled the construction of a balanced peace. In this way, we see that the embassy was an example of a sophisticated mode of intercultural communication and exchange that made a positive impact in Roman-Parthian relations.

In chapter five, Jason Schlude and Andrew Overman investigate another aspect of Parthian-Roman intercultural communication. While there were indeed many direct engagements and exchanges between Romans and Parthians, we must not forget the role of local peoples and elites in the Near East in Roman-Parthian relations. It stands to reason that elites in border territories were not interested in only being passive victims of Roman and Parthian imperialism, but rather had their own interests and sought to secure those interests by actively manipulating Roman-Parthian relations to their own advantage. Schlude and Overman argue that Herod the Great, king of Judaea (40–4 BCE), serves as an excellent case study of this dynamic and reveals a great deal about the character of Roman-Parthian relations in the Near East at this time. Contrary to most scholarship, which routinely focuses on the power of Rome in the Near East during Herod's life and so limits its analysis to Herod's relationship to Rome, Schlude and Overman point out how in 40 BCE Orodes II managed to take control of a large portion of the "Roman East," from Idumea in the south through Caria in the north. Even though Rome retook the region between 39 and 38 BCE, the Parthians had demonstrated the extent of their power and reach – and locals in the area had to negotiate, or in certain cases could manipulate, their position between Rome and Parthia. Herod, for example, used the events of 40 BCE to secure the kingship of Judaea from the Romans. And later in 36 BCE, in an enhanced position of power, he would deal in direct diplomacy with Orodes' successor, Phraates IV, winning his favor with gifts and securing benefits such as the return of Hyrcanus, the ranking member of the Jewish Hasmonean dynasty, whom the Parthians carried off to Mesopotamia after their campaign of 40 BCE. The custody of this figure gave Herod added security in his own position as king, and he took advantage of it when he killed Hyrcanus shortly after the conclusion of the Roman civil war between Octavian and Antony – a time of particular uncertainty for Herod. Here then we have a local elite using the Roman-Parthian dynamic to his own ends.

Evidence suggests that elites of northern Mesopotamia also eyed their own interests when Rome and the Arsacids fought for control of that region in the second century and early third centuries CE. As Peter Edwell describes in chapter six, Trajan's Parthian campaign of 114–117 CE indicated that Roman imperial interests were aggressively moving once again into Mesopotamia. And though this campaign did not result in lasting territorial gains east of the Euphrates, Lucius Verus in the 160s CE, Septimius Severus in the 190s CE, and Carcalla in the 210s CE all indicated that those interests were not fleeting, but persisted for a century and, in the cases of Verus and Severus, resulted in territorial gains and the expansion of Roman power and influence in northern Mesopotamia and the middle Euphrates. This competitive imperial context in Mesopotamia gave local elites with an interest in power leverage in their negotiations with Rome and Parthia. Of particular interest to Edwell is the region of Oshroene and its capital city Edessa. Utilizing the coinage arising from mints in Edessa, Edwell shows how the Abgarid dynasty opportunistically positioned itself in these circumstances. Ma'nu VIII, for example, who came to the throne of Edessa in 139 CE, saw the potential for a shift in the geopolitics of northern Mesopotamia even before Verus' campaign materialized. Having bet then on Rome, Ma'nu found himself deposed by the Arsacid Vologases IV in 163 CE, who supported the installation of a certain Wael. But with Verus' victory over the Parthians in 165 CE, Ma'nu found the backing necessary to return to the throne, which he then held till his death in 179 CE. Wishing to make clear his allegiance to Rome, he took the title *Philoromaios*, present on several of his silver coins. And his son Abgarus VIII employed a similar strategy, at least until the civil war following the demise of Commodus in 192 CE. Indeed a bronze series features his portrait paired with that of either Septimius Severus or Commodus and sports a titulature for Abgarus VIII that incorporates the names of these emperors. Yet upon the death of Commodus and outbreak of Roman civil war, Osrhoene (and presumably Abgarus VIII) turned on Rome and attacked its garrison in Nisibis. Such action is instructive; it indicates that the actions of these elites were calculated, opportunistic, and assertive. Edwell's chapter also touches on other themes of this volume in his observation that Roman power in northern Mesopotamia led to the re-emergence of certain Hellenistic cultural forms, as made clear by the coinage and title of *Philoromaios* mentioned above, the appearance of Tyche on coins of northern Mesopotamia in the late second century CE, and Caracalla's appeal to the legacy of Alexander, which could have been directed at audiences in northern Mesopotamia who by that point were once again accustomed to a more western cultural orientation. As often, even as a contributor focuses on one theme of the volume, further observations are made that support another.

Finally, Björn Anderson continues to investigate local perspectives in Mesopotamia, but focuses on the city of Hatra in modern Iraq. While he reviews the political context of the city in chapter seven, he is more interested in what its art reveals about the broader cultural character and outlook of its people. As he points out, many scholars have argued that the political character of the city was fully Parthian until the demise of the Parthian empire and ascendance of the Sasanian in 224 CE, at which time it allied with Rome against the Sasanians, who attacked and ultimately defeated it in 229 CE and 240/241 CE. As for its cultural character, there has been more debate. Some have looked at its material culture from a western and Roman point of reference. Others, once again, have responded with an emphasis on its Parthian cultural identity. Anderson, however, attempts to move the discussion beyond binary approaches. The material culture of the city, its art and iconography, is richly complex, adopting and adapting a diversity of cultural elements from a range of traditions: not just Parthian, but also Greek, Syrian, Nabatean Iranian, and Gandharan. Much like the Nabateans, the Hatrans selected from the many cultural forms in the region and combined them in distinctive ways that made sense to them and spoke to their fellow Hatrans. Once more we see local peoples and local elites not helplessly dominated by Parthia and Rome in every way, but actively and creatively forging their own distinctive paths.

Scholarship on Parthia has come a long way. It started with the synthesis of fragmentary evidence and then developed into an investigation of the intercultural communication of the Parthian empire. Our collective goal is that the studies presented here will further that investigation, highlighting aspects of intercultural exchange that have not received their proper due or could benefit from additional analysis. In the end, we hope this volume will help to bring further balance to our understanding of the Parthian empire. The Arsacids adapted Achaemenid and Greek traditions (not to mention others) for their own imperialistic ends. As for their relations with Rome, they engaged in war, but also diplomacy, leading to productive periods of peace. And while both of these imperial powers dominated the Near East, local states and elites took the opportunity to use Roman and Parthian political, military, and cultural resources in their own bids for power. If our volume assists in this way, then it is a success.

Notes

1. For discussion of the source tradition, see Boyce 1983, 1151–1165; Widengren 1983, 1261–1283; Wiesehöfer 1998; Hackl, Jacobs, and Weber 2010; Dąbrowa 2012, 164–186; Potts 2013.
2. Rawlinson 1873; Debevoise 1938.
3. Shippmann 1980; Bivar 1983, 21–99.
4. Ziegler 1964.
5. Sherwin-White 1984; Linz 2009.
6. Campbell 1993, 213–240.
7. Wolski 1993; Shayegan 2011.
8. Colledge 1977.

Bibliography

Bivar, A. D. H. (1983) "The Political History of Iran under the Arsacids." In E. Yarshater (ed.) *The Cambridge History of Iran, Volume 3 (1): The Seleucid, Parthian and Sasanian Periods*, 21–99. Cambridge, Cambridge University Press.

Boyce, M. (1983) "Parthian Writings and Literature." In E. Yarshater (ed.) *The Cambridge History of Iran, Volume 3 (1): The Seleucid, Parthian and Sasanian Periods*, 1151–1165. Cambridge, Cambridge University Press.

Campbell, J. B. (1993) "War and Diplomacy: Rome and Parthia, 31 BC–AD 235." In J. W. Rich and G. Shipley (eds.) *War and Society in the Roman World*, 213–240. New York, Routledge.

Colledge, M. A. R. (1977) *Parthian Art*. Ithaca, NY, Cornell University Press.

Dąbrowa, E. (2012) "The Arsacid Empire." In T. Daryaee (ed.) *The Oxford Handbook of Iranian History*, 164–186. Oxford, Oxford University Press.

Debevoise, N. C. (1938) *A Political History of Parthia*. Chicago, University of Chicago Press.

Hackl, U., Jacobs, B. and Weber, D. (eds.) (2010) *Quellen zur Geschichte des Partherreiches: Textsammlung mit* Übersetzungen *und Kommentaren*. Göttingen, Vandenhoeck and Ruprecht.

Linz, O. (2009) *Studien zur römischen Ostpolitik im Principat*. Hamburg, Verlag Dr. Kovač.

Potts, D. T. (ed.) (2013) *The Oxford Handbook of Ancient Iran*. Oxford, Oxford University Press.

Rawlinson, G. (1873) *The Sixth Great Oriental Monarchy: Geography, History, and Antiquities of Parthia*. London, Longmans, Green, and Co.

Shayegan, M. R. (2011) *Arsacids and Sasanians: Political Ideology in Post-Hellenistic and Late Antique Persia*. Cambridge, Cambridge University Press.

Sherwin-White, A. N. (1984) *Roman Foreign Policy in the East, 168 B.C. to A.D. 1*. London, Duckworth.

Shippmann, K. (1980) *Grundzüge der Parthischen Geschichte*. Darmstadt, Wissenschaftliche Buchgesellschaft.

Widengren, G. (1983) "Sources of Parthian and Sasanian History." In E. Yarshater (ed.) *The Cambridge History of Iran, Volume 3 (2): The Seleucid, Parthian and Sasanian Periods*, 1261–1283. Cambridge, Cambridge University Press.

Wiesehöfer, J. (ed.) (1998) *Das Partherreich und seine Zeugnisse*. Stuttgart, Franz Steiner Verlag.

Wolski, J. (1993) *L'empire des Arsacides*. Leuven, E. Peeters.

Ziegler, K. H. (1964) *Die Beziehungen zwischen Rom und den Partherreich: ein Beitrag zur Geschichte de Völkerrechts*. Wiesbaden, Franz Steiner Verlag.

Chapter 1

Mithradates I and the Parthian Archer

Jeffrey D. Lerner[1]

The reverse on Parthian drachmas beginning with Arsakes I (*c*. 247–217 BCE) (Fig. 1.1) and his successors[2] depict a beardless male figure[3] wearing a bashlyk and cloak seated on a backless *diphros* turned either left or right, holding in an outstretched hand a bow with the bowstring facing outward in an unusable position. The *diphros* is substituted by an *omphalos* (Fig. 1.2) on some of the coins (drachmas, dichalkoi, triobols, diobols, and obols) of Mithradates I[4] (*c*. 171–138 BCE) until it, too, changes under Mithradates II[5] (*c*. 123–88 BCE) to a *thronos* (Fig. 1.3).

The aim of this paper is to provide a framework for understanding two aspects of early Parthian coins. The first seeks to explain why on the coins of Mithradates I the *diphros* is replaced by the *omphalos*. This in turn provides the basis for the second: determining the identity of the Parthian archer. We shall see that while Greeks may well have regarded the archer as Apollo, emphasized all the more given the adoption of the *omphalos*, the same does not ring true for Iranians.

Previous Identifications of the Parthian Archer

The interpretation of the Parthian archer depicted on the reverse of Parthian coins has taken a fairly consistent trajectory beginning with Eckhel who argued that the figure was the reigning monarch himself, on behalf of whom the coin was produced.[6] This notion was subsequently altered by others who regarded the archer as none other than the deified founder of the dynasty, Arsakes himself.[7]

Wroth slightly tweaked this argument by noting that he was not aware of any evidence indicating that both the dynasty's founder and Tiridates I were ever deified, and referred to the archer as simply a "Parthian warrior", the replacement of Apollo. Since this figure sports a diadem, Wroth asserted that he must be either Arsakes, the dynasty's founder, or the first king, Tiridates I, but with the caveat that he was never divinized.[8] He also concluded that this "Parthian archer" – as he also called him – seated as a bowman is based on the prototype of the Seleukid type of Apollo

Figure 1.1: AR drachma. Arsakes I. Mithradatkart-Nisa? Sellwood 1980: 3.1. Sunrise Collection (U. S. A.).

Figure 1.2: AR drachma. Mithradates I. Hecatompylos. Sellwood 1980: type 7.1. Sunrise Collection (U. S. A).

Figure 1.3: AR drachma. Mithradates II. Uncertain mint. Sellwood 1980: type 27.1. G. R. Assar Collection.

seated on his *omphalos*. In this respect, Wroth amplified the observation made by Babelon[9] that on Seleukid coins Apollo frequently holds an arrow in his outstretched hand and a bow in his other lowered hand, while in the Parthian version the arrow disappears altogether and in his extended hand the archer holds a bow, representing the emblem of the Parthian warrior. Wroth further observed that on some of the coins of Antiochos I and Antiochos II the bow and not the arrow is held in Apollo's outstretched hand.[10] It should be interjected at this point that recently Iossif has shown that this Apolline reverse type actually appears on more coins of Seleukid kings than Wroth had realized, although he is quick to dismiss any notion that these coins could in any way have served as models for the Parthian archer.[11] For his part, Seltman proposed that the figure based on a Seleukid prototype was none other than a clothed Apollo seated upon his *omphalos*,[12] while College saw in the beardless archer a figure that held "some religious significance," but wondered whether it represented "the deified Arsaces, some Parni god, or a resuscitation in Parthian guise of the archer of Achaemenid coins?"[13] To a large extent Koshelenko also agreed that the Parthian version represents a modification of the Seleukid prototype, but it was a version that was adopted for two reasons.[14] First, there was the tradition that affirmed the right of conquest and acquisition of the throne after having vanquished the sovereign in power, for which there were numerous precedents, such as Cyrus over Astyages, and Arsakes over Andragoras.[15] There was also a legal foundation that was not based on the principle of "the right of conquest," as much as it drew on certain arguments of a religious nature that were used to justify the dynasty in order "to vindicate through an established logical connection between royal and divine power."[16] In other words, the Arsakid concept of divine royal authority was in many ways interdependent of the exercise of political ideology. In terms of coins, Koshelenko noted that besides their use as monetary objects, they were also used as propaganda to convey certain state ideas in their legends, types, and devices. Coins thus reflected specific ideological concepts of the sovereign.[17]

It is on this last point in particular that Raevskii[18] formulated his analysis. Apollo served two roles for the Seleukids: he was their patron deity, and he was a political symbol, of which the bow was an integral attribute. For example, when only the bow appears on coins, it is understood in semantic terms as a representation of the god. On Parthian coins, the archer also conveys a symbolic political meaning. Raevskii interprets the Parthian archer's posture as indicating the moment when the bow, as the regal symbol of authority, is being transferred to the king. Either the archer is in the process of handing the bow to another or is in the act of taking it from someone. In order to determine the identities of the individuals involved in this transaction, Raevskii looked to evidence from the European Skythians who settled on the Black Sea. He asserted that the scenes on two spherical silver cups from the Kul-Oba and Voronezh kurgans represent the same creation myths of the Skythians as those recounted by Herodotos (4.5–7; 4.8–10). Both vessels contain toreutic reliefs that form, according to Raevskii, narrative scenes. The Voronezh cup contains three pairs of Skythian male figures long recognized by Rostovtzeff.[19] Raevskii interprets them as the three sons of Targitaos-Herakles, each of whom was credited with having founded the Skythian race. In both versions, the father – Targitaos and Herakles – had three sons. Raevskii argues that they are portrayed on the vessel following their trial as it is represented on the Kul-Oba flask, the youngest of whom inherited his father's bow, which the Skythians regarded as the symbol of royal authority.[20] Raevskii regarded the depiction on what he termed ritual objects, like the Voronezh vase, as proof that Skythian kings looked to figures like Targitaos-Herakles and his son as the source of the divine nature of their sovereignty, because he interpreted the scene on the Voronezh vase as Targitaos-Herakles in the guise of the bearded old warrior handing a small bow to his youngest son Kolaxais who appears as the clean-shaven youth. In terms of Parthian coins, Raevskii concluded that on the early series the figure of the archer on the reverse and the clean-shaven kings' portrait on the obverse portray the same individual – Arsakes. Later the obverse portrait is replaced by various Parthian kings who issued coins during their respective reigns, but in the early period the portrait depicted the dynasty's founder on the obverse, while the reverse represents the moment when Arsakes, like the young man on the Voronezh vase, received into his hands the symbol of divine and regal power. In this case, Arsakes, the dynasty's founder, is supposed to have been Kolaxais. On later coins, the king whose portrait appears on the obverse is cast in the role of "recipient," while Arsakes himself on the reverse acting on behalf of the higher power hands the sovereign his bow (and hence his attribute): the investiture of royal power justified by the notion of the "right of conquest" and thus the ruler's divine character.[21]

Unfortunately, Raevskii's argument is based on a highly subjective analysis of the art and its conjectured agreement with Herodotos' text. His theory suffers from a series of principal defects as outlined by Meyer. First, the artist has omitted any recognizable detail that could link these scenes with those in Herodotos' account (4.10), such as the snake-legged mother of Herakles' sons or the golden vessel decorating the end of the clasp of the belt worn by Herakles and his descendants. The figures thus appear generic. Second, Meyer[22] notes that Herodotos' version of the Skythian foundation story derives from the Greeks of the Black Sea. Yet, he asks, "how could its allied visual representation have escaped the effects of Greek selection and adaptation? Was the legend reported by Herodotos not just another story the Greeks told about the Scythians?" The implication that these questions raise is that if one accepts the links between image and text, then Raevskii undercuts his own argument, "a reconstruction of Skythian mythology, ritual, and the worldview allegedly embedded in them." Raevskii bases his argument on a highly subjective analysis of the art and its conjectured agreement with Herodotos' text. His theory suffers from a series of principal defects as outlined by Meyer: namely, the figures appear generic; Herodotos' version of the Skythian foundation story derives from Greeks and not Skythians; and propositions about Scythian worldviews are by necessity abstract and can be neither proven nor rejected, although Greco-Scythian art tells us more about the identity of the represented Scythians than the agendas of representation.

Fowler has proposed an interpretation to explain what the archer might be doing. He looked to Dio (*Historia Romana* 49.27.3–5), who explains that during the peace negotiations between Phraates IV (38–2 BCE) and the envoys of M. Antonius, the Parthian king sat on a golden chair fingering his bowstring (ἐπί τε χρυσοῦ δίφρου καθήμενος καὶτὴν νευρὰν τοῦ τόξου ψάλλων; *Historia Romana* 49.27.4). Fowler extrapolates that this is precisely the action that is rendered on all Parthian coins in which the archer appears. As a result, Dio in presenting this studied and symbolic attitude of Phraates in fact has captured an image that is "meant to epitomise "Arsacid kingship." He concludes that the coins depicting the Parthian archer are an assimilation of the *omphalos* on which Apollo sits on Seleukid coins with the image of "the king as archer" on Achaemenid coins.[23] Unfortunately, this scene as described by Dio only pertains to this passage. As a theory it is groundless, for Fowler fails to demonstrate how it relates to Parthian iconography and in particular the early Arsakid coins under discussion. As such, the connection – assuming that one exists – between Dio's passage and these coins remains at best a superficial construct without any new insight into the matter.

Recently, Koshelenko working with Gaibov has revised his earlier argument. They assert that the earliest evidence of a royal cult is to be found on two groups of sources. One consists of a series of silver drachmas that they claim were issued by Arsakes II, but has been mistakenly attributed to Mithradates I.[24] The legend reads: ΒΑΣΥΛΕΩΣ ΘΕΟΥ ΑΡΣΑΚΟΥ, "[coin] of god king Arsakes." In support of this contention, they reference a second piece of evidence: a passage in Ammianus Marcellenus (23.6.5–6):

> (5) Hence, the overweening kings of the same race permit themselves to be called brothers of the Sun and Moon and, as the title Augustus is desirable and sought after for our emperors, so to the Parthian kings – lowly and ignoble previously – they summoned the very greatest increases in status, through the happy auspices of Arsaces. (6) For this reason, they venerate and worship him like a god, with honors having grown to such an extent within living memory that, unless he is a descendant of Arsaces, no one is put forward over the rest in taking up the kingship, and in any civil strife at all, which constantly happens for them, everyone is wary, as if [it were] a sacrifice, that he not strike with his right hand an Arsacid who is bearing arms or a private citizen.[25]

Since Ammianus' text makes it clear that the deification of Arsakes was not the result of his own desire, but an act of apotheosis, Koshelenko and Gaibov conclude that Arsakes II must have been responsible for awarding his predecessor this posthumous honor. Moreover, they note that this custom did not originate from Parthian tradition, but was based on the Seleukid practice of the ruler cult. Arsakes II, they argue, was ahead of his time, for unlike contemporary practices he introduced the innovation of referring to his predecessor as "God" in the legend of his coins. The same practice would not be repeated (imitated?) on Seleukid coins until the reign of Antiochos IV several decades later. Moreover, they credit Arsakes II with another innovation in his coin legends: the use of THEOY THEOPATOR and MEGALOY, "[coin] of the great king Arsakes, [having] a divine father." For Koshelenko and Gaibov the posthumous cult of Arsakes commenced almost at the inception of the Parthian state based on a modified version of the Seleukid ruler cult. The practice, however, was presumably, temporarily interrupted during the eastern anabasis of Antiochos III in 210 BCE, who placed the Parthian mint under the control of the Seleukids, and it did not reappear on coins until the reign of Phraates II (*c.* 138–127 BCE) some seventy years later when he reinstated it for his father Mithradates I (*c.* 171–138 BCE). At this point, a note of caution should be exercised, for the appearance of the epithet THEOY THEOPATOR on the silver drachmas attributed by Koshelenko and Gaibov to the coins of Arsakes II is still a subject of much debate. Coins with epithets such as this may have in fact been issued during the reign(s) of Phriapatios, Phraates II, or even Mithradates I.[26]

The problem with this reclassification of Mithradates I's coins on the basis of the Parthian ruler cult is that the evidence for it is at best circumstantial. For example, it is assumed based on the passage from Ammianus Marcellinus above that immediately following the death of the Arsakes I, his successor, Arsakes II, deified him, albeit posthumously. In fact, Ammianus makes no such claim. He merely states: *numinis eum vice venerantur et colunt ea*, "they venerate and worship him like a god." In other words, we are not told when the cult dedicated to Arsakes I was first installed, who was responsible for it, or even where the place of worship was located. We are simply informed that he was venerated and worshipped at some point after his death. On this basis, there is no compelling reason to reassign the coins that Sellwood had attributed to Mithradates I. Furthermore, there are the additional problems of how to account for the haphazard appearance of the *omphalos* on which the archer sits, and how to explain the occasion for its introduction. It is difficult to believe that a mint(s) would produce coins in a whimsical manner: for some unknown reason the *omphalos* was introduced and for another unknown reason it was replaced by a *diphros*, only later to reappear again without a consistent pattern.

As a result, the interpretation of the Parthian archer as a reverse type rests on four important considerations: the identity of the male figure; the identification of the different types of seats upon which he sits; the meaning of the bow; and the significance of the manner in which the archer holds his bow. As a general rule, the identity of the figure of the archer is considered to be Arsakes, who wears a tiara, and was the eponymous founder of the Arsakid royal house. He is depicted seated first on a *diphros*, or backless stool, until it is transformed into the famous *omphalos* of Delphi where the Hellenic Apollo used to sit. Apparently, we should understand that the use of the *omphalos* was inspired by Seleukid coins, although no one has yet attempted to equate Arsakes with Apollo. While the use of the bow as an emblem of royal and perhaps divine authority might be traced to the reverse type of Apollo with a bow on early Seleukid coinage (Fig. 1.4), the coins of Tarkamuwa/Datames, the Achaemenid satrap of Kilikia, seem to have served as the source of inspiration for both Seleukid and Parthian coinage (Fig. 1.5).[27] Finally, as we have noted, the posture of the archer seems to suggest, at least to Fowler, that he is in the act of tweaking his bowstring.[28]

Figure 1.4: AR tetradrachma. Antiochos I. Courtesy of the American Numismatic Society.

Figure 1.5: AR stater. Tarkamuwa/Datames satrap. Kilikia, Tarsos. Courtesy of the American Numismatic Society.

A Reconsideration of the Parthian Archer

Early Parthian history begins with Arsakes, who in the mid-third century BCE as leader of the Aparni tribe conquered the country of Astauene in the upper Atrek river valley of the Seleukid province of Parthia (modern district of Quchan) from Andragoras and Seleukos II.[29] At its capital of Assak, or Arsakia, (modern Ustuva) he was crowned king, although it is not known whether he ever used the royal title, unlike his successors who did.[30] Similarly, little is known of Arsakes' religious beliefs or those of his successors, including whether or not Arsakes was ever deified.[31] What is known is that, according to Wiesehöfer, there seems to have been an association between the Parthian monarchy and Zoroastrian notions of "Gottesgnadentum"[32] (*i.e.* "divine right") that at once harkens back to the Achaemenid period, but also reflects the later practice of the Hellenistic ruler-cult and its influence on the Arsakid monarchy. The earliest indication we have that such a connection might have existed is found with Arsakes himself. According to Isidore of Charax (*Stath. Part.* 11), in the city of Assak where Arsakes was crowned king there was "an everlasting fire" that was "guarded." The implication is that this city was specifically chosen for Arasakes' coronation because it contained an important Zoroastrian fire-temple. Moreover, there are literary traditions that establish the genealogy of the Arsakids as a legitimate Iranian dynasty, traced from its founder, Arsakes.[33] This genealogy consists of no less than five different ancestors: Dārā, Isfandiyār, Kai Kavād, Ash son of Siyāvush, and Ārash.[34] Of these the famed archer Ārash is for our purpose most significant.

We have seen that for almost a century and a half, the archer on the reverse of Arsakid coins has been regarded as Arsakes. This recognition has been primarily based on the fact that Arsakes' coins portray him on the obverse as a young, clean-shaven man, wearing a diademed bashlyk, while the archer, whom some consider – perhaps as a deified – Arsakes, is seated on a backless *diphros* holding a bow in his outstretched hand (Fig. 1.1). Yet, none of these coins contain any reference to a regal title in their legend and both types remained standard until the reign of Mithradates I (Fig. 1.2).[35]

On the other hand, little attention has been paid to the Parthian archer's possible identification as Ārash,[36] the famed archer among the Aryans,[37] whose name is similar to that of Arsakes, the dynasty's founder.[38] Such an identification would mean that from the outset the Parthian moneyers, Greeks and/or Hellenized Iranians, would have looked to emissions produced by Achaemenid satraps[39] for supplying the prototypes of Arsakes' coins and, as it happened, those of his immediate successors. In order to understand the reason why Ārash might well have been chosen to serve as the reverse type of the Parthian archer, it is first necessary to turn to the *Šāh-nāma* for its explanation of how Ārash won his reputation.[40] When Afrāsiyāb invaded Ērānshahr in the kingdom of Manūchihr, he vanquished the Iranian army that met him. A peace was eventually brokered when the two combatants agreed to have Ārash shoot an arrow toward the east from the summit of Mount Damâvand to fix the borders of Manūchihr's kingdom of Iran and Afrāsiyāb's of Turan. After the arrow landed, the two kings drew up a treaty. According to al-Bīrūnī,[41] in the month of Tīr on the day of Tīr the feast of Tīragān was held in honor of Ārash for his skills at archery. Ārash also appears in the *Tištrya Yašt* in which Sirius, "flying with rapid pulsation (and) vibrant flight, who flies with such sparkle towards the Sea Vourukaša," is likened to "the celestial arrow" fired by "the vibrant-arrowed ərəxša, the most vibrant-arrowed (archer) among the Aryans launched from Mount Airyō.šiθa to Mount Xᵛanvant."[42] The recognition of ərəxša as Ārash has long been established[43] as has the hero's "strictly Miθraic features in Middle and New Iranian literature."[44] Moreover, the identification between ərəxša and Miθra is made firmer by representations of the latter having shot an arrow at a rock from which a fountain of water streams forth.[45] The religious literature thus connects Arsakes, and by extension the Arsakids, with ərəxša and Miθra by way of Ārash. The identification of Ārash as the Parthian archer is further strengthened by the other components that make up the reverse type.

The bow appears as part of the iconography on the earliest issues of Parthian coins symbolizing the military victories enjoyed by Arsakes and his followers. In this respect, the implementation of Ārash as the archer for the reverse type on coinage represents the significance that the Parthians placed on archery[46] and specifically the bow as a military weapon. The bow forged a sense of national identity among the Parthians.[47] As a symbol of power and kingship, it was regarded in much the same way as the Elamites, Assyrians, and Achaemenids had used it in art and in the case of the latter on their coins,[48] but unlike the Achaemenids for whom the bow was one of several such royal emblems, it was for the Arsakids the essential attribute. In this respect, the bow served as much as the archer's attribute – indeed it is what gave the archer his identity – as it did as the heraldic emblem of the royal dynasty of the Arsakids. Together the semantic use of the archer with his bow provided for the Parthians a national identity as indigenous Iranians and the rightful heirs of the Achaemenids.[49] Zeimal' argued that the reverse type of the Parthian archer is actually a composite representation whose origins can be traced back to the staters of the Achaemenid satrap of Kilikia, Tarkamuwa/Datames (386–362 BCE) (Fig. 1.5) whose obverse type depicts Baal of Tarsos enthroned facing right holding an eagle-tipped scepter and a corn-ear with a bunch of grapes, and a thymiateriaon is at his side. The field behind is occupied by an Aramaic legend, while beneath the throne a flower appears. A border representing battlements of the city encloses the motif. On the reverse a male figure is depicted enthroned facing right and sighting an arrow; a quiver is placed on his lap, and in the field above, a winged solar disk appears. The bow, however, that is placed at the feet of the figure was subsequently transferred on Parthian coins to the archer's outstretched right hand as a consequence of the modification made to the Achaemenid satrapal prototype.[50]

This male figure is portrayed wearing nomadic clothing comparable to that worn by Ārash seated on a *diphros*.[51] The main difference between this Achaemenid type and the Arsakid type is the presence in the former of a winged disk. In this case, the seated archer is used to connote regal authority and was an attempt by Tarkamuwa/ Datames to legitimize his self-declared regal authority by means of the Zoroastrian symbol of the winged disk, representing a *fravahr* – soul, guardian angel, or fortune – and hence bestowing divine favor onto the ruler,[52] as opposed to its representation of Ahura Mazda,[53] the uncreated spirit central to Zoroastrianism. Other Achaemenid satraps, like Pharnabazos[54] (379–374 BCE) (Fig. 1.6), also employed a *diphros* on the reverse on which was an enthroned deity, like Baal; here Baaltars is enthroned left, holding a scepter, with an astragalos under his throne (the obverse contains a helmeted head of a bearded warrior left). This type was later modified. Alexander's coins, for example, portray an enthroned Zeus holding a Nike in his outstretched right hand that is based on the Pheidian cult statue of Zeus at Olympia.[55] This same type was repeated on various coinages throughout the Hellenistic period, especially on those of the Seleukids[56] and the Greek-Baktrians,[57] among others.

The action or posture of the Parthian archer in the guise of Ārash with his extended arm holding the bow is derivative of similar gestures on the coins of Achaemenid satraps that over time became ubiquitous with deities holding forth their attribute, rather than a direct imitation of coins struck by Alexander and his successors,

Figure 1.6: AR stater. Pharnabazos satrap. Kilicia, Tarsos. Courtesy of the American Numismatic Society.

including the Seleukids, although the type of *diphros* that appears on Arsakid coins may have originated from the Greek and Hellenistic model.[58] As a result, there is no evidence to substantiate the claim of an association of the Parthian archer with the Voronezh vase and the creation myths of the Skythians as related by Herodotos. The vase contains three different peaceful scenes of Skythian life that were long ago explained by Rostovtzeff: warriors holding a conference, a Skythian camp, and, most important for our purpose, "an old warrior instructing a youth in the use of the bow."[59] There is nothing about any of these scenes, particularly the latter, that would suggest that they are anything other than what they depict, and certainly there is nothing about them that suggests a connection with the divine or the Parthian archer. That the bearded old man appears to be represented in a position that is similar to the Parthian archer, can easily be explained as chance and nothing more. In so far as a connection between the Parthian archer and the stories of Skythian genesis and the importance of the bow, there is no disagreement with the notion that the bow was important to Skythians and Parthians, but to extrapolate from this some sort of closer association is no more than belief based on speculation.

During the reign of Mithradates I the diphros was replaced by an *omphalos*, or as it has also been termed an "up-turned basket."[60] On coins the Hellenic god Apollo, who is usually portrayed nude, is often depicted sitting on his *omphalos*, in association with one or more of his attributes, an arrow(s), bow, and lyre, among others. On Parthian coins the archer Ārash remains dressed in his nomadic attire holding his bow in an outstretched hand, except that now he sits atop an *omphalos*. The appropriation of the *omphalos* has traditionally been regarded as the manifestation of the king's authority to rule over territory taken "by right of conquest" from the Seleukids until the reign of Mithradates II when the *thronos*, or high-backed throne, perhaps derived from Achaemenid prototypes, replaced it.[61] It is important to stress that without a key to a Parthian understanding of the identity of the archer Ārash in the guise of Apollo, reproduction of Greek art forms could take on a non-Greek meaning for the Parthians.

The event that quite likely precipitated this iconographic change was Mithradates' first expedition (Fig. 1.7) outside the Parthian realm that resulted in the kingdom's enlargement dated variously between 163 and 150 BCE.[62] The campaign was directed eastward against the Greek-Baktrian realm of Eukratides I[63] (c. 171/170–c. 145 BCE), which was still experiencing or had just recently undergone a series of rebellions. It seems that shortly before Mithradates' incursion into the country, Eukratides had left on his own expedition into India. The result proved successful for Mithradates who presumably marched as far east as Baktra or its environs and was able to incorporate the satrapies of Aspionos/Aspiones and Tourioua. In the course of the campaign, he defeated the son of Eukratides, whom he had appointed as co-regent prior to his departure. It is unknown, however, whether Eukratides' son swore an oath of allegiance to the Parthian king. Upon his triumphant return, Eukratides was slain by this same son who then ascended to the throne.[64] We have no indication from any Greek-Baktrian coin or any other piece of evidence that Mithradates had ever incorporated Baktria as a satrapy. He had, however, accomplished the goal of extending his kingdom eastward to include Areia (the satrapy of Tourioua/Tapuria) in the south, the extreme western portion of Baktria in the east, and Margiana (the satrapy of Aspionos/Aspiones) in the north. It was not until 148/147 BCE[65] that Mithradates turned his attention westward and succeeded in annexing Media, assigning Bagasis or Vacasis, perhaps his brother, as the satrap of both Media and Atropatene prior to his return to Hyrkania.[66]

As a result, the appearance of the *omphalos* connoted different meanings to different audiences. Certainly, from a Greek perspective the introduction of the *omphalos* transformed the Parthian archer into the Hellenic god Apollo, although in an Orientalized manner and portrayed differently than he had appeared on Seleukid coins. Seen from this perspective these coins seem to suggest that this change was prompted by Mithradates in an attempt to placate the Greeks who comprised substantial numbers in the newly acquired cities that had formerly been part of the Seleukid kingdom. Hellenistic iconography was thus used for propagandistic purposes.[67] But one also can view this innovation from an Iranian, and hence Parthian, point of view. Certainly, when one takes into account the overall history of this period, Mithradates' conquest marks a significant turning point for the Parthian kingdom, because it represents the first stage of how this little state developed into a great empire. But at the time no one could have known this and it does not explain why the *omphalos* was used. Ārash sits atop an *omphalos* representing semantically the lands that Mithradates had just conquered in the east from the Greek-Baktrians: Areia, Baktria, and Margiana. In other words, the use of this "Greek throne" was intended for domestic consumption and, if there was any thought of what it might signify to the Greeks, it mattered no more than as an after-thought. In this regard, the change held both a political and religious connotation intended for an Iranian audience. It is all the more understandable if the moneyers who produced this coinage were Greek or Hellenized Iranians, because the *omphalos* used as a symbol of imperialism signified the conquest of the East and hence the reestablishment of the ancient frontiers of

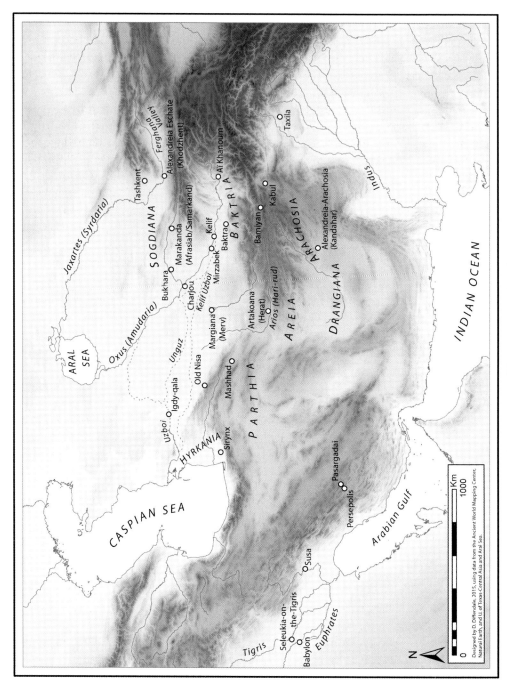

Figure 1.7: Map of the eastern Iranian plateau.

Iran. The connection is made firmer by the assimilation of Tīr and the Mesopotamian god of writing Nabu, who had himself been assimilated first with Apollo, then with the Tīr in the Parthian period.[68] The link between Tīr and the Arsakids is made firmer by his veneration in Central Asia. For example, there are discoveries at Old Nisa, subsequently Mithradatkirt, of several personal names containing his theonym on ostraca formed with Tīr,[69] which appears in Khorasmia in Khorasmian personal names,[70] while in Sogdiana (Sog. *tydr*) his popularity is attested by his wide spread use in personal names.[71] If Grenet and Marshak are correct, he also may have been depicted as the war-like deity who served as the guardian and consort of Nana.[72]

In this sense, Mithradates' coins cast Eukratides in the role of Afrāsiyāb, the Greeks his followers, and Baktria as Turan, but themselves as the defenders of Ērānshahr. The coins portray Ārash after he had let loose his arrow eastward to fix the borders of Iran and Turan, just as Mithradates had fixed the borders of Parthia and Greek-Baktria. The archer sits on Apollo's *omphalos*, symbolizing the Parthian conquest of the Greek lands in the east that had been held by Eukratides I and his nameless son. It is a statement of rule "by right of conquest" to his fellow Iranians and not meant to placate his newly acquired Greek subjects. He is posed with his outstretched hand holding his bow in a gesture reminiscent of depictions of gods and men on coins from the Achaemenid period, and still very much in vogue, but now reserved for deities both Hellenistic and Iranian. It is not difficult to imagine that the celebration of this political triumph with its Zoroastrian connotations would have been held in the month of Tīr on the day of Tīr, the feast of Tīragān.

Conclusion

By way of conclusion it should be noted that the appearance of the *omphalos* as the chief attribute of Apollo makes perfect sense given the Olympian's status throughout the Seleukid kingdom. He was after all the patron deity of the Seleukids and his widespread popularity is testified by numerous coins and other forms of art depicting the deity, as well as inscriptions referring to Apollo as the royal family's ancestor, and various literary accounts.[73] Throughout his reign and afterward, Seleukos was associated with Zeus and his son, Antiochos I with Apollo.[74] In 281 BCE the relationship had become so well established that the Ilians welcomed a cult of Seleukos I, his ancestor Apollo, and subsequently Antiochos I. The implications are clear enough: Apollo was credited as the founder (ἀρχηγὸς τοῦ γένους) of the Seleukid dynasty.[75] Yet, it was Antiochos I who replaced the hitherto dominant types of Herakles and Zeus on the coins of Seleukos I with new types, most notably Apollo, and to have done so in such a way as to place the Seleukids as the natural inheritors of the eastern tradition of monarchy; they proclaimed divine kinship with Apollo/Helios/Mithra and portrayed him as the divine *Toxartes*.[76] By 197 BCE, the filial bond between the Seleukids and the Apolline triad had become a matter of fact. In an inscription found in Leto's sanctuary, the "Great King Antiochos III" consecrated the city of Xanthos to Leto, Apollo, and

Artemis, because of their *syngeneia*, "the kinship" that existed between the Seleukids and Apollo, and by extension Leto and Artemis.[77]

In terms of the Upper Satrapies, we know that Demodamas of Miletos participated in numerous campaigns during Antiochos I's co-regency in the Upper Satrapies. According to Pliny (*NH* 6.49), Demodamas crossed the Tanais (*i.e.* Jaxartes) and erected altars to Apollo of Didyma (*... transcendit eum amnem [scil. Tanain] Demodamas, Seleuci et Antiochi regum dux, quem maxime sequimur in his, arasque Apollini Didymaeo statuit*). His autobiography also seems to have served as the source of Pliny and Strabon for information about the colonizing and refounding activities undertaken by Antiochos I in Central Asia at such sites as Antioch-in-Margiana (Pliny, *NH* 6.47; Strabo 11.10.2), Achaïs-in-Margiana (Pliny, *NH* 6.48), and Antioch-in-Aria (Pliny, *NH* 6.93.). The idea to set up altars to Apollo, who would have been understood by the local populace as Mithra in the Upper Satrapies, was part of a policy encouraged by Apama – the daughter of Spitamenes, wife of Seleukos I, and the mother of Antiochos I – as a way to win over the Asiatic Greeks and the Persians.[78] In addition, in the main temple dedicated to Apollo within the walls of Aï Khanoum, initially built by Antiochos I and where subsequently a newer temple was constructed in its place by Antiochos III during his eastern *anabasis* in Baktria in 208–206 BCE, the remains of a cultic statue of Apollo were found. Moreover, this temple of Apollo places in context the Delphic Maxims that were found at the *temenos* of Kineas, the city's founder.[79] The main temple also yielded a number of locally manufactured cultic figurines, including a metal plaque with the representation of Kybele standing in her chariot pulled by lions in association with various deities,[80] including Helios. In a peculiar twist of irony, the last Greek-Baktrian kings to have issued a coinage, Eukratides II and Platon, depict as their reverse type Apollo and Helios, respectively, reminiscent of the Seleukids.[81] Moreover, among the objects found during excavations of the Temple of the Oxos at the site of Takhti-Sangin was a silver plaque of Helios in radiant nimbus.[82] Finally, long after Greek rule in the region had ended the Kushans issued their own coins among which were included Helios-Mioro, corresponding with Mithra.[83] It comes as no surprise, therefore, that Ārash the Parthian archer who appears on the coins of Mithradates I was also closely identified with Ɂrəxša and Mithra. The latter had already been fused with Apollo/Helios. The result was a syncretized deity whose identity was fused as much with a Persian national identity as it was with an eastern Hellenic identity formed by the Seleukids.

Notes

1   This paper benefitted from the comments and suggestions on earlier drafts of this paper from Vesta Sarkhosh Curtis and Marek J. Olbrycht. Any errors are the sole responsibility of the author.

2. Sellwood 1980, types 1–6.1. Sellwood's classification in recent years has been questioned by a number of scholars exercising different points of view. Assar, for example, has argued that the obverse types portraying the ruler in a kyrbasia or bashlyk should be assigned to Arsakes I, Arsakes II, Friyapat (=Phriapatius), Phraates I, and the early emissions of Mithradates I (*e.g.*

Assar 2004, 77–89; Assar 2006, 75–78). Given the disenchantment with the current arrangement of early Arsakid coins, a reassessment of Sellwood's work is clearly needed. Unfortunately, such a study falls outside the scope of this work.

3. In a concise study of Hellenistic portraits on the obverse of coins, Günther has recently explored the notion that males sporting beards tend generally to be representations of gods, while beardless ones represent rulers (Günther 2011).

4. Sellwood 1980, types 7, 8.1, 9, 10, 11.1–5, and 12.1–5.

5. Sellwood 1980, types 26.1–25, 27.1–5, 28.1–7, 29.

6. Eckhel 1828, 544–546, 549–550.

7. Longpérier 1853, 29–30; Gardner 1877, 18; Gutschmid 1888, 32; Марков 1892a, 272 *et passim*; Марков 1892b, 6 *et passim*; Newell 1938, 476; Simonetta 1950, 23; Зограф 1951, 80–81 (*cf.* Zograf 1977); Simonetta 1955, 116; Le Rider 1964, 312, 320; Кошеленко 1968, 58 *et passim*; Кошеленко 1971, 215.

8. Wroth 1964, lxviii–lxix.

9. Babelon 1890, lix.

10. Wroth 1964, lxvii–lxviii; *cf.* Gardner 1963, 14; Newell 1938, 476; Кошеленко 1968, 54–56; Le Rider 1964, 312–324.

11. Iossif has extended the period of their production from Antiochos I to Seleukos IV, including the short reign of Antiochos V, and has posited the notion that they were emitted from as many as a dozen different mints (Iossif 2010, 232–234; Iossif 2011, 262–264).

12. Seltman 1955, 236.

13. College 1967, 103.

14. Кошеленко 1968, 58.

15. Кошеленко 1971, 214–215. The basis of this portion of the argument derives from Neusner 1963.

16. Кошеленко 1971, 216.

17. Кошеленко 1971, 212.

18. Раевский 1977a, 83–85; Раевский 1977b, 125–128.

19. Ростовцев 1914, 79–93.

20. Раевский 1970, 90–95; Раевский 1977b, 30–36.

21. Раевский 1977a, 84–85. Raevskii notes that after he had formulated his theory and shortly before the article was to be published he learned of two articles that had appeared much earlier. László (1951, 100) and Harmatta (1951, 128) argued that the scene on the Voronezh vase of the old man handing the younger man a small bow represents a ritual transference power with the bow itself symbolizing the insignia of sovereignty. They also regard the stone pile on which the old man sits as an *omphalos*. Harmatta suggests that the Parthian archer was Arsakes I.

22. Meyer 2013, 26–28.

23. Fowler 2005, 147–148; *cf.* Iossif 2011, 273. Dąbrowa 2010, 129, proposes 36 BCE as the date of the conference.

24. The assertion is based on Sellwood 1980, 34–35, type 10. Кошеленко 1968, 66–68, no. 2; Кошеленко and Гаибов 2010, 172–174; for an elaboration on their thesis, Кошеленко and Гаибов 2012, 27–31.

25. (5) *Unde ad id tempus reges eiusdem gentis praetumidi appellari se patiuntur Solis fratres et Lunae, utque imperatoribus nostris Augusta nuncupatio amabilis est et optata, ita regibus Parthicis abiectis et ignobilibus antea, incrementa dignitatum felicibus Arsacis auspiciis accessere vel maxima. (6) Quam ob rem numinis eum vice venerantur et colunt ea usque propagatis honoribus ut ad nostri memoriam non nisi Arsacides is sit, quisquam in suscipiendo regno cunctis anteponatur, et in qualibet civili concertatione, quae adsidue apud eos eveniunt, velut sacrilegium quisque caveat ne dextra sua Arsaciden arma gestantem feriat vel privatum.* See Seyfarth 1978 for a complete list of all editions, and Boeft, Drijvers, Hengst, and Teitler 1995 and 1998 for the commentary.

26. In addition to n. 2 above, see Assar 2004, 69–93, 82; Curtis 2012, 68–70; Martinez-Sève 2014, 131–137.
27. This view was first expressed by Zeimal' 1982 and has become foundational in subsequent studies, *e.g.* Curtis 1998, 66; Wiesehöfer 2003, 173–185; Curtis 2007, 414–417. The Aramaic name *TRKMW* or Tarkumwa that appears on coin legends is a rendering of the indigenous Luwian Tarḫu[nt]-mu(u̯a)ta (Nöldeke 1884, 298; Six 1884, 114–117; Harrison 1982, 321–336; Casabonne 2001), of which the prefix Tarḫu[nt] is the vernacular of the sky-god of the Tauros Mountains (Hutter 2003, 220–224). For comparisons of the portrait on the obverse of early Arsakid coins with the Persian satraps Tissaphernes and Autophradates of the fourth century BCE, Curtis 2007, 416–417, figs. 5–6.
28. Fowler 2005, 147–148.
29. For an overview of the particulars, see Olbrycht 1996, 147–169; Olbrycht 1998, 51–76; Lerner 1999, 13–43; Luther 2006–2007, 39–55.
30. Isidore of Charax, *Stath. Part.* 11; Justin 41.5.5–8; Wolski 1969, 212 *et passim*; Olbrycht 1998, 61; Chaumont 1973, 198; Gaslain 2005a, 221–222; Gaslain 2005b, 13; Dąbrowa 2010, 124. Olbrycht 2013, 69, suspects that Arsakes probably used the Iranian royal title *šāh.*
31. *Cf.* Drijvers 1999, 198–199.
32. Wiesehöfer 1996, 62; *cf.* Gnoli 1998.
33. There is a small but growing body of literature on the nomadic heritage of the Arsakids. One of the best is Olbrycht 2003 for a concise survey with ample bibliography.
34. Yarshater 1983, 475; von Stackelberg 1904, 853–854, 858.
35. For a discussion on the apotheosis of Arsakes, Invernizzi 2011. Mithradates is credited with having been the first king to install the ruler-cult, *e.g.,* Gariboldi 2004, 374–375; Dąbrowa 2009. The reasons he did so, however, remain unclear. See Dąbrowa 2011, 230, with n. 40. The title ΒΑΣΙΛΕΩΣ first appeared on the Alexander tetradrachmas in 325 BCE in Babylon (Kontes 2000).
36. Lukonin 1983, 686, with n. 2, in which he cites the coin published in Morgan 1923–1936, 50, fig. 27, noting that "the figure of Apollo sitting on the omphalos [is] replaced by the figure of the legendary ancestor of the Arsakid dynasty, Ārish" – an idea that he attributes parenthetically to Zeimal'.
37. von Stackelberg 1891, 622–624; Bartolomae 1904, 203–204; Firdawsi, Warner, and Warner 1912, 197; *cf.* Кошеленко 1968, 65–68.
38. Gutschmid 1880, 743.
39. Thus Dayet 1949.
40. Mir Khvand and Shea 1832, 175; Nöldeke 1881, 445; Yarshater 1983, 372–373; Tafażżolī and Hanaway 2011.
41. al-Bīrūnī 1879, 20.
42. Panaino 1990, *Tištrya* no. 36 (p. 60); *cf.* no. 6 (p. 32); p. 76.
43. Nöldeke 1881, 445–447; von Stackelberg 1904, 853–854; Panaino 1990, 91, n. 5.
44. Panaino 1995, 52–53; *cf.* Panaino 1990, *Tištrya* no. 7 and 38; Panaino 1988.
45. Panaino 1990: 53, n. 24. In later tradition this act appears in the panels of numerous mithraea that decorate the walls, known as the "Miracle of the Water;" for a discussion with bibliography, Méndez 2006, 10–11. Tīr is associated with water and rain in the *Avesta* (Gray 1929, 115–116).
46. On the symbolic content of archery from a comparative perspective, see Coomaraswamy 1943.
47. Alram 1987, 117–118; pl. 13, no. 52–75; Vardanyan 2001, 27, 99–100, 106; Assar 2005, 36–46, fig. 6–15, 17; Fowler 2005, 147–149.
48. Winkelmann 2006, 131–132, 137, 139–141. For an overview of the significance of the archer in Achaemenid art and coins, see Garrison 2010, 337–356, and Lintz 2010, 370, 373–377; Nitschke 2013, 261–264; *cf.* Dąbrowa 2010, 128.
49. Зеймаль 1982, 48.
50. Зеймаль 1982, 47–48. Followed by Vardanyan 2001, 106; Iossif 2011, 272; Curtis 1996, 233. It is difficult to agree with Curtis' assignment that a similar reverse type exists on some of the coins

of Mazaios (361–333 BCE), the successor of Tarkamuwa/Datames at Tarsos, referenced to Hill 1900, pl. 30.9.

51. Opinion about the source of the *diphros* is divided: Zervos 1982, 168; Price 1982, 184–185 with n. 12.
52. Shahbazi 1974, 143–144; Shahbazi 1980, 140–145; *cf.* Vardanyan 2001, 100.
53. See Moysey 1986, 20.
54. For a concise history of the satrapy of Daskyleion, including the family of Pharnabazos, see Bakir 2001, 169–180.
55. On the identification of Zeus with Baal from the time of Alexander based on an analysis of these coins, see Wright 2010, 57–63.
56. Houghton, Lorber, and Hoover 2002–2008.
57. Bopearachchi 1991.
58. Curtis 1996, 233–234, 243; Alram 1996, 88–98.
59. Rostovtzeff 1922, 114.
60. Curtis 1996, 234.
61. Curtis 1996, 235, 243.
62. Кошеленко 1972, 97–98, and Rtveladze 2011, 149, date the event 160–150 BCE; Olbrycht 2010, 237, prefers 163–155 BCE with n. 42 for references to dates proposed by others in close proximity. For a discussion on 140–138 BCE proposed by Altheim and Stiehl 1970, 581–583, see Jenkins 1951, 16–17; Кошеленко 1972, 97; *cf.* Sève 2013, 219; *contra*, Dąbrowa, who, while in agreement that this expedition might have been Mithradates' first as king, concludes that no date reasonably can be attached to it (Dąbrowa 1998, 36–37; Dąbrowa 2005, 75; Dąbrowa 2006, 38).
63. Narain 1957, 53–58, 64, 69–73; Bopearachchi 1991, 66–73, 85–86; Smirnova 1992.
64. Knowledge about these events derive primarily from Justin 41.6.1–5; Strabon 11.11.2 [516–517]; and Moses of Khorene 2.68. For an overview of the campaign, see Lerner 2015.
65. Justin 41.6.7. On the date of the conquest of Media, Bivar 1983, 33.
66. Assar 2001a, 41; Assar 2001b, 17–22. The evidence largely depends on a Babylonian document dated to "about 165 B.C." that mentions Pilinusu, "the *strategos* of Akkad," went to Media to report to the "brother of the king" Bāgā-Asā (*i.e.* the Vacasis of Justin 41.6.7), Simonetta and Widemann 1978, 162, n. 9.
67. *Cf.* Curtis 2007, 418; Dąbrowa 2008, 27–29.
68. Boyce 1982, 21–22, 204–206; Panaino 1995, 108; Bernard 1990, 57–62.
69. Diakonoff and Livshits 2001, no. 1060.5, 1646.2.
70. Лившиц 2004, 191; Иванчик and Лурье 2013, 287.
71. Lurje 2010, no. 1004, 1277, 1278(?), 1279, 1289, 1291, 1292, 1294.
72. Grenet and Marshak 1998, 10–15.
73. Concise surveys of the evidence are presented in Iossif 2010; Iossif 2011; Iossif and Lorber 2009.
74. *OGIS* 245; *cf.* the parchment cited by Rostovtzeff 1935; Rostovtzeff 1939, 283–284.
75. Frisch 1975, no. 33.
76. Iossif 2010; Iossif 2011, 248–250, 252–257; *cf.* Iossif and Lorber 2011, 26–29 for a discussion on the solar imagery of Seleukos IV and Antiochos IV. Erickson 2011, 52, n. 6, argues that Apollo as a principal Seleukid deity did not appear on coins until 288 after Antiochos was well into his co-regency of the Upper Satrapies.
77. *OGIS* 212, 237, 219; Musti 1963, 225–239; Bresson 2001, 234–240; Ma 1999, 323–324, no. 22, and see also 84, 110. The first known Seleukid to pronounce the *syggeneia*, a variant of *syngeneia*, with Apollo was Seleukos II in 246/245 BCE in an inscription extending his gratitude to the citizens of Miletos and the sanctuary of Apollo Didymaios (Bringmann and von Steuben 1995, no. 282 E). It may have been at Didyma that the divine filiation between the Seleukids and Apollo was first announced with Seleukos I being proclaimed son or descendant of the god and where later Antiochos II received his epithet, *Theos* (Fontenrose 1988, 18, 168).

78. Müller 2013, 206–209.
79. *E.g.* Lerner 2003–2004, 391–395.
80. Bernard 1970, 339–347, fig. 31; Francfort 1984, 93–104, pl. XLI; Пичикян 1991, 256–259; Francfort 2007, 516–517. On an identical object found at Takht-i Sangin, see Пичикян 1987, 618; Литвинский and Пичикян 2000, 84 (no. 1174), *cf.* 285.
81. Bopearachchi 1991, 217–221. Curiously, their supposed contemporary, Heliokles I, did not (Bopearachchi 1991, 222–225).
82. Литвинский 2000.
83. Errington and Cribb 1992, 68.

Bibliography

al-Bīrūnī. (1879) *The chronology of ancient nations.* Translated and edited by C. E. Sachau. London, H. W. Allen & Co.

Alram, M. (1987) "Die Vorbildwirkung der arsakidischen Münzprägung." *Litterae Numismaticae Vindobonenses* 3, 117–146.

Alram, M. (1996) "Die Geschichte Irans von den Achaimeniden bis zu den Arsaciden (550 v. Chr.-224 n. Chr.)." In W. Seipel (ed.) *Weihrauch und Seide: alte Kulturen an der Seidenstraße: Kunsthistorisches Museum Wien, 21. Jänner bis 14. April 1996,* 73–98. Milan, Skiro.

Altheim, F. and Stiehl, R. (1970) *Geschichte Mittelasiens im Altertum.* Berlin, Walter de Gruyter.

Assar, G. F. (2001a) "Recent Studies in Parthian History: Part II. The Celator." *Journal of Ancient and Medieval Coinage* 15.1, 17–27, 41.

Assar, G. F. (2001b) "Recent Studies in Parthian History: Part III. The Celator." *Journal of Ancient and Medieval Coinage* 15.2, 17–22.

Assar, G. F. (2004) "Genealogy and coinage of the early Parthian rulers I." *Parthica* 6, 69–93.

Assar, G. F. (2005) "Genealogy and coinage of the early Parthian rulers, II: A revised stemma." *Parthica* 7, 29–63.

Assar, G. F. (2006) "Moses of Chorene and the early Parthian chronology." In E. Dąbrowa (ed.) *Greek and Hellenistic Studies.* Electrum 11, 61–86. Kraków, Wydawn, Uniwersytetu Jagiellonskiego.

Babelon, E. (1890) *Les rois de Syrie, d'Arménie et de Commagéne.* Paris, Rollin et Feuardent.

Bakir, T. (2001) "Die Satrapie in Daskyleion." In T. Bakir, H. Sancisi-Weerdenburg, G. Gürtekin, P. Briant, and W. Henkleman (eds.) *Achaemenid Anatolia. Proceedings of the first International Symposium on Anatolia in the Achaemenid Period, Bandirma 15-18 August 1997,* 169–180. Leiden, E. J. Brill.

Bartolomae, C. (1904) *Altiranisches Wörterbuch.* Strassburg, K. J. Trübner.

Bernard, P. (1970) "Communication. Campagne de fouilles 1969 à Aï Khanoum en Afghanistan." *Comptes Rendus de l'Académie des Inscriptions et Belles-Lettres,* 301–349.

Bernard, P. (1990) "Vicissitudes ay gré de l'histoire d'une statue en bronze d'Heraclès entre Séleucie du Tigre et la Mésène." *Journal des savants,* 3–68.

Bivar, A. D. H. (1983) "The Political History of Iran under the Arsacids." In E. Yarshater (ed.) *Cambridge History of Iran 3.1: The Seleucid, Parthian and Sasanian Periods,* 21–99. Cambridge, Cambridge University Press.

Boeft, J. den and Hengst, D. den (1995) *Philological and Historical Commentaries on Ammianus Marcellinus XXII.* Groningen, Wolters.

Boeft, J. den and Jonge, P. de (1998) *Philological and Historical Commentaries on Ammianus Marcellinus XXIII.* Groningen, Wolters.

Bopearachchi, O. (1991) *Monnaies gréco-bactriennes et indo-grecques: catalogue raisonné.* Paris, Bibliothèque nationale.

Boyce, M. (1982) *A history of Zoroastrianism, vol. 2: Under the Achaemenians.* Leiden, E.J. Brill.

Bresson, A. (2001) "Dédicace de Xanthiens à Antiochos III." In A. Bresson and R. Descat (eds.) *Les cités d'Asie Mineure occidentale au IIe siècle a.c.,* 234–240. Bordeaux, Ausonius.

Bringmann, K. and von Steuben, H. (1995) *Schenkungen hellenistischer Herrscher an griechische Städte und Heiligtümer. I. Zeugnisse und Kommentare.* Berlin, Akademie Verlag.

Casabonne, O. (2001) "De Tarse à Mazaka et de Tarkumuwa à Datâmes: D'une Cilicie à l'autre?" In É. Jean, A. M. Dinçol, and S. Durugönül (eds.) *La Cilicie. Espaces et pouvoirs locaux (2e millénaire av. J.-C. - 4e siècle ap. J.-C.): Actes de la table ronde internationale d'Istanbul, 2-5 novembre 1999,* 243–263. Paris, De Boccard.

Chaumont, M.-L. (1973) "Études d'histoire parthe, II: Capitales et residences des premiers Arsacides (IIIe–Ier s.av. J.-C.)." *Syria* 50, 197–222.

Colledge, M. A. R. (1967) *The Parthians. Ancient peoples and places.* New York, Praeger.

Coomaraswamy, A. K. (1943) "The symbolism of archery." *Ars Islamica* 10, 105–119.

Curtis, V. S. (1996) "Parthian and Sasanian furniture." In G. Herrmann and N. Parker (eds.) *The furniture of Western Asia ancient and traditional: papers of the conference held at the Institute of Archaeology, University College London, June 28 to 30, 1993,* 233–244. Mainz, Philipp von Zabern.

Curtis, V. S. (1998) "The Parthian costume and headdress." In J. Wiesehöfer (ed.) *Das Partherreich und seine Zeugnisse. The Arsacid Empire: Sources and Documentation. Beiträge des Internationalen Colloquiums, Eutin 27-30 June 1996).* Historia. Einzelschriften 122, 61–73. Stuttgart, F. F. Steiner Verlag.

Curtis, V. S. (2007) "Religious iconography on ancient Iranian coins." In J. Cribb and G. Herrmann (eds.) *After Alexander: Central Asia before Islam.* Proceedings of the British Academy 133, 413–434. Oxford, Oxford University Press.

Curtis, V. S. (2012) "Parthian coins: kingship and divine glory." In P. Wick and M. Zehnder (eds.) *The Parthian empire and its religions. Studies in the dynamics of religious diversity. Das Partherreich und seine Religionen. Studien zu Dynamiken religiöser Pluralität.* Pietas, vol. 5, 67–81. Gutenberg, Computus Druck Satz & Verlag.

Dąbrowa, E. (1998) "Philhellên. Mithridate Ier et les Grecs." *Electrum* 2, 35–44.

Dąbrowa, E. (2005) "Les aspects politiques et militaires de l'invasion de la Mésopotamie par les Parthes." *Electrum* 10, 73–88.

Dąbrowa, E. (2006) "The conquests of Mithradates I and the numismatic evidence." *Parthica* 8, 37–40.

Dąbrowa, E. (2008) "The political propaganda of the first Arsacids and its targets (from Arsaces I to Mithradates II)." *Parthica* 10, 25–31.

Dąbrowa, E. (2009) "Mithradates I and the beginning of the ruler-cult in Parthia." *Electrum* 15, 41–51.

Dąbrowa, E. (2010) "The Parthian Kingship." In G. B. Lanfranchi and R. Rollinger (eds.) *Concepts of kingship in antiquity. Proceedings of the European science foundation exploratory workshop held in Padova, November 28th-December 1st, 2007.* History of the Ancient Near East, Monographs 11, 123–134. Padova, S. A. R. G. O. N. Editrice e Libreria.

Dąbrowa, E. (2011) "ΑΡΣΑΚΕΣ ΕΠΙΦΑΝΗΣ. Were the Arsacids deities 'revealed'?" In B. Virgilio (ed.) *Studi Ellenistici* 24, 223–230. Pisa-Roma, Giardini editori e stampatori in Pisa.

Dayet, M. (1949) "Monnaies arsacides à bonnet satrapal." *Revue numismatique* 1949, 9–26, pl. II.

Diakonoff, I. M. and Livshits, V. A. (2001) *Parthian economic documents from Nisa, Texts I.* London, Lund Humphreys.

Drijvers, J. W. (1999) "Ammianus Marcellinus' image of Arsaces and early Parthian history." In J. W. Drijvers and D. Hunt (eds.) *The Late Roman World and Its Historian. Interpreting Ammianus Marcellinus,* 193–206. London, Routledge.

Eckhel, J. (1828) *Doctrina Numorum Veterum,* vol. 3.1. Vindobonae, Sumptibus Iosephi Vincentii Degen [tum] sumptibus Friderici Volke.

Erickson, K. (2011) "Apollo-Nabû: the Babylonian policy of Antiochus I." In K. Erickson, G. Ramsey, and C. E. Ghita (eds.) *Seleucid dissolution: the sinking of the anchor,* 51–65. Wiesbaden, Harrassowitz.

Firdawsi, Warner, A. G. and Warner, E. (1912) *The Sháhnáma of Firdausí,* vol. 6. London, Taylor and Francis.

Fontenrose, J. (1988) *Didyma: Apollo's oracle, cult, and companions.* Berkeley, University of California Press.

Fowler, R. (2005) "'Most fortunate roots': Tradition and legitimacy in Parthian royal ideology." In O. Hekster and R. Fowler (eds.) *Imaginary kings. Royal images in the ancient Near East, Greece and Rome*. Oriens et Occidens 11, 125–155. Stuttgart, F. F. Steiner Verlag.

Francfort, H.-P. (1984) *Le sanctuaire du temple à niches indentées. 2. Les trouvailles*. Mémoires de la Délégation Archéologique Française en Afghanistan 27. Fouilles d'Aï Khanoum 3. Paris, Klincksieck.

Francfort, H.-P. (2007) "Archéologie de l'Asie intérierure de l'âge du bronze à l'âge du fer." *École pratique des hautes etudes. Section des sciences historiques et philogiques. Livret-Annuaire* 21, 511–520.

Frisch, P. (1975) *Die Inschriften von Ilion*. Bonn, Habelt.

Gardner P. (1877) *The parthian coinage*. International numismata Orientalia, 5. London, Trübner.

Gariboldi, A. (2004) "Royal ideological patterns between Seleucid and Parthian coins: the case of θεοπάτωρ." In R. Rollinger and C. Ulf (eds.) *Commerce and monetary systems in the ancient world: means of transmission and cultural interaction. Proceedings of the Fifth Annual Symposium of the Assyrian and Babylonian Intellectual Heritage Project held in Innsbruck, Austria, October 3rd–8th 2002*. Melammu symposia 5, 366–384. Stuttgart, F. F. Steiner Verlag.

Garrison, M. B. (2010) "Archers at Persepolis: The emergence of royal ideology at the heart of the empire." In J. Curtis and St. J. Simpson (eds.) *The world of Achaemenid Persia: history, art and society in Iran and the ancient Near East. Proceedings of a conference at the British Museum 29th September–1st October 2005*, 337–359. London, British Museum.

Gaslain, J. (2005a) "Arsaces I, the First Arsacid King? Some Remarks on the Nature of Early Parthian Power." In В.П. Никоноров (ed.) *Центральная Азия от Ахеменидов сделать Тимуридов: археология, история, этнология, культура: Материалы международной научной конференции, посвященной 100-летию со дня рождения Александра Марковича Беленицкого, Санкт-Петербург, 2-5 ноября 2004 года*, 221–224. Санкт-Петербург, Институт Истории материальной культуры РАН.

Gaslain, J. (2005b) "Le bachlik d'Arsace Ier ou la representation du nomade-roi." *Bulletin of Parthian and Mixed Oriental Studies* 1, 9–30.

Gnoli, Gh. (1998) "L'Iran tardoantico e la regalità sassanide." *Mediterraneo Antico* 1.1, 115–139.

Gray, L.H. (1929) *The foundations of the Iranian religions*. Bombay.

Grenet, F. and Marshak, B.I. (1998) "Le myth de Nana dans l'art de la Sogdiane." *Arts Asiatiques* 53, 5–18.

Günther, L.-M. (2011) "Herrscher als Götter – Götter als Herrscher? Zur Ambivalenz hellenistischer Münzbilder." In L.-M. Günther und S. Plischke (eds.), *Studien zum vorhellenistischen und hellenistischen Herrscherkult*. Oikumene Studien zur antiken Weltgeschichte 9, 98–113. Berlin, Verlag Antike.

Gutschmid, A. von (1880) "Bemerkungen zu Tabari's Sasanidengeschichte übersetzt von Th. Nöldeke." *Zeitschrift der morgenlandischen Gesellschaft* 34, 721–748.

Gutschmid, A. von. (1888) *Geschichte Irans und seiner Nachbarländer von Alexander dem Grossen bis zum Untergang der Arsaciden*. Tübingen, H. Laupp.

Harmatta, J. (1951) "The golden bow of the Huns." *Acta archaeologica Academiae Scientiarum Hungaricae* 1.1–2, 114–149.

Harrison, C. M. (1982) Coins of the Persian satraps. Unpublished thesis, University of Pennsylvania.

Hill, G. F. (1900) *Catalogue of the Greek coins of Lycaonia, Isauria, and Cilicia*. London, The Trustees.

Houghton, A., Lorber, C. C. and Hoover, O. D. (2002–2008) *Seleucid coins: a comprehensive catalogue*, vol. 1.1–2.2. New York, The American Numismatic Society; London, Classical Numismatic Group.

Hutter, M. (2003) "Aspects of Luwian religion." In H. C. Melchert (ed.), *The Luwians*, 211–280. Leiden, E. J. Brill.

Invernizzi, A. (2011) "Royal cult in Arsakid Parthia." In P. P. Iossif, A. S. Chankowski, and C. C. Lorber (eds.) *More than Men, Less than Gods: Studies on Royal Cult and Imperial Worship. Proceedings of the international colloquium organized by the Belgian school at Athens (November 1-2, 2007).* Studia Hellenistica 51, 649–690. Leuven, Peeters.

Iossif, P. P. (2010) "Imago mundi: expression et representation de l'idéologie royale séleucide. La procession de Daphné." *Electrum* 18, 121–152.

Iossif, P. P. (2011) "Apollo Toxotes and the Seleukids: Comme un air de famille." In P. P. Iossif, A. S. Chankowski, and C. C. Lorber (eds.) *More than Men, Less than Gods: Studies on Royal Cult and Imperial Worship. Proceedings of the international colloquium organized by the Belgian school at Athens (November 1-2, 2007).* Studia Hellenistica 51, 229–291. Leuven, Peeters.

Iossif, P. P. and Lorber, C. C. (2009) "The cult of Helios in the Seleucid East." *Topoi* 16, 19–42.

Jenkins, G. K. (1951) "Notes on Seleucid Coins." *Numismatic Chronicle*, ser. 6, 11, 1–21.

Kontes, Z. S. (2000) "The dating of the coinage of Alexander the Great." Brown University's Institute for Archeology and the Ancient World, http://www.brown.edu/Departments/Joukowsky_Institute/publications/papers/alexander_coinage/alexander.html#f15.

László, G. (1951) "The Significance of the Hun Golden Bow." *Acta archaeologica Academiae Scientiarum Hungaricae* 1.1–2, 91–106.

Le Rider, G. (1964) *Suse sous les Séleucides et les Parthes: les trouvailles monétaires et l'histoire de la ville.* Mémoires de la Mission archéologique en Iran, 38. Paris, P. Geuthner.

Lerner, J. D. (1999) *The impact of Seleucid decline on the eastern Iranian plateau. The foundations of Arsacid Parthia and Graeco-Bactria.* Historia. Einzelschriften 123. Stuttgart, F. Steiner Verlag.

Lerner, J. D. (2003–2004) "Correcting the early chronology of Āy Kānom." *Archäologische Mitteilungen aus Iran und Turan* 35–36, 373–410.

Lerner, J. D. (2015) "Mithradates I's Conquest of Western Greek-Baktria." Проблемы истории, филологии, культуры = *Journal of historical, philological, and cultural Studies* 47.1, 45–55.

Lintz, Y. (2010) "The archer coins: a closer examination of Achaemenid art in Asia Minor." In J. Curtis and St. J. Simpson (eds.) *The world of Achaemenid Persia: history, art and society in Iran and the ancient Near East. Proceedings of a conference at the British Museum 29th September-1st October 2005*, 369–377. London, I. B. Tauris.

Longpérier, A. de (1853) *Mémoires sur la chronologie et l'iconographie des rois parthes Arsacides.* Paris, É. Leroux.

Lukonin, G. (1983) "Political, social and administrative institutions: taxes and trade." In E. Yarshater (ed.) *The Cambridge History of Iran. Vol. 3.2: The Seleucid, Parthian and Sasanian periods*, 681–746. Cambridge, Cambridge University Press.

Lurje, P. B. (2010) *Personal names in Sogdian texts.* Wien, Verlag der Osterreichischen Akademie der Wissenschaften.

Luther, A. (2006–2007) "Zur Genealogie der frühen Partherkönige." *Iranistik. Deutschsprachige Zeitschrift für Iranistische Studien* 5, 39–55.

Ma, J. (1999) *Antiochos III and the cities of western Asia Minor.* Oxford, Oxford University Press.

Martinez-Sève, L. (2014) "Remarques sur la transmission aux Parthes des pratiques de gouvernement séleucides: modalités et chronologie." *Ktèma: civilisations de l'Orient, de la Grèce et de Rome antiques* 39, 123–142.

Méndez, I. C. (2006) "Continuity and Change in the Cult of Mithra." *Mithras Journal: an academic and religious journal of Greek, Roman and Persian Studies* 1, 5–22.

Meyer, C. (2013) *Greco-Scythian art and the birth of Eurasia.* Oxford, Oxford University Press.

Mir Khvand, M. ibn Khavandshah and Shea, D. (1832) *History of the early kings of Persia: from Kaiomars, the first of the Peshdadian dynasty, to the conquest of Iran by Alexander the Great.* London, Oriental Translation Fund of Great Britain and Ireland.

Morgan, J. J. M. de. (1923–1936) *Manuel de numismatique orientale de l'Antiquité et du Moyen Age,* vol. 1. Paris, Paul Geuthner.

Moysey, R. A. (1986) "The silver stater issues of Pharnabazos and Datames from the mint of Yarsus in Cilicia." *American Numismatic Society Museum Notes* 31, 7–62.

Müller, S. (2013) "The female element of the political self-fashoning of the Diadochi: Ptolemy, Seleucus, Lysimachus, and their Iranian wives." In A. T. Víctor and E. M. Anson (eds.) *After Alexander: the time of the Diadochi (323–281 BC)*, 199–214. Oxford, Oakville, CT.

Musti, D. (1963) "Sull'idea di syngeneia in iscrizioni greche." *Annali della Scuola. Normale di Pisa*, ser. 2, 32, 225–239.

Narain, A. K. (1957) *The Indo-Greeks*. Oxford, Clarendon Press.

Newell, E. T. (1938) "The coinage of the Parthian." In A. U. Pope, P. Ackerman, and T. Bestermann (eds.) *A survey of Persian art from prehistoric times to the present,* vol. 1, 475–492. Oxford, Oxford University Press.

Neusner, J. (1963) "Parthian political ideology." *Iranica Antiqua* 3.1, 40–59.

Nitschke, J. L. (2013) "Interculturality in Image and Cult in the Hellenistic East: Tyrian Melqart Revisited." In E. Stavrianopoulou (ed.) *Shifting social imaginaries in the Hellenistic period: narrations, practices, and images*. Mnemosyne supplements, vol. 363, 253–282. Leiden, E. J. Brill.

Nöldeke, Th. (1881) ""Der beste der arischen Pfeilschützen" im Awestâ und im Tabarî." *Zeitschrift der Deutschen Morgenländischen Gesellschaft* 35, 445–447.

Nöldeke, Th. (1884) Review of Krumholz, P. *De Asiae minoris satapis persicis' Göttingische gelehrte Anzeiger* 8, 290–300.

Olbrycht, M. J. (1996) "Die Beziehungen der Steppennomaden Mittelasiens zu den hellenistischen Staaten (bis zum Ende des 3. Jahrhunderts vor Chr.)." In B. Funck (ed.), *Hellenismus. Beiträge zur Erforschung von Akkulturation und politischer Ordnung in den Staaten des hellenistischen Zeitalters*, 147–169. Tübingen, J. C. B. Mohr.

Olbrycht, M. J. (1998) *Parthia et ulteriores gentes: die politischen Beziehungen zwischen dem arsakidischen Iran und den Nomaden der eurasischen Steppen*. Quellen und Forschungen zur antiken Welt, 30. Munich, Tuduv-Verlagsgesellschaft.

Olbrycht, M. J. (2003) "Parthia and nomads of Central Asia. Elements of steppe origin in the social and military development of Arsacid Iran." *Orientwissenschaftliche Hefte* 12, 69–109.

Olbrycht, M. J. (2010) "Mithradates I of Parthia and his conquests up to 141 B.C." In E. Dąbrowa, M. Dzielska, M. Salamon, and S. Sprawski (*eds.*), *Hortus Historiae. Księga pamiątkowa ku czci profesora Józefa Wolskiego w setną rocznicę urodzin*, 229–245. Kraków, Towarzystwo Wydawnicze "Historia Iagellonica."

Olbrycht, M. J. (2013) "The titulature of Arsaces I, king of Parthia." *Parthica* 15, 63–74.

OGIS = Dittenberger, W. (ed.) (1903–1905) *Orientis Graeci Inscriptiones Selectae*. Leipzig.

Panaino, A. (1990) *Tištrya. Part 1: The Avestan hymn to Sirius*. Serie Orientale Roma 68.1. Rome, Istituto italiano per il Medio ed Estremo Oriente.

Panaino, A. (1995) *Tištrya. Part 2: The Iranian myth of the star Sirius*. Serie Orientale Roma 68.1. Rome, Istituto italiano per il Medio ed Estremo Oriente.

Panaino, A. (1988) "Tištrya e Miθra." *Annali della Facoltà di Lettere e Filosofia dell'Università degli Studi di Milano* 41.3, 229–242.

Price, M. J. (1982) "2. Alexander's reform of the Macedonian regal coinage." In O. H. Zervos and M. J. Price. "Debate. The earliest coins of Alexander the Great." *Numismatic Chronicle* 142, 166–190, pls. 43–47 (specifically 180–190, pls. 46–47).

Rostovtzeff, M. I. (1922) *Iranians Greeks in South Russia*. Oxford, Clarendon Press.

Rostovtzeff, M. (1935) "Progonoi." *Journal of Hellenic Studies* 55, 56–66.

Rostovtzeff, M. (1939) "Some remarks on the monetary and commercial policy of the Seleukids and Attalids." In W. M. Calder and J. Keil (eds.) *Anatolian studies presented to W. H. Buckler*, 277–298. Manchester, Manchester University Press.

Rtveladze, E. V. (2011) "Parthians in the Oxus valley. Struggle for the Great Indian Road." *Anabasis: Studia classica et orientalia* 2, 149–168.

Seltman, C. (1955) *Greek coins. A history of metallic currency and coinage down to the fall of the Hellenistic kingdoms*. 2nd ed. London, Methuen.

Sève, L. M. (2013) "Données historiques." In G. Lecuyot, *L'habitat,* with contributions from P. Bernard, H.-P. Francfort, B. Lyonnet, and L. M. Sève. Fouilles d'Aï Khanoum 9. Mémoires de la Délégation archéologique française en Afghanistan 34, 213–220. Paris, De Boccard.

Seyfarth, W. (1978) *Ammiani Marcellini Rerum Gestarum libri qui supersunt,* vol. 1–2. Berlin, B. G. Teubner.

Shahbazi, A. Sh. (1974) "An Achaemenid symbol, I. A farewell to 'Fravahr' and 'Ahuramazda.'" *Archaeologische Mitteilungen aus Iran.* Neue Folge 7, 135–144.

Shahbazi, A. Sh. (1980) "An Achaemenid symbol, II. Fravahr (god given) fortune symbolized." *Archaeologische Mitteilungen aus Iran.* Neue Folge 13, 119–147.

Simonetta, B. (1950) "A proposito di monete arsacidi con 'Berretto satrapale.'" *Numismatica* 19, 22–25.

Simonetta, B. (1955) "A proposito di monete arsacidi con "Berretto satrapale."" Translated by H. A. Murray. *New Zealand Numismatic Journal* Sep–Dec 1955, 115–120.

Simonetta, M. and Widemann, F. (1978) "The Chronology of the Gondopharean Dynasty." *East and West* 28.1–4, 155–187.

Six, J. P. (1884) "Le satrap Mazaios." *Numismatic Chronicle* 4, 97–159.

Smirnova, N. (1992) "Coins of Eucratides in Museum Collections." *East and West* 42.1, 85–102.

Stackelberg, R. von (1891) "Iranica." *Zeitschrift der Deutschen Morgenländischen Gesellschaft* 45, 620–628.

Stackelberg, R. von (1904) "Die iranische Schützensage." *Zeitschrift der Deutschen Morgenländischen Gesellschaft* 58, 853–858.

Tafażżolī, A. and Hanaway, Jr., W. L. (2011) "ĀRAŠ." *Encyclopedia Iranica,* updated. http://www.iranicaonline.org/articles/aras-avestan-erexsa.

Vardanyan, R. (2001) "Tendenzene culturali e ideologiche nell'impero portico riflesse dalla Monetazione." *Parthica* 3, 25–132.

Wiesehöfer, J. (1996) "'King of Kings' and 'Philhellên': Kingship in Arsacid Iran." In P. Bilde, T. Engberg-Pedersen, L. Hannestad, and J. Zahle (eds.) *Aspects of Hellenistic Kingship.* Aspects of Hellenistic Kingship 7, 55–66. Aarhus, Aarhus University Press.

Wiesehöfer, J. (2003) "Tarkumuwa und das Farnah." In W. Henkelman and A. Kuhrt (eds.) *A Persian perspective. Essays in memory of Helleen Sancisi-Weerdenburg.* Achaemenid History 13, 173–187. Leiden, E. J. Brill.

Winkelmann, S. (2006) "Waffen und Waffenträger auf parthischen Münzen." *Parthica* 8, 131–152.

Wolski, J. (1969) "Der Zusammenbruch der Seleukidenherrschaft im Iran im 3. Jahrhundert v.Chr." In F. Altheim and J. Rehork (eds.) *Der Hellenismus in Mittelasien,* 188–254. Darmstadt, Buchges.

Wright, N. L. (2010) Religion in Seleukid Syria: gods at the crossroads (301–64 BC). Unpublished thesis, Macquarie University.

Wroth, W. W. (1964 [reprinted 1903 ed.]) *Catalogue of the coins of Parthia. A Catalogue of the Greek coins in the British Museum.* Bologna, A. Forni.

Yarshater, E. (1983) "Iranian national history." In E. Yarshater (ed.) *The Cambridge History of Iran. Vol. 3.1: The Seleucid, Parthian and Sasanian periods,* 359–477. Cambridge, Cambridge University Press.

Zervos, O. H. (1982) "1. Notes on a book by Gerhard Kleiner." In O. H. Zervos and M. J. Price. "Debate. The earliest coins of Alexander the Great." *Numismatic Chronicle* 142, 166–190, pls. 43–47 (specifically 166–179, pls. 43–45).

Zervos, O. H. and Price, M. J. (1982) "Debate. The earliest coins of Alexander the Great." *Numismatic Chronicle* 142, 166–190, pls. 43–47.

Zograf, A. N. (1977) *Ancient coinage.* Translated by H. B. Wells. BAR supplementary series, 33. Oxford, British Archaeological Reports.

Зеймаль, Е. В. (1982) "Парфянский лучник и его происхождение." *Сообщения Государственного Эрмитажа* 47, 46–49.

Зограф, А. Н. (1951) *Античные монеты.* Материалы и исследования по археологии СССР 16. Москва, Искусство.

Иванчик, А.И. and Лурье, П.Б. (2013) "Две надписи из Чирик-работа." In С. Р. Тохтасьев and П. Б. Лурье (eds.) *Commentationes Iranicae. Сборник статей к 90-летию Владимира Ароновича Ливщица*, 286–295. Санкт Петербург, Нестор-История.

Кошеленко, Г. А. (1968) "Некоторые вопросы истории ранней Парфии." *Вестник древней истории* 1968.1, 53–71.

Кошеленко, Г. А. (1971) "Царская власть и её обоснование в ранней Парфии." In Б. Г. Гафуров (отв. ред.) *История Иранского государства и культуры (к 2500-летию Иранского государства)*, 212–218. Москва, Наука.

Кошеленко, Г. А. (1972) "Монетное дело Парфи и при Митридате I." *Нумизматика и эпиграфика* 10, 79–102.

Кошеленко, Г. А. and Гаибов, В. А. (2010) "Нумизматические данные по проблеме царского культа в Парфии." *Вестник древней истории* 3, 169–178.

Кошеленко, Г. А. and Гаибов, В. А. (2012) "Монетное дело Парфии пре Аршаке II." *Проблемы истории, филологии, культуры. Памяти Бориса Анатольевича Литвинского* 4.38, 24–33.

Ливщиц, В. А. (2004) "Надписи и документы." In В. И. Вайнберг (ed.) *Калалы-Гыр II. Культовый центр в древнем Хорезме IV-II вв. до н.э.*, 188–213. Москва, Восточная лит-ра РАН.

Литвинский, В. А. (2000) "Гелиос в храме Окса." *Вестник древней истории* 230.1, 57–65.

Литвинский, В. А. and Пичикян, И. Р. (2000) *Эллинистический храм Окса в Бактрии (Южный Таджикистан). Т. 1. Раскопки. Архитектура. Религизная жизнь*. Москва, Vostochnaia лит-ра РАН.

Марков, А. К. (1892a) "Неизданные арсакидские монеты." *Записки Восточного отделения Русского археологического общества* 6, 265–304, pl. 3.1.

Марков, А. К. (1892b) *Неизданные арсакидские монеты*. Санкт-Петербург, Типография Императорской Академии Наук.

Пичикян, И. Р. (1987) "Раскопки на Тахти-Сангине." *Археологическое открытия 1985 года*, 618.

Пичикян, И. Р. (1991) *Культура Бактрии (ахеменидский и эллинистический периоды)*. Москва, Наука.

Раевский, Д. С. (1970) "Скифский мифологический сюжет в искусстве и идеологии царства Атея." *Советская археология* 1970.3, 90–101.

Раевский, Д. С. (1977a) "К вопросу об обосновании царской власти в Парфии («Парфянский лучник» и его семантика)." In Б. Г. Гафурова and Б. А. Литвинского (eds.) *Средняя Азия в древности и средневековье (история и культура)*, 81–86. Москва, Наука.

Раевский, Д. С. (1977b) *Очерки идеологии скифо-сакских племен*. Москва, Главная редакция восточной литературы издательства "Наука."

Ростовцев, М. И. (1914) "Воронежский серебряный сосуд." *Материалы по археологии России, издаваемые Императорской археологической комиссией* 34, 79–93.

Chapter 2

The Seleucids Imprisoned: Arsacid-Roman Hostage Submission and Its Hellenistic Precedents

Jake Nabel

From around 200 BCE, the chief political development in the ancient Mediterranean and Near East was the defeat and annexation of the Hellenistic kingdoms by two groups of barbarians, each at the head of an expansionist empire: the Parthians in the east and the Romans in the west. In the following centuries these two powers steadily conquered their way towards one another and, ultimately, carved up nearly the entire Greek world between them – a world that exerted profound influence even as the political formations that ruled it collapsed.

Long before Rome and Parthia shared a border along the Euphrates, then, the two empires were already connected through their mutual experiences with the Hellenistic monarchies, first and foremost as their conquerors, but also as the students and adapters of their ruling strategies and cultural practices.[1] The most direct aspect of this connection was their common engagement with the Seleucid empire, the most expansive of all the Hellenistic polities and a victim of both Parthian and Roman imperialism. Both Rome and Parthia fought the Seleucids, they both negotiated with the Seleucids, and they both – as this contribution examines – took members of the Seleucid royal family as hostages and prisoners.

The following discussion investigates whether and to what extent a shared historical experience with captive Seleucid monarchs prefigured Roman-Parthian relations during the Julio-Claudian period. From *c.* 30 BCE to 66 CE, numerous members of the Arsacid family (Parthia's ruling dynasty) were held captive in Rome for extended periods of time; in several cases, individuals from this group returned to Parthia, where they sought the Arsacid kingship.[2] How did the Seleucid prisoners of Rome and Parthia shape later ideas about how captive dynasts were to be used? Were the Arsacid hostages of the Julio-Claudian period cut from the same cloth as the Seleucids of the Hellenistic era, or were they something different?

Much of the literature on Seleucid prisoners has described them as the tools of imperialism, a way of subordinating the Seleucid kingdom to a Parthian or Roman imperial order through the creation of an obedient and submissive client king.[3] But if such logic did underpin the Roman and Parthian utilization of their royal captives, there were distinct grounds for disappointment: released Seleucid hostages and prisoners do not seem, on balance, to have done much to further the interests of their former captors. So while there were some similarities between the imprisoned Seleucids of the Hellenistic era and the Arsacid hostages of early imperial Rome, the royal prisoner's poor performance as an agent of empire in the former period may have contributed to an important change in the latter. In a world divided between Rome and Parthia, the royal prisoner became a way for leaders in both empires to pursue domestic political goals through their counterparts across the Euphrates, sustaining an international connection that was built on the mutual pursuit of internal objectives.

The Prisoners

The evidence for Seleucid and Arsacid hostages and prisoners is collected in the following tables, which include all members of these families held involuntarily and under compulsion in either Parthian or Roman custody. Cases of doubtful historicity are indicated with an asterisk. The disparities in the level of documentation are considerable. Since almost all the relevant evidence is Greco-Roman and literary, there is much less information available on Seleucid-Parthian relations. The lack of Parthian literary sources means that Greco-Roman accounts of Arsacid "hostages" (Greek ὅμηροι, Latin *obsides*) cannot be taken at face value. A Sasanian inscription from the late third century CE preserves the Parthian word for hostage (*nēpāk*).[4] But there is no way to know whether the Arsacids would have used this term for the members of their family who went to Rome. As discussed below, their understanding of the exchange may have been considerably different.

Although several cases are obscure, it is clear that a relatively high number of Seleucids spent time in captivity. Most conventional chronologies count 26 kings from the founder Seleucus I Nicator to Antiochus XIII, whose dethronement by Pompey in 65/64 BCE is usually understood to mark the end of the dynasty.[5] Of these kings, four were held in custody in either Rome (Antiochus IV, Demetrius I) or Parthia (Demetrius II, Demetrius III). There are an additional three (Seleucus II, Seleucus V, Antiochus X) whose stories are unclear or ambiguously reported in the sources, but they too may have been prisoners among the Parthians. Ultimately, at least 15% of the monarchs who sat on the Seleucid throne were captives in either Rome or Parthia at some point during their lives, and the figure may well be higher.

No cases of Parthian kings held captive among the Seleucids are known. Their absence from the historical record might simply be due to the meagerness of the ancient sources for Seleucid-Parthian affairs. On the other hand, the Seleucids were on the back foot against the Parthians for most of the two empires' coexistence,

Table 2.1: Seleucids in Parthia

Name	Date	Sources
Seleucus II*	c. 236 BCE	Athen., *Deip.* 12.438, 153a–b = Posidonius, *BNJ* 87 F 12; *cf.* Just. 41.4.9–5.2; Strab. 11.8.8; Lerner 1999, 35–37; Plischke 2014, 239
Demetrius II	139/138 BCE	Just. 36.1.1–6, 38.9.2–3; Sachs and Hunger 1996, no. –137 'Rev.' 8'–11' (=p. 160–161); Joseph., *AJ* 13.184–186; App., *Syr.* 67; *1 Maccabees* 14.1–3; Euseb., *Chron.* 117.1–124.5 [Karst] = Porphyry, *BNJ* 260 F 32 = *FrGH* 260 F 32.16; Diod. 33.28; Oros. 5.4.18; Moses Khorenats'i 2.2 (= Thomson 1978, 131–132)
Seleucus, son of Antiochus VII*	129 BCE	Euseb., *Chron.* 117.1–124.5 [Karst] = Porphyry, *BNJ* 260 F 32 = *FrGH* 260 F 32.19–20
Daughter of Antiochus VII	129 BCE	Just. 38.10.10
Seleucus V*	129 BCE	Ath., *Deip.* 12.438, 153a–b = Posidonius, *BNJ* 87 F 12; *cf.* Bouché-Leclercq 1913–1914, 1.386, 1.393, n. 2, 2.600
Antiochus X*[i]	c. 90–88 BCE	Euseb., *Chron.* 117.1–124.5 [Karst] = Porphyry, *BNJ* 260 F 32 = *FrGH* 260 F 32.27f; *cf.* Joseph., *AJ* 13.370–371; App., *Syr.* 69
Demetrius III	c. 88/87 BCE	Joseph., *AJ* 13.384–386

[i]Porphyry has Antiochus X going into exile with the Parthians, not imprisonment. I include him in the table here on the grounds that, if he did reach the Parthians, his position at the Arsacid court presumably would have been similar to that of Demetrius III, who according to Josephus was a Parthian captive (if one held in honor).

Table 2.2: Seleucids in Rome

Name	Date	Sources
Antiochus IV	189/188 BCE	Polyb. 21.43.22; Liv. 38.38.15; Diod. 29.10; Ascon., *In Pison.* p. 13 [Clark] = Atticus, fr. 6P = FRH 33 F 7; App., *Syr.* 39; Memnon, *FrGH* 434 F 18.9 = *BNJ* 434 F 1.9; Just. 34.3.2; *1 Maccabees* 1.10
Demetrius I	178 BCE	Polyb. 31.2, 31.11–15; Liv., *Per.* 46.12; Diod. 31.18; App., *Syr.* 45; Just. 34.3.6; Granius Licinianus 28.39.1–40.1 [Criniti]; Euseb., *Chron.* 117.1–124.5 [Karst] = Porphyry, *BNJ* 260 F 32 = *FrGH* 260 F 32.14

so their failure to capture an Arsacid dynast would be understandable.[6] There is of course no royalty to speak of in the Roman Republic. But a member from one of Rome's most prestigious families was temporarily a prisoner among the Seleucids: Lucius Cornelius Scipio, son of the famous Publius Scipio Africanus, was captured by Antiochus III during the run-up to Magnesia.[7] Antiochus treated him generously and returned him to Africanus with no conditions attached. Africanus' political enemies would later highlight this kindness while prosecuting the commander for collusion with Antiochus, among other crimes.[8] A charge of collaboration with his son's former captor – whether true or not – helped bring down one of the most illustrious figures in Roman politics. This sort of accusation was frequently encountered by royal hostages and prisoners, as discussed below.

Rome hosted a considerable number of Arsacids during the early empire. Precise figures are rarely available, but an estimate of one or two dozen seems reasonable as

Table 2.3: Arsacids in Rome

Name	Date	Sources
Son of Phraates IV	*c.* 30 BCE	Dio 51.18.2–3, 53.33.1–2; Just. 42.5.6–9; *cf. Mon. Anc.* 32.1
Vonones, Phraates, Seraspadanes, Rhodaspes, two wives, four sons	*c.* 19–10 BCE	*Mon. Anc.* 32.2; Vell. Pat. 2.94.4; Strab. 6.4.2, 16.1.28; Joseph., *AJ* 18.42; Tac., *Ann.* 2.1.2; Suet., *Aug.* 21.3; Just. 42.5.11–12; Fest. 19.4; Oros. 6.21.29; Eutrop. 7.9; *CIL* 6.1799
Darius	*c.* 36/37 CE	Joseph., *AJ* 18.96, 18.101–5; Suet., *Calig.* 14.3; *Vit.* 2.4; Dio 59.27.2–3
Several Arsacids	55 CE	Tac., *Ann.* 13.9.1
Daughter of Tiridates,[i] other Arsacids*	63 CE	Tac., *Ann.* 15.30.2; Dio 62.23.4
Several Arsacids	66 CE	Dio 63.1.2; *cf.* Plin., *HN* 6.23
Daughter of Osroes, other Arsacids*[ii]	*c.* 114 CE	SHA, *Had.* 13.8; Aurel. Vict., *Lib. Caes.* 13.3
Zalaces*[iii]	*c.* 117 CE	Juv. 2.164

[i]Tiridates' daughter may only have remained a hostage until peace was ratified: Elbern 1990, 100, 140.
[ii]This hostage transfer (Aurel. Vict., *Lib. Caes.* 13.3) is not mentioned in any of the other extant sources for Trajan's Parthian campaign, and it is quite possibly not historical.
[iii]Zalaces appears only in Juvenal's second Satire, which was written near the end of Trajan's reign or the beginning of Hadrian's: Syme 1984, 1135–1157; Braund 1996, 16. It cannot be determined when his hostageship began or ended. He may have been an Arsacid; see Wheeler 2002, 290; Ferguson 1987, 249. On the passage, see further Courtney 1980, 149–150; Braund 1996, 164–167; Isaac 2004, 232–233.

a ballpark figure. Royal women were among them, which means that at least some contenders for the Parthian throne were born and raised at Rome.[9] Over the course of the Julio-Claudian period the emperors released one Arsacid at the request of a Parthian king, and four at the request of certain Parthian noblemen.[10] Of those released, three (Vonones I, Tiridates II, Meherdates) would hold brief kingships. The evidence for continued Arsacid hostage submission after the reign of Nero is slight, and it may have ceased altogether.

No Arsacid king ever captured his Roman counterpart; the Sasanian Shapur I's seizure of Valerian in 260 CE was the only time an emperor fell into enemy hands.[11] Arsacid-Roman hostage submission was apparently not reciprocal: there is no record of any Roman dynast, Julio-Claudian or otherwise, imprisoned in Nisa or Ctesiphon. A few non-royal but still high-ranking Romans are occasionally seen in Parthian custody. But these seem to have been temporary arrangements and far less consequential than the Arsacids at Rome.[12] Upon the collapse of his regime in 218 CE, the emperor Macrinus is said by Dio to have dispatched his son and co-ruler Diadumenian to the Parthian king Artabanus V. Had Diadumenian lived, it is conceivable that his position at the Arsacid court might have resembled that of the Seleucid captives of an earlier age. But he was caught and killed in Roman territory.[13] The gaps in the historical record may conceal similar cases, but this can be no more than speculation.

Royal Prisoners and Foreign Policy

What was a royal prisoner or hostage good for? Many ancient sources and modern discussions provide one answer: they were a way to project power and integrate territory into a new imperial order. After a lengthy captivity, the royal prisoner's release and installation on the throne of his native land would – in theory – subordinate his kingdom's possessions to the interests of his former captors. His acquiescence, it is sometimes thought, was insured through a process of acculturation to the norms and views of his hosts, a transformation that helped reconcile him with their imperial project and expansionist aims. These arguments are found most frequently in the literature on royal hostages and prisoners in the Roman Republic and Principate, but they have been applied to Parthian history as well. For both Parthia and Rome, Seleucid captives supply important case studies.[14]

But if this logic did underpin the Parthian and Roman use of their Seleucid captives, it is difficult to see the practice as a strategic masterstroke. The Seleucids who took the throne after confinement in either the Arsacid court or in Rome do not appear to have been the pawns of their former captors. And while it is safe to assume that these prisoners and hostages were profoundly shaped by their years of confinement, it is less clear that their transformations obtained any benefits for Parthia or Rome in the realm of international politics.

The hostageship of Antiochus IV is an illustrative example for the Roman side. Antiochus became a hostage in compliance with the terms of the Peace of Apamea, signed in 189/188 BCE. Among other conditions, the treaty required Antiochus III to furnish twenty hostages between 18 and 45 years of age who were to be exchanged every three years.[15] It is not entirely clear whether Antiochus met these age requirements, since the year of his birth cannot be firmly established. But the stipulation that the hostages be switched after three years clearly did not apply to him. He would not leave Rome until 178/177 BCE, when Seleucus IV sent his son Demetrius to take his place.[16]

While at Rome, Antiochus moved in the highest circles of power. A house was erected for him at public expense, and since the wealthy poet Lucilius lived there a few decades later, the dwelling was probably a comfortable one and commensurate with Antiochus' royal status.[17] Polybius' description of the Roman life of Antiochus' successor Demetrius – a personal acquaintance of the historian – shows that Seleucid hostages enjoyed several amenities. Demetrius could roam within the city and even outside of it at will; slaves attended him; he owned dogs and nets for hunting trips in the nearby town of Circeii. He apparently was not guarded. After his escape to Syria, it took four days for his absence to arouse any suspicion.[18] Antiochus probably lived under similar conditions. A Seleucid envoy would later exclaim before the Senate that, during Antiochus' time at Rome, "he was treated by all classes as a king, not as a hostage." The context of the speech is diplomatic and Antiochus had reasons to lay it on thick, but the claim might not have been too far from the truth.[19]

Privilege meant not only material comforts, but also contact with Rome's ruling elite and exposure to Roman political life. The ancient sources give the impression that association with the powerful left its mark on the hostage, who is said to have later adopted certain Roman customs. After his return to Syria, Antiochus would sometimes exchange his kingly attire for a simple toga, canvass the neighborhoods of Antioch for votes, and dispense judgments from a curule chair. He is also supposed to have built a temple for Jupiter Optimus Maximus in Antioch and staged Roman gladiatorial displays.[20]

It is unclear where these reports originated, and whether they are reliable. The evidence permits no firm conclusions, but it may be useful to consider a range of possibilities. Antiochus' Romanized habits could simply be the invention of Polybius, who may have fabricated or exaggerated such behavior to support his portrayal of a mad and undignified king.[21] Another suggestion is that Antiochus really did mimic Roman customs, but as "gentle mockery rather than serious imitation" of his former captors.[22] It is also worth noting, though, that the negative reports of Romanized behavior are all tied to Antioch near Daphne. The connection suggests that the tales of the king's Roman antics might have originally come from Antiochenes hostile to his regime.[23] The possibility exists, therefore, that certain inhabitants of the Seleucid kingdom used Antiochus' hostageship to caricature him as a Romanized quisling.

The idea that Antiochus' enemies within the Seleucid realm used his Roman hostageship as a propaganda weapon against him is supported by comparanda. The most pertinent case from Hellenistic history is the successful campaign of the Antigonid Perseus to cast his younger brother Demetrius – a hostage at Rome from 197–191 BCE – as a traitor and a Roman collaborator.[24] Although the evidence for Demetrius' treason was meager, Perseus was nevertheless able to convince their father Philip V of his brother's guilt, and Demetrius lost his life.[25] At one point during an interrogation, Livy has Demetrius complain that the favor shown to him by the Romans as a result of his hostageship was more of a detriment than an asset once he returned home.[26] He was right; their support left him vulnerable to accusations of betrayal that eventually got him killed. Antiochus was never thrust into a position quite so dire, but the reports of his "madness" at Antioch highlight the possibility that his enemies, too, tried to tar the former hostage with the brush of Romanization.

Whatever the truth about Antiochus' Roman habits, one thing about his kingship is reasonably clear: his years at Rome did not prevent him from later pursuing an independent and aggressive foreign policy, even to Rome's displeasure.[27] It is possible that Rome supported Antiochus' suspiciously quick installation on the Seleucid throne, and some scholars have seen the king's adoption of Roman customs as an intention to reform along Roman lines.[28] But if the Romans expected their hostage's acculturation to lead to political subservience, they must have been disappointed. In short order, Antiochus set about flouting the terms of the very treaty that had brought him to Rome. Apamea forbid the Seleucid possession of elephants and warships as well as the recruitment of mercenaries from Roman territories. Antiochus violated all of these conditions.[29] To be sure, the king made no secret of these transgressions, which evidently did not alarm the Romans overmuch, and it is unclear whether the treaty signed by Antiochus III was still binding for his son.[30] But the Romans later referenced Apamea to justify their intervention in 163/162 BCE against Antiochus V, so it would appear that compliance with the treaty still mattered.[31]

Antiochus' independence was most on display during the Sixth Syrian War and the "Day of Eleusis" that marked its climax. The king's invasion of Egypt was embedded in a long-running struggle between the Seleucids and Ptolemies and showed that a hostageship in Rome did little to diminish the Hellenistic drive for spear-won land. In the end Antiochus did back down, of course, and Popilius Laenas' ultimatum had its intended effect. But Antiochus yielded because of credible Roman threats to use force, not because he was a former hostage. It was the hard power of Rome's military, not the soft power of cultural imperialism, that ended Antiochus' adventure in Egypt.[32]

For the Romans, Antiochus' case would have shown that confinement in their city and association with Republican elites were no guarantee that a former hostage would help to create the sort of international order that Rome wanted to see. Moreover, if the negative reports of Antiochus' Roman behavior indeed originated in Antioch, then the Romans might have learned a second lesson: Antiochus' hostageship had left him vulnerable to accusations from his subjects that he was a Romanized quisling. As a tool of empire, Antiochus had performed poorly. The record of Rome's first Seleucid hostage as an agent of Roman imperialism was marked by distinct shortcomings.

Much the same can be said of the Parthian experience with captive Seleucid monarchs. In 139 BCE, Demetrius II turned aside from his kingdom's domestic conflicts in order to deal with the Parthian threat in the east.[33] Having campaigned successfully against the Greco-Bactrians in central Asia, the Arsacid king Mithridates I was now encroaching on Seleucid possessions in Media and Mesopotamia.[34] In the first few clashes between the Parthian and Seleucid armies Demetrius appears to have had the upper hand, but whether by treachery or battlefield defeat he was eventually taken alive by his Parthian opponents along with several of his closest friends and advisors.[35]

Mithridates' first move was to put the captive king on display for local populations. Several sources report dissatisfaction in Mesopotamia and Iran with the initial imposition of Arsacid control, and the exhibition of a defeated and humiliated Seleucid monarch may have been meant to discourage further resistance.[36] Demetrius was then brought to a royal palace in Hyrcania, where his close proximity to the king meant that he no doubt remained a visible sign of Arsacid military prowess. This practice is paralleled in Rome, where there is evidence for the participation of hostages in the triumphs of conquering generals.[37] In both cases, the exhibition of royal prisoners enhanced the prestige of the commanders who captured them. Success on the battlefield led to a strengthened domestic position.

Like Antiochus at Rome, Demetrius' treatment during his decade-long Hyrcanian captivity was commensurate with his royal rank. He was held in honor and provided with the comforts due to a king. Mithridates even married Demetrius to his daughter, Rhodogune. How willingly Demetrius entered into this union is impossible to say, though his two attempts to escape Parthian custody in the following years might provide some indication. Still, the pair had children together. Demetrius' bids for freedom ended in failure, and he was returned to his Parthian family both times. Like his father, the Roman hostage Demetrius I, the Seleucid captive grew restless and unhappy in his imprisonment. Unlike his father, he could not escape.[38]

What was the motive behind the Arsacid treatment of their prisoner? Justin's epitome of Trogus is clearest: the Parthians had designs on the kingdom of Syria and intended to use Demetrius as a tool against Antiochus VII, who had taken the Seleucid throne in his absence. Demetrius' involuntary incorporation into the Arsacid family has accordingly been seen as an effort to subordinate the Seleucid territories to an expanding Parthian imperial order.[39] The marrying of Arsacid royal women to local dynasts is attested in other contexts, though to be sure these matrimonial ties went both ways.[40] And just as intermarriage was one practice in the Arsacid imperial toolkit, so too was the cultivation of potential client-kings at the Arsacid court. Tigranes II of Armenia is a clear case in point. Kamnaškiri the Younger of Elam and Artabazos of Characene are other possibilities.[41]

But in Demetrius' case, the course of events seems to have forced Phraates' hand, and the eventual release of his Seleucid captive was calculated less to add to the Arsacid empire than to disrupt the Seleucid one. Antiochus VII gathered an army and in 131 BCE won a series of battles against the Parthian forces in Mesopotamia. The Arsacids, who were also beset on their eastern frontier by nomadic incursions, buckled and nearly broke.[42] Peace talks began. But Antiochus grew overconfident, demanding not only the release of Demetrius but also the return of all territories taken from the Seleucids and the resumption of Parthian tribute payments. This was too much for Phraates, who broke off the negotiations.[43]

It was just at this point that the Arsacid king decided to release Demetrius "so that in this way Antiochus would be recalled from Parthia to protect his own possessions."[44] In view of the dire military situation, Phraates' immediate goal at this point was probably not at the annexation of Syria but rather the derailment of Antiochus' campaign through the fomenting of domestic strife.[45] But the tactic proved unnecessary. Antiochus VII died in a decisive battle with the Parthians in 130/129 BCE; his daughter and perhaps also a son fell into the hands of the enemy. Too late Phraates realized his release of Demetrius had been to no purpose, but an attempt to recapture him failed. Demetrius reached Syria, where after a ten-year interregnum he resumed his kingship.[46]

Demetrius' Parthian captivity left an indelible mark on his second reign. In a departure from established numismatic traditions, the king now wore a full beard on his coins. Several motives have been proposed for the innovation, but it is often explained as a consequence of his captivity among the Arsacids, who usually wore beards in their own coin portraits.[47] His subjects may also have noticed a change. According to Justin, the residents of Antioch revolted, "upbraiding the arrogance of the king, which because of his association with the Parthians had become unbearably cruel."[48] It is unclear whether this explanation for the change in Demetrius' nature was part of Antiochene propaganda or is an authorial interjection of Justin or Trogus, whose history he epitomated.[49] The former is at least a possibility, which means that the Antiochenes may have justified their rebellion against Demetrius on the grounds that his Parthian captivity had rendered him an unsuitable ruler. Demetrius' nickname "Seripides/Siripides" may also be relevant in this context.[50] The epithet could be a diminutive of the Aramaic *'swr* and mean "the little bound prisoner." It might also be a corruption of the Greek Σιδηρίτης, "iron-man," a likely reference to chains.[51] In either case, the contemptuous reference to Demetrius' captivity is clear.

But despite these Parthian connections both real and imagined, it would be a mistake to see Demetrius' second reign as an incorporation of Seleucid Syria into the Arsacid empire. Phraates himself had no illusions about Demetrius' independence; he reportedly contemplated an invasion of Syria, which was only prevented by a massive rebellion in his army.[52] Almost immediately upon his return, Demetrius set out for Egypt to intervene in a Ptolemaic civil war.[53] This campaign, a manifestation of the kingdom's deep-seated tendency to pursue gain at the expense of the Ptolemies, showed that traditional Seleucid priorities were what mattered to Demetrius, not Parthian ones. Moreover, Demetrius' wife Cleopatra Thea was reportedly incensed by his marriage to Rhodogune, though neither the Arsacid princess nor her children returned with the king to Syria. Her anger led her to abandon Demetrius and, in some accounts, to plot his murder. Appian attributes the deed to jealousy, though one suspects that Cleopatra – wife to three kings, mother to two, and murderer of two – acted from political rather than personal motives.[54]

From an Arsacid point of view, then, Demetrius' record as an agent of Parthian imperialism left much to be desired. The king showed no sign of accepting Parthian vassalage once back in power, and if the Parthians did have immediate designs on Syria, he did nothing to advance them. Worse still, Demetrius' Parthian captivity was used as a political weapon against him. The Antiochenes may have used it to explain what they perceived as the king's cruelty, or at least as a justification for rebellion. And Cleopatra Thea may have taken umbrage at his marital connections to the Arsacid family for either personal or political reasons. In short, with Demetrius the Parthians may have incurred the resentment of empire-building without the tangible benefits that the addition of new territory usually brought.

As tools of foreign policy, Seleucid hostages and prisoners had come up short for both the Romans and the Parthians during the second century BCE. But one aspect of the Parthian experience with Demetrius held an important lesson: royal prisoners might create unrest on the domestic level if returned to their native kingdom at the right moment. That observation helps explain the continuity between the Seleucid captives of the Hellenistic period and the Arsacid hostages of Julio-Claudian Rome – and also the more consequential changes.

Royal Prisoners and Domestic Politics

For the Arsacids, the lesson from Demetrius' captivity was that it was easier to use royal prisoners to destroy than to use them to build: they were better as the tools of disruption than the instruments of an imperial order. One student who seems to have learned this lesson well was not an Arsacid king, but a Roman emperor.

After Parthia and Rome completed their respective conquests of the Hellenistic world in the mid-first century BCE, the new status quo between the two empires took shape in the old Seleucid territories. In Syria, the Euphrates provided a surprisingly stable boundary that endured to the days of Trajan and beyond. But Armenia remained a point of contention, and sparring between the two empires for prestige and influence was a frequent occurrence there.[55] One such conflict began in 35 CE, when the Parthian king Artabanus II invaded Armenia and installed his son Arsaces on the Armenian throne.[56] The move violated the Roman-Parthian settlement concluded under Augustus and Phraates IV, and Rome had to take action.

But the emperor Tiberius had two things that allowed him to deal with the crisis without resorting to military force. The first was an embassy from certain Parthian noblemen asking him for assistance against Artabanus, who Dio says "was treating the Parthians in an arrogant manner."[57] The second was a group of Arsacid family members living in captivity in the city of Rome, several of whom were viable candidates for the Arsacid throne. The delegation from the nobility was asking for one of them to be released as a replacement for the reigning Arsacid, an event that had happened once already during the reign of Augustus.[58] Tiberius consented. The first choice was Phraates, the eldest remaining son of Phraates IV who had now been at Rome for some 40 years, but he died in Syria on the way to his native land. A replacement was quickly found in Tiridates, a young Arsacid who probably had been born at Rome.[59]

As Tiridates approached the Euphrates, Artabanus' campaign in Armenia collapsed. The Syrian governor Lucius Vitellius escorted the young Arsacid to the river, where he built a bridge and released him to his Parthian supporters. Although Rome provided no further military assistance, the rumor of a Roman war and Tiridates' considerable support among the Parthian nobles led to mass desertions in Artabanus' army. The king fled to central Asia, where he would bide his time and gather new forces. Meanwhile Tiridates claimed the Arsacid throne to what seemed like broad acclaim.[60]

Just a few months later, Artabanus was back on the throne, and Tiridates had fled to Roman territory.[61] What had gone wrong? Tiridates, it turned out, was vulnerable to the accusations of acculturation that a returning hostage often faced: his captivity had imparted a "foreign effeminacy;" he was a tool of those that installed him on the throne (in this case, the Parthian nobleman Abdagaeses); and – a charge frequently leveled in Parthia – he effectively had lost Arsacid status by virtue of his hostageship in Rome.[62] This invective against Tiridates is reported only by Tacitus, and to be sure, its inclusion is part of the author's literary designs.[63] But it also reveals a typical domestic political reaction against a returning royal captive. As seen above, the argument that a royal hostage or prisoner had become a puppet of his former captors was a useful weapon in political discourse; it gave the dynast's enemies a means of discrediting him and a justification for rebelling against his reign. The fate of Tiridates' kingship was decided on the battlefield, of course. But the Parthian rhetoric preserved in Tacitus suggests that criticism of his hostageship played a role in uniting the forces that defeated him.

Should the release of Tiridates accordingly be reckoned a failure on Tiberius' part? Just the opposite. The emperor had deftly used an Arsacid hostage to eject the Parthians from Armenia without committing Roman legions to the cause – a successful application of his preference for "managing foreign affairs through plots and stratagem, and keeping arms at a distance."[64] Tiberius' expectations of what Tiridates would accomplish within Parthia were probably modest: his release would trigger a civil war, create domestic disturbance, and undercut Artabanus' expansionist campaign by striking at the base of his power. And while Artabanus did recover his throne in the end, his designs on Armenia did not return with him. He patched up relations with Rome at a conference on the Euphrates with Vitellius, and even handed over hostages to seal the deal.[65]

In Tiberius' use of Tiridates, then, some continuity between Seleucid and Arsacid royal captives is evident. Just as Phraates II released Demetrius to distract Antiochus Sidetes from his Parthian campaign, so Tiberius' repatriation of Tiridates was a measure designed to foment dynastic strife to foil a Parthian initiative in Armenia. Tiberius had learned a lesson that both the Roman and the Parthian experience with Seleucid prisoners could have taught him: if royal prisoners were poor tools of imperial expansion, their return to their native lands was a reliable way to stir up domestic chaos.

But while there were some similarities between the Seleucids of the Hellenistic period and the Arsacids of Julio-Claudian Rome, there were also differences between them that, in the end, count for more. The realization that royal prisoners operated first and foremost at the domestic level brought to the fore a function that, while not unprecedented, now assumed a new significance: both the Parthians and the Romans began to use Arsacid hostages for their own domestic political purposes. The royal prisoner's traditional deployment as an instrument of foreign policy was superseded by applications in the realm of internal affairs – though, to be sure, the international dimension of hostage submission remained relevant.

This development began with political conditions within the Parthian kingdom, where a persistent tension between the Arsacid king and recalcitrant factions of the Parthian nobility was a central dynamic throughout the empire's history. The contours of these domestic struggles appear only in their barest outlines in the

Greco-Roman literary sources.[66] Neither the Arsacid family nor the Parthian nobility was a monolithic entity, and throughout Parthian history actors from both of these groups will have arranged themselves in constellations that can only be guessed at in the absence of detailed literary narratives. But one aspect of their relationship is reasonably clear: on occasion, factions of Parthian nobles acting in concert would conspire to unseat an unpopular Arsacid monarch only to replace him with another member of the dynasty. Fear of such plots sometimes led to purges within the Arsacid family as the reigning king systematically assassinated his relatives and rivals.[67] Such dynastic strife was not unique to the Arsacids, of course, though in their case the problem may have been compounded by royal polygamy and the large families that this custom produced.[68]

It is against this backdrop that the beginning of Arsacid-Roman hostage submission must be understood. The first coordinated transfer of Arsacid hostages to Augustus was primarily an event in Parthian domestic politics: Phraates IV sent his family members to his Roman counterpart in an effort to deprive his political enemies of a suitable Arsacid rival who might supplant him. The paramount importance of Parthian domestic politics is highlighted in Strabo, Josephus, and Tacitus, and while their assessments differ in certain respects, their collective emphasis on Phraates' agency is nonetheless clear.[69] That is not to say that Rome played no part whatsoever; although the date of the hostage submission cannot be securely determined, it seems to have happened while Roman legions were active on Parthia's western frontier, and Phraates may have been looking to head off a potential Roman invasion.[70] But no source – not even the *Res Gestae* of Augustus himself – reports a Roman demand for Parthian hostages. If Phraates acted to avoid Roman aggression, he did so in a manner of his own choosing and, in a way, that dealt simultaneously with domestic and external challenges to his position.[71]

Artabanus' submission of his son Darius at the Euphrates conference in 36/37 CE was more closely connected to international affairs; in this case, the Roman emperor did demand hostages from his Parthian counterpart.[72] But in the next major hostage transfer under Vologaeses I in 55 CE, Arsacid initiative was again the primary factor. Vologaeses had installed his brother on the Armenian throne and started another war with the Romans, but he was forced to withdraw to deal with an internal rebellion by another Arsacid.[73] According to Tacitus, at this point Vologaeses gave hostages "in order to prepare war from an advantageous position – or, in the name of 'hostages' to remove those suspected of rivalry."[74] Vologaeses' hostage transfer was a purge of Arsacid rivals rather than a legitimate concession to Roman demands.[75] As a negotiating ploy, it was all the more effective for playing on Roman expectations that, once hostages were surrendered, Parthia's contestation for Armenia would be over.[76] The fact that the Armenian war would drag on for another eight years shows that the submission of hostages did not indicate political or military submission.

It is true, of course, that while the Arsacid kings could shore up their domestic position by shipping rivals to Rome, the Roman emperor could always send those rivals back to Parthia. But with the exception of Tiberius, the emperors do not seem to have used their Arsacid hostages in an offensive capacity. Two of the three Arsacid kings who submitted hostages (Phraates IV and Vologaeses I) never had to deal with the threat of an Arsacid rival returning from Rome. Artabanus II faced this situation twice, but both cases were before he sent his son Darius to Rome. After his conference with Vitellius in 37 CE, he would not have to deal with the problem a third time. Moreover, no emperor ever released a hostage without a request from the Parthian king or nobility.[77] When the former hostage Vonones returned to Parthia in *c.* 8 CE, the Arsacid throne was empty. And when Claudius released Meherdates in 49 CE, his opponent Gotarzes had spent virtually his entire kingship fighting civil wars; he posed little or no threat to Rome.[78] The idea that the Romans used their Arsacid hostages to keep Parthia weak and divided is difficult to reconcile with such cases.

But if the Romans didn't simply use their Arsacid hostages to enfeeble their imperial neighbor, how else did they employ them? An important part of the answer is once again to be found in the domestic political arena. The Arsacids of Rome were showpieces, a way for the emperors to proclaim Rome's supremacy over the Parthian empire in absence of the military success that had fueled the imperialism of the late Republic. Not long after the first Arsacids arrived in Rome, Augustus made a prominent display of them at one of his many public spectacles, leading them through the middle of the arena and then seating them prominently above him in the second row.[79] Presumably clad in Parthian costume, Phraates IV's children would have offered the Romans a living example of the subdued Parthian, a caricature they knew through the coins, poetry, and art of the Augustan period.[80] The arena spectacle would have recalled the display of hostages in the triumphs of the middle and late Republic, where the exhibition of captive royalty was a sign of the conquering general's power over the kingdoms from which they had been taken.[81] But there was a key difference: Augustus never defeated Parthia militarily. Hostages created the appearance of Roman domination in the east, even though the realities of power on the ground were much different.

The staging of spectacles featuring the Arsacids of Rome was continued under later emperors. Caligula's famous Baiae procession in 39 CE made prominent use of Darius, the son of Artabanus II who had recently arrived in Italy. Whether as an honored guest or as the *spolia* of a triumph (the sources do not agree), the Arsacid prince accompanied the emperor as he traversed his massive pontoon.[82] Darius took part on the second day of the procession as Caligula rode from Baiae to Puteoli. The fact that he was once again traversing a bridge from east to west suggests that Caligula's spectacle was, among other things, a recreation of Vitellius' pontoon over the Euphrates – the very structure Darius crossed, from east to west, in order to enter Roman custody.[83] Once again, the prominent display of a hostage celebrated Roman success against Parthia in the east, even though the status quo with Parthia remained basically the same.

Finally, Nero may have made use of a fresh shipment of hostages during the famous "Golden Day" of 66 CE.[84] The event celebrated the arrival of the Arsacid Tiridates, the brother of Vologaeses I who was to be crowned king of Armenia by Nero.[85] In his retinue Tiridates brought not only his own children, but numerous others from the Arsacid family.[86] Dio does not say whether they stayed on in Rome after Tiridates' departure, but a reference in Pliny to a group of royal hostages from Corbulo's campaigns suggests that at least some were detained.[87] While the highlight of the day was Tiridates' obeisance to Nero, the prostration of the entire Arsacid retinue is supposed to have drawn a loud roar of acclamation from the crowd of onlookers.[88] To the extent that the status quo had changed, it was in Parthia's favor; an Arsacid now held the Armenian throne. But the apparent subservience of Tiridates and the hostages that came with him allowed the emperor to maintain the appearance of Roman domination in the east. And for Nero especially, the glitter of prestige may have mattered rather more than the reality of political control.[89]

The repeated use of Arsacid hostages in Roman *spectacula* shows that these dynasts were indispensable tools for crafting an image of Roman supremacy over Parthia. It mattered little that this image was, by and large, illusory. The Arsacids of Rome were props with which the emperor played to a domestic audience. They were not just a tool through which Parthian policy was carried out; they were an end at which that policy aimed. Arsacid hostages were a resource obtained from across the Euphrates, but put to work at the center of Roman imperial power.

To be sure, domestic applications were not unprecedented, and the international dimension remained significant. As discussed above, hostages and prisoners graced the triumphs of victorious generals during the Republic, boosting their captor's prestige in the intense competition among Roman aristocrats for honor and advancement. Details are unavailable for the Parthian side, but Mithridates' exhibition of Demetrius II suggests that the Arsacids too may have made use of such displays. Moreover, hostages were involved in nearly every Roman-Parthian interaction throughout the Julio-Claudian period. An Arsacid captive could be used to ward off Parthian aggression, as Tiberius' release of Tiridates shows, or to mend and preserve ties between the two empires, as Augustus may have done by returning Phraates IV's young son in *c.* 23 BCE.[90] The dynastic prisoner still played a part in international politics.

Yet with Parthian and Roman conquests halted at the Euphrates, the royal captive's role in the realm of internal affairs now took on a new importance. While the submission of Arsacid hostages was a key feature of the Roman-Parthian relationship, this international connection was forged and sustained largely because it suited the domestic political interests of the major players on both sides of the Euphrates. Such exploitation of the royal captive for domestic gain by both the surrendering and the receiving party represented a real break from the Hellenistic past and was a new feature of the Roman-Parthian status quo. Through hostages, each empire had become part of the internal functioning of the other.

Conclusion

Seleucid clashes with the growing empires of both Parthia and Rome led to the imprisonment of several members of the kingdom's royal family. Much scholarship holds that these captive dynasts were the instruments of imperialism, a means for the Romans and Parthians to shape the international order to their liking. But if this was the end that Seleucid hostages and prisoners were meant to achieve, there were grounds for disappointment. Released Seleucids did not help either empire bend the Seleucid kingdom to its will. They acted independently, pursuing traditional Seleucid agendas. And they may in some cases have stirred up anti-Roman and anti-Parthian sentiment, particularly in the key Seleucid city of Antioch.

As Parthia and Rome completed their conquest of the Hellenistic world, the stage was therefore set for a change in how the royal prisoner was used in relations between empires. To be sure, there were continuities. Tiberius' release of Tiridates to stir up civil war within Parthia echoed the repatriation of Demetrius by Phraates II as a way to derail Antiochus Sidetes' eastern campaign. The Seleucids of the Hellenistic period showed that, if it was difficult to build an international order with royal prisoners, it was easier to unleash dynastic strife by releasing them at the right moment. Tiberius' management of the Armenian crisis in 35 CE was a skillful application of this lesson.

But the changes were more significant. As leaders in both Rome and Parthia looked east or west at where the Seleucid kingdom used to be, the dismal record of Seleucid captives as tools of foreign policy may have suggested new uses for the royal prisoner in the domestic political arena. The Arsacid kings used hostage submission for their own purposes, shoring up their hold on power by shipping potential rivals to Rome. The emperors then used these hostages to project an image of Roman suzerainty over Parthia to an internal audience. The Arsacid royal prisoner became, for both the Parthians and the Romans, a way of managing internal political problems through the international medium of hostage submission.

Long after the Seleucid empire was gone, then, the legacy of Rome and Parthia's Seleucid prisoners lived on, underpinning a new kind of relationship between the joint conquerors of the Hellenistic world's largest polity. Even in decline, even as hostages, prisoners, and captives, the Seleucid royal family shaped the age to come.

Notes

* I thank Benjamin Rubin, Jason Schlude, and Barry Strauss for comments that greatly improved this piece. All translations are my own unless otherwise noted.
1. Some key studies in the large literature on the Greek world's influence on Rome: Gruen 1984, 250–272; Zanker 1988; Wallace-Hadrill 2008, 17–37; Spawforth 2012. Parthia's engagement with Hellenism is less studied, but was no less consequential; see Wolski 1983b; Wiesehöfer 2000; Fowler 2005, 151–155.
2. For previous discussions of Rome's Arsacids, see Dąbrowa 1987; Wiesehöfer 2010; Nedergaard 1988; Strothmann 2012; Gregoratti 2015.
3. See below, n. 18 for literature.

4. The Parthian word *nyp'k/nēpāk* is found in the inscription of Narseh at Paikuli (section 94 = Skjærvø 1983, 73, 114). See also Durkin-Meisterernst 1998, 239, for the word in Manichaean Middle Persian and Parthian.

5. This reckoning excludes the usurper Tryphon and the Armenian king Tigranes II on the grounds that, although they both ruled Seleucid territory for a time, neither was a member of Seleucid family. For Antiochus XIII as the last king, see, *e.g.* Green 1990, 724; Ehling 2008, 263.

6. *Cf.* Elbern 1990, 131; Álvarez Pérez-Sostoa 2012, 385, on the general absence of Roman hostages in the sources – largely, if not entirely, attributable to Rome's military superiority.

7. Polyb. 21.15.2–3; Liv. 37.34.4–6; Diod. 29.8.1; Val. Max. 2.10.2, 3.5.1; Plin. *HN* 35.22; Dio, fr. 62.2 = 19.20.2; App. *Syr.* 29 (who confuses this Scipio with the later Scipio Aemilianus). This son was probably Lucius rather than Publius, Africanus' other son: Balsdon 1972, 228; Walbank 1979, 107–108; Briscoe 1981, 339. The accounts vary on the exact date and manner of his capture.

8. Liv. 38.51.2: *filium captum sine pretio redditum.* The ancient sources for Africanus' trial are listed in Scullard 1973, 290, n. 1; Briscoe 2008, 170. For discussion, see Kienast 1954, 57–67; Scullard 1970, 210–224; 1973, 290–303; Ruebel 1977; Briscoe 2008, 170–179. Lucius himself was later expelled from the Senate: Liv. 41.27.2. There is no indication in Livy that his former captivity was a factor, but in Valerius Maximus (3.5.1) his Seleucid imprisonment is mentioned in the same context as his political failure. On Lucius' career, see further Liv. 41.21.1 with Briscoe 2012, 109; Val. Max. 4.5.3. The gifts of Antiochus VII to Scipio Aemilianus (Liv., *Per.* 57.8) might be evidence for continued ties between the two families in the later second century BCE.

9. *E.g.* the wives who accompanied the sons of Phraates IV (Strab. 16.1.28). On Arsacid royal women generally, see Hartmann and Huber 2006; Bigwood 2004; 2008.

10. See below, n. 81.

11. Sources for the capture of Valerian: ŠKZ 18–22; SHA, *Valeriani Duo* 1–4.2; Eutrop. 9.7; Lactantius, *De Mortibus Persecutorum* 5; Aurel. Vict., *Epit. de Caes.* 32.5–6; al-Ṭabarī in Bosworth 1999, 29–31. For discussion, see Kettenhofen 1982, 97–100; Potter 2004, 255–256; Ando 2012, 167–170; Dignas and Winter 2007, 180–182.

12. Pompey's envoy C. Lucilius Hirrus was imprisoned by Orodes II: Caes., *BC* 3.82; Dio 41.55.3–4, 42.2.5; Debevoise 1938, 104–105. But Hirrus evidently supplied fish for Caesar's triumph in 45 BCE (Plin., *HN* 9.171), so his captivity cannot have been long. In 63 CE the general Corbulo sent his stepson Annius Vinicianus and the knight Tiberius Alexander into the Parthian camp as hostages: Tac., *Ann.* 15.28.3. But both are later found active in Roman territory (Dio 62.23.6; Suet., *Ner.* 36.1; Joseph., *BJ* 2.309), and their term as hostages was almost certainly limited to the duration of the battlefield negotiations (*cf.* Elbern 1990, 101).

13. Dio 79.39–40; *cf.* Ziegler 1964, 135; Potter 2004, 151–152. The other ancient sources (SHA, *Macr.* 10.3–6; *Diad.* 9.4; Herod. 5.4.12) do not mention the attempted flight to Artabanus and report that father and son died together.

14. Hostages and prisoners as part of Roman imperialism, especially via acculturation or education: Matthei 1905, 231–243; Lécrivain 1916, 131; Aymard 1961, 140–142; Moscovich 1974, 425–426; 1983, 299; Walker 1980, 42, 119, 207–209; Braund 1984, 12–17; Elbern 1990, 118–124; Lee 1993, 366–367; Ndiaye 1995, 154–155; Noy 2000, 106–109; Burns 2003, 100–101; Allen 2006, 34, 149–177. As part of Parthian imperialism: Wolski 1980, 257–267; 1987, 169; 1993, 82; Dąbrowa 2011a, 24; Shayegan 2003, 92–97; 2011, 140–150.

15. Polyb. 21.43.22; Liv. 38.38.15; Diod. 29.10; App. *Syr.* 39; Memnon *FrGH* 434 F 18.9 = *BNJ* 434 F 1.9. For discussion of the settlement and its impact, see Mørkholm 1966, 22–32; Gruen 1984, 640–643; Green 1990, 421–423; Sherwin-White and Kuhrt 1993, 210–216; Ma 1999, 247–250; Austin 2003, 131–132. For discussions of the regular exchange of hostages (*mutatio obsidum*), see Allen 2006, 15, n. 46 with references.

16. Antiochus' age and birthdate: Mittag 2006, 32–37. Exchange with Demetrius: App., *Syr.* 45. The date of Antiochus' release from Rome depends in part on an inscription that may put him in Athens in 178/177 BCE: Tracy 1982, 61–62; but *cf.* now Scolnic 2014; Knoepfler 2014.
17. Ascon., *Pis.* 13C = Atticus, fr. 6P = *FRH* 33 F 7; Walker 1980, 106 and n. 31; Mittag 2006, 37–40; 2014, 119–121.
18. Demetrius' amenities: Polyb. 31.14.1–3; *cf.* Diod. 31.18.1; Walker 1984, 120. His escape from Roman captivity: Polyb. 31.15.6; Mørkholm 1966, 39; Braund 1984, 13–14; Matthews 1989, 39–40. Like Demetrius, the Arsacid Vonones would later attempt to escape Roman custody while under guard in Pompeiopolis under the pretense of a hunting expedition: Tac., *Ann.* 2.68.1.
19. Liv. 42.6.9: *ut pro rege non pro obside omnibus ordinibus fuerit.* Gruen 1984, 648–650 highlights Antiochus' desire for Roman support in his looming conflict with the Ptolemies. Walker 1980, 199, holds that Livy's version of the speech plays up Roman civility and generosity. Antiochus also had to excuse a late tribute payment due to financial difficulties: Liv. 42.6.6; *cf.* 2 Macc. 8:10; Briscoe 2012, 173.
20. Polyb. 26.1.5–6 = Athen. 10.439a; Liv. 41.20.1, 41.20.9–13; Dio. 29.32; *cf.* Heliodorus, *FrGH* 373 F 8 = *BNJ* 373 F 8. Granius Licinianus writes that Antiochus erected two colossi, one for Olympian and the other for Capitoline Jupiter (28.10.1–11.1; *cf.* Briscoe 2012, 107). On the lack of archaeological evidence for a Jupiter temple in Antioch, see Allen 2006, 168–169. For the festival at Antioch near Daphne, which featured (among other attractions) men armed in Roman fashion and gladiators, see Polyb. 30.25–26; Diod. 31.16.2–3.
21. See Mittag 2006, 334; Mørkholm 1966, 183–188; Green 1990, 437–438; Grainger 1990, 156 and n. 80; *cf.* MacMullen 2000, 16. It is usually assumed that Polybius' friendship with Demetrius I darkened his portrayal of Antiochus, but *cf.* Paltiel 1979b, who argues for a friendly relationship between the two Seleucid hostages.
22. Gruen 1984, 662.
23. *Cf.* Mittag 2006, 147, 335. Green 1990, 432, 437 sees Antiochenes behind the pun on Antiochus' epithet (*Epimanes*/"Madman" for *Epiphanes*/"Manifest"). On Antioch near Daphne (also known as Antioch on the Orontes) see Downey 1961, especially 112–118; Cohen 2006, 80–93.
24. For the background on Demetrius' hostageship and return to Macedon, see Edson 1935; Allen 2006, 1–13.
25. The "smoking gun" was a letter from Flamininus to Philip V, which at any rate contained nothing overtly incriminating: Liv. 40.23.7–8; *cf.* Diod. 29.25. The ancient sources held this document to be a forgery, on which point see Walbank 1940, 251; Briscoe 1972, 25–26; 2008, 469; Gruen 1974, 243–244; Pfeilschifter 2005, 358–359; Newey 2009, 79–83.
26. Liv. 40.12.6.
27. Allen 2006, 166–169. Gruen 1984, 665, makes the same point for Antiochus' successor and fellow hostage, Demetrius I.
28. Antiochus installed with Roman help: Will 1979–1982, 2.256–257; Walbank 1979, 285; but *cf.* Green 1990, 429 and n. 156. Roman-inspired reforms: Goldstein 1976, 104–125.
29. Elephants: Polyb. 21.42.12 (treaty); Polyb. 30.25.11; *1 Maccabees* 1.17, 3.34; Joseph. *AJ* 12.295 (violation). Ships: Polyb. 21.42.13 (treaty); Liv. 44.19.9, 45.11.9; *1 Maccabees* 1.17; *2 Maccabees* 4.18–20 (violation). See McDonald and Walbank 1969 for a discussion of the naval clauses. Mercenaries: Polyb. 21.42.15 (treaty); Polyb. 30.25.4–5; *1 Maccabees* 6.29; *cf. 2 Maccabees* 5.24 (possible violations). The treaty of Apamea forbid Seleucid mercenary recruitment from territories under Roman rule, but it is not clear how far Rome's writ extended: see Paltiel 1979a, 32, for discussion.
30. Popilius Laenas seems to have seen the Seleucid navy personally in Egypt and Cyprus without taking any punitive action: Liv. 45.12.7; Polyb. 29.27.9–10. Polyaenus (4.21) even reports that Antiochus presented the Romans with war elephants before Pydna, though this seems to conflict with Livy (45.13.3) and has been rejected: see Mørkholm 1966, 66, n. 7. On whether the Treaty

of Apamea remained in force during Antiochus IV's reign, see Paltiel 1979a, 41; Morgan 1990, 48 and n. 49.

31. That Rome used the violation of Apamea as grounds for destroying the Seleucid navy and elephants in 162 is clear in App., *Syr.* 46 and Dio 20.25, but absent from earlier sources (Polyb. 31.2.9–11; Cic., *Phil.* 9.2.4). If the treaty could be used as a pretext for intervention even after his reign, Antiochus clearly ran a risk in ignoring its provisions. For discussion, see Mittag 2006, 224.

32. *Cf.* Green 1990, 431–432, 437–438. On the Sixth Syrian War in general, see the sources and discussion in Fischer-Bovet 2014, 219–242; Grainger 2010, 288–308. Sources for the Day of Eleusis: Polyb. 29.27.1–10; Liv. 45.12.3–8; Cic., *Phil.* 8.23; Vell. Pat. 1.10.1; Diod. 31.2; Val. Max. 6.4.3; Just. 34.3.1–4; Plin., *HN* 34.24; Plut., *Mor.* 202f; App., *Syr.* 66; Porphyry, *BNJ* 260 F 50; Zon. 9.25; for discussion, see Gruen 1984, 657–663; Morgan 1990. On an evident reference to Antiochus' departure in Egyptian evidence, see Fischer-Bovet 2014, 230–231.

33. Demetrius' motive for marching east is debated; see the discussion in Shayegan 2003, 86, with references.

34. Parthian war with Greco-Bactria under Mithridates I: Just. 41.6.1–3; Strab. 11.11.2; Wolski 1993, 79–80. A Greek inscription at Behistun dating to 148 BCE "for the welfare of Kleomenes, commander of the upper satrapies," may reflect Seleucid apprehension over an impending Parthian attack: see Hackl *et al.* 2010, 2.476 (III.1.3.F.3).

35. See Table 2.1 for the sources, which do not agree on how Demetrius came into Arsacid captivity. Justin has him treacherously double-crossed by the Parthians during a peace conference, while Josephus and *1 Maccabees* say he was captured after losing a battle. For discussion of the campaign, see Dąbrowa 2011b; Ehling 2008, 182–186; Shayegan 2003, 84–87.

36. Just. 36.1.3–5, 38.10.5; Joseph., *AJ* 13.186; Dąbrowa 2011a, 17; Kosmin 2014, 173. For a more nuanced story of local reactions to Arsacid invasion based partly on the evidence from the Babylonian astronomical diaries, see Shayegan 2011, 81; and Potts 1999, 388, noting that the Elymaeans were opposed to both Arsacid and Seleucid suzerainty.

37. *E.g.* at Flamininus' triumph in 193 BCE: Liv. 34.52.9; Eutrop. 4.2.3; Oros. 4.20.2; and at Pompey's in 61 BCE: Plut., *Pomp.* 45.4; App., *Mith.* 117. Walker 1980, 98, plausibly suggests that other generals may have followed suit. On Pompey's triumphs, see further Beard 2007, 7–41.

38. Demetrius' generous treatment and marriage to Rhodogune: Just. 36.1.6, 38.9.3; App., *Syr.* 67–68; Hartmann and Huber 2006, 500. On the apparent contradiction between Justin and Appian as to the giver of the Arsacid princess, see Shayegan 2003, 85. Escape attempts and despair in captivity: Just. 38.9.4–9. On Demetrius I's escape from Rome, see Gruen 1984, 663–667; Allen 2006, 210–212.

39. Just. 38.9–10. See Dąbrowa 2011a, 18; Wolski 1993, 82; Shayegan 2003, 97.

40. The Arsacid king Phraates III married his daughter to Tigranes, son of Tigranes II the Great of Armenia, whom he attempted to put on the Armenian throne: Dio 37.6.4; *cf.* 36.51; App., *Mith.* 104. For marriages between the daughters of local dynasts and the Arsacid kings, see Hartmann and Huber 2006, especially 502.

41. Hostageship of Tigranes: Just. 38.3.1; *cf.* Sachs and Hunger 1996, no. –95 C ´obv.´ 5´–7´; no. –95 C ´rev.´ 12´; no. –95 D ´obv.´ 11´ (=p. 418–423). Kamnaškiri: see the arguments in Shayegan 2003, 94; 2011, 77–94. Artabazos of Characene: see Lucian, *Macr.* 16; Schuol 2000, 310–312, with Shayegan 2011, 92.

42. Antiochus' campaign and initial success: Just. 38.10.5–6; Joseph., *AJ* 13.250–252; *BJ* 1.50, 1.62; Poseidonius, *BNJ* 87 F 9a = Ath. 540b–c; Val. Max. 9.1.ext.4; Oros. 5.10.8. For the Parthian struggle against eastern invaders at this point, see Dąbrowa 2011a, 19–20; Ehling 2008, 203, n. 743; Olbrycht 1998, 85–88.

43. Diod. 34/35.15; App., *Syr.* 68; *cf.* Green 1990, 536.

44. Just. 38.10.7: *ut eo pacto Antiochus ad sua tuenda a Parthia revocaretur*; *cf.* App., *Syr.* 68; Euseb., *Chron.* 117.1–124.5 [Karst] = Porphyry, *BNJ* 260 F 32 = *FrGH* 260 F 32.19.

45. It was probably fear of this tactic that had prompted Antiochus to demand Demetrius' return: see Debevoise 1938, 31.
46. Death of Antiochus VII: Just. 38.10.10; Diod. 34/35.16–17; Joseph., *AJ* 13.253 (death in battle); App., *Syr.* 68; Ael., *NA* 10.34 (suicide after defeat); *cf.* Poseidonius, *BNJ* 87 F 11. Capture of Antiochus' daughter: Just. 38.10.10. Capture of a son named Seleucus: Euseb., *Chron.* 117.1–124.5 [Karst] = Porphyry, *BNJ* 260 F 32 = *FrGH* 260 F 32.19–20; for discussion, see Shayegan 2003, 94–96. Failed attempt to recapture Demetrius: Just. 38.10.11.
47. Dürr 1979, 8; Green 1990, 536–537; Ehling 2008, 206–207, with n. 777 for further literature.
48. Just. 39.1.3: *execrantes superbiam regis, quae conversatione Parthicae crudelitatis intolerabilis facta erat.*
49. Grammatically speaking, one would expect a subjunctive verb in the relative clause if the claim were part of the speaker's original statement, whereas *facta erat* is indicative. But this may be an overly subtle reading of a text that has been substantially reworked from the original, and at any rate the two possibilities are not mutually exclusive. On Justin's relationship to Trogus, see the introduction in Yardley and Heckl 1997, especially 15–19.
50. The name survives only in Armenian sources: Euseb., *Chron.* 117.1–124.5 [Karst] = Porphyry, *BNJ* 260 F 32 = *FrGH* 260 F 32.16; Moses Khorenats'i 2.2 (=Thomson 1978, 131–132). On Moses' misreporting of the name as Siripindēs ("with bound feet") see Thomson 1978, 132, n. 8.
51. For the Aramaic derivation, see Kosmin 2014, 173; for the Greek, see Toye 2015. Another case of a possible Aramaic nickname for a Seleucid king is Alexander Balas, whose epithet "Zabinas" is Aramaic for "The Bought One" – a likely Antiochene reference to their "purchase" of Alexander from Ptolemy Physcon. See Bevan 1902, 2.249; Green 1990, 540.
52. Diod. 34/35.18; Just. 42.1.1–5.
53. Just. 39.1.2; Euseb., *Chron.* 117.1–124.5 [Karst] = Porphyry, *BNJ* 260 F 32 = *FrGH* 260 F 32.21; *cf.* Ehling 2008, 208–209.
54. Cleopatra Thea's jealousy and murder of Demetrius: App., *Syr.* 68; Liv., *Per.* 60.11; but *cf.* Just. 39.1.8; Joseph., *AJ* 13.268; Euseb., *Chron.* 117.1–124.5 [Karst] = Porphyry, *BNJ* 260 F 32 = *FrGH* 260 F 32.21.
55. On the Euphrates boundary, see Edwell 2013. On the role of Armenia, see Wolski 1983a; Wheeler 2002, 287.
56. Tac., *Ann.* 6.31.1; Joseph., *AJ* 18.96; Dio 58.26.1. *Cf.* Philost., *Vit. Apoll.* 2.2, who mentions an Armenian king named Arsaces. On possible mentions of this campaign in later sources, see Wiesehöfer 1986, 179–180. This Artabanus used to be reckoned the third of his name but is now generally acknowledged as the second: see Fowler 2005, 125, n. 1.
57. Dio 58.26.1: ὑπερηφανώτερον καὶ τοῖς Πάρθοις ἐχρῆτο.
58. The first Arsacid to return from Rome was Vonones in *c.* 8 CE: see *Mon. Anc.* 33; Joseph., *AJ* 18.46; Tac., *Ann.* 2.2.1.
59. Tac. *Ann.* 6.31–2; Dio 58.26.2. On Tiridates' youth, *cf.* Tac., *Ann.* 6.43.3. If Tiridates had been part of Phraates IV's hostage submission between 19 and 10 BCE, he could hardly qualify as young in 35/36 CE, even in the reckoning of a political enemy like Hiero. The inclusion of Arsacid women in Phraates IV's submission (Strab. 16.1.28) further supports the idea that he was born at Rome.
60. Tac., *Ann.* 6.36–37; Debevoise 1938, 158–160; Ziegler 1964, 60–62. On Vitellius' use of the language of paternalism, see Allen 2006, 136.
61. Tac., *Ann.* 6.44; Dio 58.26.3. Tiridates then disappears from the historical record.
62. Tac., *Ann.* 6.43.3.
63. Namely, the critique of the Principate through a Parthian mouthpiece. On the literary aspects of Tacitus' Parthian digressions, see Keitel 1978; Martin 1981, 179–180; Gowing 1990; Malloch 2013, 114–175; Clark 2011.
64. Tac., *Ann.* 6.32.1: *destinata retinens, consiliis et astu res externas moliri, arma procul habere. Cf. Ann.* 2.26.3. On Tiberius' non-expansionism in general, see Levick 1976, 142–144; Seager 2005, 147–150.

65. Joseph., *AJ* 18.96, 101–105; Suet., *Calig.* 14.3; *Vit.* 2.4; Dio 59.27.2–3; Debevoise 1938, 162–163; Bivar 1983, 73–74; Allen 2006, 117–118. Contradictions in the sources make it difficult to date this conference precisely, and it is unclear whether Tiberius or Caligula was emperor when it took place: see Täubler 1904, 33–40; Garzetti 1956.

66. On the Parthian nobility and their representation in the Greco-Roman literary sources, see Hauser 2005, 185–199; Dąbrowa 2013. Evidence for the nobility in the Sasanian period might shed some light on how the Parthian nobility was structured: see Lukonin 1983, 698–699; Hauser 2005, 193–194.

67. Instances of Arsacid dynastic strife: Orodes II: Dio 39.56.2; *cf.* Just. 42.4.1–4. Phraates IV: Plut., *Crass.* 33.5; *Ant.* 37.1; Dio 49.23.3–4; Just. 42.4.16, 42.5.1–2. Artabanus II: Tac., *Ann.* 6.31.2. Gotarzes II: Tac., *Ann.* 11.8.2, 12.10.1. On the hostility of the nobility to Arsacid kin-slaying, see, *e.g.* Just. 42.5.2, where the nobility becomes angry at Phraates IV for this reason. *Cf.* Dąbrowa 1983, 75; Ehrhardt 1998, 298; Bigwood 2004, 45–46.

68. Orodes II, for example, is supposed to have had 30 sons among his various concubines: Justin 42.4.14. On royal polygamy, *cf.* Scheidel 2009, 272–295.

69. Strab. 16.1.28 (but *cf.* 6.4.2 and n. 74 below); Joseph., *AJ* 18.42; Tac., *Ann.* 2.1.2; *cf.* Taylor 1936, 162; Ziegler 1964, 51–52; Nedergaard 1988, 107. Josephus assigns the initiative to Phraates' Italian wife Thea Musa and her desire to secure the succession for her son, Phraataces. But Musa's agency and that of Phraates IV need not be mutually exclusive. On Musa, see further Bigwood 2004; Strugnell 2008; Hartmann and Huber 2006, especially 495.

70. See esp. Vell. Pat. 2.94.4. In contrast to his other assessment of the event, Strab. 6.4.2 attributes Phraates' hostage submission to Parthian subservience; see further Allen 2006, 146–147 on this inconsistency. On the date, see the discussion in Rose 2005, 36–38.

71. *Cf.* Wiesehöfer 2010, 187. On Augustus' account of Phraates' hostage submission, see Lerouge 2007, 105–115.

72. Joseph., *AJ* 18.96. For the date and problems with the source tradition, see the literature cited above, n. 69.

73. The identity of this rival is unclear due to textual uncertainties in Tac., *Ann.* 13.7.2, but most identify him as an unnamed son of the earlier Arsacid king Vardanes: see Kahrstedt 1950, 23, and n. 23; Sinisi 2012, 16; Wiesehöfer 2015, 338; Schottky 1991, 117.

74. Tac., *Ann.* 13.9.1: *quo bellum ex commodo pararet, an ut aemulationis suspectos per nomen obsidum amoveret.* On the date of this hostage submission, see Wheeler 1997, 385.

75. *Cf.* Heil 1997, 79.

76. Gilmartin 1973, 588–589; Dąbrowa 1983, 137; Wheeler 1997, 385.

77. Augustus returned Phraates IV's young son at the king's request: Dio 53.33.2; Just. 42.5.9. Embassies from the nobility for the return of Vonones: *Mon. Anc.* 33; Joseph., *AJ* 18.46; Tac., *Ann.* 2.2.1. Phraates: Tac., *Ann.* 6.31.2; Dio 58.26.2. Tiridates: Tac., *Ann.* 6.32.2–3; Dio 58.26.2. Meherdates: Tac., *Ann.* 11.10.4, 12.10–11.

78. For Meherdates' contest with Gotarzes, see Debevoise 1938, 172–174; Schippmann 1980, 53–54; Olbrycht 1997, 94–95; Malloch 2011, 114–131; Braund 2015, 130.

79. Suet., *Aug.* 43.3–4. These were probably the hostages sent by Phraates IV between 19 and 10 BCE rather than the young son that arrived with Tiridates some ten years earlier: see Wardle 2014, 328–329.

80. Sonnabend 1986, 256–257; Wiesehöfer 2010, 188. For the subdued Parthian on coins, see, *e.g.* RIC 1 (Sutherland and Carson 1984) 62, no. 287; Rose 2005, 23. Poetry: Meyer 1961, 52–53; Wissemann 1982. Art: Zanker 1988, 186–192; Schneider 1986, 18–97; 2007, 61–72.

81. For the use of hostages and prisoners in Roman triumphs, see Beard 2007, 107–142; Östenberg 2009, 128–167; and above, n. 41.

82. Suet., *Calig.* 19.2 may imply that Caligula acted as Darius' charioteer: see Allen 2006, 122. But Dio (59.17.5; *cf. Epit. de Caes.* 3.9) puts Darius walking behind Caligula as though he were spoils,

which suggests a triumphal procession: Hurley 1993, 74; Barrett 1989, 211; Winterling 2011, 128; but *cf.* Wardle 1994, 192; Malloch 2001, 211. Seneca (*De Brev. Vit.* 18.5) mentions the Baiae procession, but not Darius' participation.

83. Hurley 1993, 74. Vitellius' pontoon over the Euphrates: Joseph., *AJ* 18.102–103.
84. For the decorations that gave the day its name, see Dio 63.4.1–6.1; Plin., *HN* 33.54; Champlin 2003, 119. *Cf.* Suet., *Ner.* 13; Tac., *Ann.* 16.23.2.
85. Tac., *Ann.* 15.24.2; Dio 62.22.3; Campbell 1993, 230–231.
86. Dio 63.1.2. Tiridates' retinue included the children of Vologaeses I, his brother Pacorus, and Monobazus, the last of whom was not an Arsacid but the king of Adiabene.
87. Plin., *HN* 6.23. On these hostages as a source for Pliny's research on eastern geography, see Matthews 1989, 40.
88. Dio 63.4.3–5.1.
89. The Golden Day as a loss for Rome: Fest., *Brev.* 20; Wolski 1987, 175. Loss concealed by theatrics: Wheeler 2002, 289; *cf.* Champlin 2003, 233–234; Braund 2015, 126. See also Heil 1997, 78–80 on Nero's response to the Parthian hostage submission in 55 CE.
90. See Schlude and Rubin in chapter four in this volume, and above, n. 81.

Bibliography

Álvarez Pérez-Sostoa, D. (2010) "Opsides abdoucit: la toma de rehenes en la latina." *Epigraphica* 72, 169–189.

Álvarez Pérez-Sostoa, D. (2012) "Conflits autour des otages romains pendant les guerres civiles." In H. Ménard, P. Sauzeau, and J. Thomas (eds.) *La pomme d'Eris: le conflit et sa représentation dans l'Antiquité*, 383–397. Montpellier, Presses Universitaires de la Méditerranée.

Ando, C. (2012) *Imperial Rome AD 193 to 284: The Critical Century*. Edinburgh, Edinburgh University Press.

Austin, M. (2003) "The Seleukids and Asia." In A. Erskine (ed.) *A Companion to the Hellenistic World*, 121–133. Malden, MA, Blackwell Publishing.

Aymard, A. (1961) "Les otages barbares au debut de l'empire." *Journal of Roman Studies* 51, 136–142.

Balsdon, J. P. V. D. (1972) "L. Cornelius Scipio: A Salvage Operation." *Historia: Zeitschrift für Alte Geschichte* 21.2, 224–234.

Barrett, A. (1989) *Caligula: The Corruption of Power*. New Haven, Yale University Press.

Beard, M. (2007) *The Roman Triumph*. Cambridge, MA, Belknap Press of Harvard University Press.

Bevan, E. (1902) *The House of Seleucus*, vol. 1–2. London, Edward Arnold.

Bigwood, J. M. (2004) "Queen Mousa, Mother and Wife(?) of King Phraatakes of Parthia: A Re-Evaluation of the Evidence." *Mouseion* 3.4, 35–70.

Bigwood, J. M. (2008) "Some Parthian Queens in Greek and Babylonian Documents." *Iranica Antiqua* 43, 235–274.

Bosworth, C. E. (1999) *The History of Al-Ṭabarī. Vol. 5: The Sāsānids, the Byzantines, the Lakhmids, and Yemen*. Albany, State University of New York Press.

Bouché-Leclercq, A. (1913) *Histoire des Séleucides (323-64 J.-C.)*, vol. 1–2. Paris, E. Leroux.

Braund, D. (1984) *Rome and the Friendly King: The Character of the Client Kingship*. London, St. Martin's Press.

Braund, D. (2015) "Kings beyond the Claustra: Nero's Nubian Nile, India and the Rubrum Mare (Tacitus, *Annals* 2.61)." In E. Baltrusch and J. Wilker (eds.) *Amici - Socii - Clientes? Abhängige Herrschat Im Imperium Romanum*, 123–159. Berlin, Edition Topoi.

Braund, S. (1996) *Juvenal, Satires Book I*. Cambridge, Cambridge University Press.

Briscoe, J. (1972) "Flamininus and Roman Politics, 200–189 B.C." *Latomus* 31.1, 22–53.

Briscoe, J. (1981) *A Commentary on Livy, Books XXXIV–XXXVII*. Oxford, Oxford University Press.

Briscoe, J. (2008) *A Commentary on Livy, Books 38-40*. Oxford, Oxford University Press.

Briscoe, J. (2012) *A Commentary on Livy, Books 41-45*. Oxford, Oxford University Press.

Bunge, J. G. (1974) "'Theos Epiphanes': Zu den ersten fünf Regierungsjahren Antiochos' IV. Epiphanes." *Historia: Zeitschrift für Alte Geschichte* 23.1, 57–85.

Burns, T. (2003) *Rome and the Barbarians: 100 B.C.-A.D. 400*. Baltimore, Johns Hopkins University Press.

Campbell, B. (1993) "War and Diplomacy: Rome and Parthia, 31 BC–AD 235." In J. Rich and G. Shipley (eds.) *War and Society in the Roman World*, 213–240. London and New York, Routledge.

Champlin, E. (2003) *Nero*. Cambridge, MA, Belknap Press.

Clark, A. (2011) "Vologaeses as Mirror." *Histos* 5, 208–231.

Cohen, G. M. (2006) *The Hellenistic Settlements in Syria, the Red Sea Basin, and North Africa*. Berkeley, University of California Press.

Courtney, E. (1980) *A Commentary on the Satires of Juvenal*. London, Athlone Press.

Dąbrowa, E. (1983) *La politique de l'Etat parthe à l'égard de Rome, d'Artaban II à Vologèse I (ca 11-ca 79 de n.e.) et les facteurs qui la conditionnaient*. Kraków, Nakł, Uniwersytetu Jagiellońskiego.

Dąbrowa, E. (1987) "Les Premiers 'Otages' Parthes à Rome." *Folia Orientalia* 24, 63–71.

Dąbrowa, E. (2011a) "Könige Syriens in der Gefangenschaft der Parther. Zwei Episoden aus der Geschichte der Beziehungen zwischen Seleukiden und Arsakiden." In *Studia Graeco-Parthica: Political and Cultural Relations between Greeks and Parthians*, 15–25. Wiesbaden, Harrassowitz Verlag.

Dąbrowa, E. (2011b) "L'Expédition de Démétrios II Nicator contre les Parthes (139–138 avant J.-C.)." In *Studia Graeco-Parthica: Political and Cultural Relations between Greeks and Parthians*, 49–57. Wiesbaden, Harrassowitz Verlag.

Dąbrowa, E. (2013) "The Parthian Aristocracy: Its Social Position and Political Activity." *Parthica* 15, 53–62.

Debevoise, N. (1938) *A Political History of Parthia*. Chicago, University of Chicago Press.

Dignas, B. and Winter, E. (2007) *Rome and Persia in Late Antiquity: Neighbours and Rivals*. Cambridge, Cambridge University Press.

Downey, G. (1961) *A History of Antioch in Syria: From Seleucus to the Arab Conquest*. Princeton, Princeton University Press.

Durkin-Meisterernst, D. (1998) *Dictionary of Manichaean Middle Persian and Parthian*. Turnhout, Brepols.

Dürr, N. (1979) "Das Horn des Demetrios II." *Schweizer Münzblätter* 29, 7–9.

Edson, C. (1935) "Perseus and Demetrius." *Harvard Studies in Classical Philology* 46, 191–202.

Edwell, P. (2013) "The Euphrates as a Boundary between Rome and Parthia in the Late Republic and Early Empire." *Antichthon* 47, 191–206.

Ehling, K. (2008) *Untersuchungen zur Geschichte der späten Seleukiden (164-63 v. Chr.): Vom Tode des Antiochos IV. bis zur Einrichtung der Provinz Syria unter Pompeius*. Stuttgart, Franz Steiner.

Ehrhardt, N. (1998) "Parther und parthische Geschichte bei Tacitus." In J. Wiesehöfer (ed.) *Das Partherreich und seine Zeugnisse = The Arsacid Empire - Sources and Documentation: Beiträge des internationalen Colloquiums, Eutin (27.-30. Juni 1996)*, 295–307. Stuttgart, Franz Steiner.

Elbern, S. (1990) "Geiseln in Rom." *Athenaeum* 68, 97–140.

Ferguson, J. (1987) *A Prosopography to the Poems of Juvenal*. Brussels, Latomus.

Fischer-Bovet, C. (2014) "Est-il facile de conquérir l'Égypte? L'invasion d'Antiochos IV et ses conséquences." In C. Feyel and L. Graslin-Thomé (eds.) *Le projet politique d'Antiochos IV*, 209–259. Nancy, ADRA.

Fowler, R. (2005) "'Most Fortunate Roots': Tradition and Legitimacy in Parthian Royal Ideology." In O. Hekster and R. Fowler (eds.) *Imaginary Kings: Royal Images in the Ancient Near East, Greece and Rome*, 125–155. Stuttgart, Franz Steiner.

Garzetti, A. (1956) "La data dell'incontro all'eufrate di Artabano III e L. Vitellio, legato di Siria." In *Studi in Onore di Aristide Calderini e Roberto Paribeni*, vol. 1, 211–229. Milan, Ceschina.

Gilmartin, K. (1973) "Corbulo's Campaigns in the East: An Analysis of Tacitus' Account." *Historia: Zeitschrift Für Alte Geschichte* 22.4, 583–626.

Gowing, A. (1990) "Tacitus and the Client Kings." *Transactions of the American Philological Association* 120, 315–331.

Grainger, J. (1990) *The Cities of Seleukid Syria*. Oxford, Clarendon Press.

Grainger, J. (2010) *The Syrian Wars*. Leiden, Brill.

Green, P. (1990) *Alexander to Actium: The Historical Evolution of the Hellenistic Age*. Berkeley, University of California Press.

Gregoratti, L. (2015). "The Parthians of the Roman Empire." In P. Militello and H. Oniz (eds.) *Soma 2011: Proceedings of the 15th Symposium on Mediterranean Archaeology, Held at the University of Catania, March 3-5th, 2011*, vol. 2, 731–735. Oxford, British Archaeological Reports.

Gruen, E. (1974) "The Last Years of Philip V." *Greek, Roman and Byzantine Studies* 15.2, 221–246.

Gruen, E. (1984) *The Hellenistic World and the Coming of Rome*, vol. 1–2. Berkeley, University of California Press.

Hackl, U., Jacobs, B. and Weber, D. (2010) *Quellen zur Geschichte des Partherreiches: Textsammlung mit Übersetzungen und Kommentaren*, vol. 1–3. Göttingen and Oakville, CT, Vandenhoeck & Ruprecht.

Hartmann, U. and Huber, I. (2006) "'Denn ihrem Diktat vermochte der König nicht zu widersprechen ...' Die Position der Frauen am Hof der Arsakiden." In A. Panaino and A. Piras (eds.) *Proceedings of the 5th Conference of the Societas Iranologica Europæa, Ravenna, 6-11 Oct. 2003*, vol. 1, 485–517. Milan, Mimesis.

Hauser, S. (2005) "Die ewigen Nomaden: Bemerkungen zu Herkunft, Militär, Staatsaufbau und nomadischen Traditionen der Arsakiden." In B. Meißner, O. Schmitt, and M. Sommer (eds.) *Krieg-Gesellschaft-Institutionen: Beiträge zu einer vergleichenden Kriegsgeschichte*, 163–208. Berlin, Akademie Verlag.

Heil, M. (1997) *Die orientalische Außenpolitik des Kaisers Nero*. München, Tuduv-Verlagsgesellschaft.

Hoover, O. (2007) "A Revised Chronology for the Late Seleucids at Antioch (121/0–64 BC)." *Historia: Zeitschrift für Alte Geschichte* 56.3, 280–301.

Hurley, D. (1993) *An Historical and Historiographical Commentary on Suetonius' Life of C. Caligula*. Atlanta, GA, Scholars Press.

Isaac, B. (2004) *The Invention of Racism in Classical Antiquity*. Princeton, Princeton University Press.

Kahrstedt, U. (1950) *Artabanos III. und seine Erben*. Bern, A. Francke.

Keitel, E. (1978) "The Role of Parthia and Armenia in Tacitus Annals 11 and 12." *American Journal of Philology* 99.4, 462–473.

Kettenhofen, E. (1982) *Die römisch-persischen Kriege des 3. Jahrhunderts n. Chr. nach der Inschrift Šāpuhrs I. an der Ka'be-ye Zartošt (ŠKZ)*. Wiesbaden, Reichert.

Kienast, D. (1954) *Cato der Zensor: Seine Persönlichkeit und seine Zeit*. Heidelberg, Quelle & Meyer.

Knoepfler, D. (2014) "L'ami princier de la plus démocratique des cités: Antiochos IV, Athènes et Délos à la lumière du nouveau recueil des décrets attiques (IG II³ 1,5)." In C. Feyel and L. Graslin-Thomé (eds.) *Le projet politique d'Antiochos IV*, 75–116. Nancy, ADRA.

Kosmin, P. (2014) *The Land of the Elephant Kings: Space, Territory, and Ideology in the Seleucid Empire*. Cambridge, MA, Harvard University Press.

Lécrivain, M. C. (1916) "L'institution des ôtages dans l'antiquité." *Mémoirs de l'Académie des Sciences de Toulouse* 11.4, 115–139.

Lerner, J. (1999) *The Impact of Seleucid Decline on the Eastern Iranian Plateau: The Foundations of Arsacid Parthia and Graeco-Bactria*. Stuttgart, Franz Steiner.

Lerouge, C. (2007) *L'image des Parthes dans le monde gréco-romain*. Stuttgart, Franz Steiner.

Levick, B. (1976) *Tiberius the Politician*. London, Thames and Hudson.

Lukonin, V. G. (1983) "Political, Social, and Administrative Institutions, Taxes and Trade." In E. Yarshater (ed.) *The Cambridge History of Iran*, vol. 3.1, 681–746. Cambridge, Cambridge University Press.

MacMullen, R. (2000) *Romanization in the Time of Augustus*. New Haven, Yale University Press.

Ma, J. (1999) *Antiochos III and the Cities of Western Asia Minor*. Oxford, Oxford University Press.

Malloch, S. J. V. (2001) "Gaius' Bridge at Baiae and Alexander-Imitatio." *Classical Quarterly, New Series*, 51.1, 206–217.

Malloch, S. J. V. (2013) *The Annals of Tacitus: Book 11*. Cambridge, Cambridge University Press.

Martin, R. (1981) *Tacitus*. Berkeley, University of California Press.

Matthaei, A. (1905) "Das Geiselwesen bei den Römern." *Philologus* 64, 224–247.

Matthews, J. (1989) "Hostages, Philosophers, Pilgrims, and the Diffusion of Ideas in the Late Roman Mediterranean and Near East." In F. Clover and R. Humphreys (eds.) *Tradition and Innovation in Late Antiquity*, 29–50. Madison, University of Wisconsin Press.

McDonald, A. H. and Walbank, F. W. (1969) "The Treaty of Apamea (188 B.C.): The Naval Clauses." *Journal of Roman Studies* 59.1/2, 30–39.

Meyer, H. (1961) *Die Außenpolitik des Augustus und die augusteische Dichtung*. Köln, Böhlau.

Mittag, P. (2006) *Antiochos IV. Epiphanes: Eine politische Biographie*. Berlin, Akademie Verlag.

Mittag, P. (2014) "Die diplomatischen Beziehungen zwischen Antiochos und Rom." In C. Feyel and L. Graslin-Thomé (eds.) *Le projet politique d'Antiochos IV*, 117–135. Nancy, ADRA.

Morgan, M. (1990) "The Perils of Schematism: Polybius, Antiochus Epiphanes and the 'Day of Eleusis.'" *Historia: Zeitschrift für Alte Geschichte* 39.1, 37–76.

Mørkholm, O. (1966) *Antiochus IV of Syria*. Copenhagen, Gyldendal.

Moscovich, M. (1974) "Hostage Regulations in the Treaty of Zama." *Historia: Zeitschrift für Alte Geschichte* 23.4, 417–427.

Moscovich, M. (1983) "Hostage Princes and Roman Imperialism in the Second Century B.C." *Echos du monde classique* 27, 297–309.

Newey, P. (2009) "Flamininus and the Assassination of the Macedonian Prince Demetrius." *Revue belge de philologie et d'histoire* 87.1, 69–83.

Ndiaye, S. (1995) "Le recours aux otages à Rome sous la République." *Dialogues d'histoire ancienne* 21.1, 149–165.

Nedergaard, E. (1988) "The Four Sons of Phraates IV in Rome." In T. Fischer-Hansen (ed.) *East and West: Cultural Relations in the Ancient World*, 102–115. Copenhagen, Museum Tusculanum Press.

Noy, D. (2000) *Foreigners at Rome: Citizens and Strangers*. London, Duckworth.

Olbrycht, M. (1997) "Vardanes contra Gotarzes II. – Einige Überlegungen zur Geschichte des Partherreiches ca. 40–51 n. Chr." *Folia Orientalia* 33, 81–100.

Olbrycht, M. (1998) *Parthia et Ulteriores Gentes: Die politischen Beziehungen zwischen dem arsakidischen Iran und den Nomaden der eurasischen Steppen*. Munich: Tuduv-Verlagsgesellschaft.

Östenberg, I. (2009) *Staging the World: Spoils, Captives, and Representations in the Roman Triumphal Procession*. Oxford, Oxford University Press.

Paltiel, E. (1979a) "Antiochos IV and Demetrius I of Syria." *Antichthon* 13, 42–47.

Paltiel, E. (1979b) "The Treaty of Apamea and the Later Seleucids." *Antichthon* 13, 30–41.

Paltiel, E. (1982) "Antiochos Epiphanes and Roman Politics." *Latomus* 41.2, 229–254.

Pfeilschifter, R. (2005) *Titus Quinctius Flamininus: Untersuchungen zur römischen Griechenlandpolitik*. Göttingen, Vandenhoeck & Ruprecht.

Plischke, S. (2014) *Die Seleukiden und Iran*. Wiesbaden, Harrassowitz.

Potter, D. S. (2004) *The Roman Empire at Bay, AD 180–395*. London and New York, Routledge.

Potts, D. T. (1999) *The Archaeology of Elam: Formation and Transformation of an Ancient Iranian State*. Cambridge, Cambridge University Press.

Rose, C. (2005) "The Parthians in Augustan Rome." *American Journal of Archaeology* 109.1, 21–75.

Ruebel, J. (1977) "Cato and Scipio Africanus." *The Classical World* 71.3, 161–173.

Sachs, A. J. and Hunger, H. (1996) *Astronomical Diaries and Related Texts from Babylonia. Vol. 3: Diaries from 164 B.C. to 61 B.C.* Vienna, Verlag der Österreichischen Akademie der Wissenschaften.

Scheidel, W. (2009) "Sex and Empire: A Darwinian Perspective." In I. Morris and W. Scheidel (eds.) *The Dynamics of Ancient Empires: State Power From Assyria to Byzantium*, 255–324. New York, Oxford University Press.

Schneider, R. (1986) *Bunte Barbaren: Orientalenstatuen aus farbigem Marmor in der römischen Repräsentationskunst.* Worms, Wernersche Verlagsgesellschaft.

Schneider, R. (2007) "Friend and Foe: The Orient in Rome." In V. S. Curtis and S. Stewart (eds.) *The Age of the Parthians,* 50–86. London, I. B. Tauris.

Schippmann, K. (1980) *Grundzüge der parthischen Geschichte.* Darmstadt, Wissenschaftliche Buchgesellschaft.

Schottky, M. (1991) "Parther, Meder, und Hyrkanier: Eine Untersuchung der dynastischen und geographischen Verflechtungen im Iran des I. Jhs. c. Chr." *Archaeologische Mitteilungen aus Iran* 24, 61–134.

Schuol, M. (2000) *Die Charakene: Ein mesopotamisches Königreich in hellenistisch-parthischer Zeit.* Stuttgart, Franz Steiner.

Scolnic, B. (2014) "When Did the Future Antiochos IV Arrive in Athens?" *Hesperia: The Journal of the American School of Classical Studies at Athens* 83.1, 123–142.

Scullard, H. H. (1970) *Scipio Africanus: Soldier and Politician.* Ithaca, NY, Cornell University Press.

Scullard, H. H. (1973) *Roman Politics, 220-150 B.C.* Oxford, Clarendon Press.

Seager, R. (2005) *Tiberius.* Second edition. Malden, MA, Blackwell Publishing.

Shayegan, M. (2003) "On Demetrius II Nicator's Arsacid Captivity and Second Rule." *Bulletin of the Asia Institute, New Series,* 17, 83–103.

Shayegan, M. (2011) *Arsacids and Sasanians: Political Ideology in Post-Hellenistic and Late Antique Persia.* Cambridge and New York, Cambridge University Press.

Sherwin-White, S. and Kuhrt, A. (1993) *From Samarkhand to Sardis: A New Approach to the Seleucid Empire.* Berkeley, University of California Press.

Sinisi, F. (2012) *Sylloge Nummorum Parthicorum. Vol. 7: Vologaeses I - Pacorus II.* Vienna, Verlag der Österreichischen Akademie der Wissenschaften.

Skjærvø, P. O. (1983) *The Sassanian Inscription of Paikuli. Part 3.1. Restored Text and Translation.* Wiesbaden, Reichert.

Spawforth, A. (2012) *Greece and the Augustan Cultural Revolution.* Cambridge, Cambridge University Press.

Strothmann, M. (2012) "Feindeskinder an Sohnes Statt. Parthische Königssöhne im Haus des Augustus." In P. Wick and M. P. Zehnder (eds.) *The Parthian Empire and Its Religions: Studies in the Dynamics of Religious Diversity = Das Partherreich und seine Religionen: Studien zu Dynamiken religiöser Pluralität,* 83–102. Gutenberg, Computus Druck Satz & Verlag.

Strugnell, E. (2008) "Thea Musa, Roman Queen of Parthia." *Iranica Antiqua* 43, 275–298.

Syme, R. (1984) *Roman Papers,* vol. 3. Oxford, Clarendon Press.

Täubler, E. (1904) *Die Parthernachrichten bei Josephus.* Inaugural dissertation, Friedrich–Wilhelms–Universität zu Berlin.

Taylor, L. R. (1936) "M. Titius and the Syrian Command." *Journal of Roman Studies* 26, 161–173.

Thomson, R. W. (1978) *Moses Khorenats'i: History of the Armenians.* Cambridge, MA, Harvard University Press.

Toye, D. L. (2015) "Porphyry (260)." In I. Worthington (ed.) *Brill's New Jacoby.* Brill Online.

Tracy, S. (1982) "Greek Inscriptions from the Athenian Agora Third to First Centuries B. C." *Hesperia: The Journal of the American School of Classical Studies at Athens* 51.1, 57–64.

Walbank, F. W. (1940) *Philip V of Macedon.* Cambridge, Cambridge University Press.

Walbank, F. W. (1979) *A Historical Commentary on Polybius. Vol. 3: Commentary on Books XIX-XL.* Oxford, Oxford University Press.

Walker, C. (1980) *Hostages in Republican Rome.* Unpublished thesis, University of North Carolina.

Wallace-Hadrill, A. (2008) *Rome's Cultural Revolution.* Cambridge, Cambridge University Press.

Wardle, D. (1994) *Suetonius' Life of Caligula: A Commentary.* Brussels, Latomus.

Wardle, D. (2014) *Suetonius: Life of Augustus.* Oxford, Oxford University Press.

Wheeler, E. L. (1997) "The Chronology of Corbulo in Armenia." *Klio* 79.2, 383–397.

Wheeler, E. L. (2002) "Roman Treaties with Parthia: Völkerrecht or Power Politics?" In P. Freeman, J. Bennett, Z. T. Fiema, and B. Hoffmann (eds.) *Limes XVIII: Proceedings of the XVIIIth International Congress of Roman Frontier Studies, Held in Amman, Jordan (September 2000)*, vol. 1, 287–292. Oxford, Archaeopress.

Wiesehöfer, J. (1986) "Iranische Ansprüche an Rom auf ehemals achaimenidische Territorien." *Archäologische Mitteilungen aus Iran* 19, 177–185.

Wiesehöfer, J. (2000) "'Denn Orodes war der griechischen Sprache und Literatur nicht unkundig'. Parther, Griechen und griechische Kultur." In R. Dittmann (ed.) *Variatio Delectat. Iran und der Westen. Gedenkschrift für Peter Calmeyer*, 703–721. Münster, Ugarit Verlag.

Wiesehöfer, J. (2010) "Augustus und die Parther." In R. Aßkamp and T. Esch (eds.) *Imperium-Varus und seine Zeit: Beiträge zum internationalen Kolloquium des LWL-Römermuseums am 28. und 29. April 2008 in Münster*, 187–195. Münster, Aschendorff Verlag.

Wiesehöfer, J. (2015) "Greek Poleis in the Near East and Their Parthian Overlords." In A. Kemezis (ed.) *Urban Dreams and Realities in Antiquity*, 328–346. Leiden, Brill.

Will, E. (1979) *Histoire politique du monde hellénistique (323-30 av. J.-C.)*. Second edition, vol. 1–2. Nancy, Université de Nancy.

Winterling, A. (2011) *Caligula: A Biography*. Berkeley, University of California Press.

Wissemann, M. (1982) *Die Parther in der augusteischen Dichtung*. Frankfurt am Main, P. Lang.

Wolski, J. (1980) "L'Arménie dans la politique du Haut-Empire Parthe (env. 175–87 av. n.è.)." *Iranica Antiqua* 15, 251–267.

Wolski, J. (1983a) "Les rapports romano-parthes et la question de l'Arménie (1er siècle av. J.-C.-1er siècle ap. J.-C.)." *Ktema* 8, 269–277.

Wolski, J. (1983b) "Sur le 'philhellénisme' des Arsacides." *Gerion* 1, 145–156.

Wolski, J. (1987) "Le couronnement de Tiridate par Vologèse Ier comme roi de l'Arménie: échec de Néron et de l'empire romain." In *Neronia III: Actes du IIIe Colloque international de la Société internationale d'études néroniennes, Varenna, juin 1982*, 167–179. Rome, "L'Erma" di Bretschneider.

Wolski, J. (1993) *L'Empire des Arsacides*. Leuven, Peeters.

Yardley, J. C. and Heckel, W. (1997) *Justin: Epitome of the Philippic History of Pompeius Trogus*. Oxford, Clarendon Press.

Zanker, P. (1988) *The Power of Images in the Age of Augustus*. Ann Arbor, University of Michigan Press.

Ziegler, K. (1964) *Die Beziehungen zwischen Rom und dem Partherreich: Ein Beitrag zur Geschichte des Völkerrechts*. Wiesbaden, Franz Steiner.

Chapter 3

Marcus Antonius' Median War and the Dynastic Politics of the Near East

Kenneth R. Jones[1]

It is the nearly unanimous opinion of writers both ancient and modern that Mark Antony embarked on a war with the Parthians in 36 BCE and that it was a total disaster.[2] It is the argument of the present paper that this understanding is wrong. Not only did Antony not undertake a war with the Parthians, but the campaign of 36 was ultimately successful. The difficulty with this line of argument is that it runs counter to all of our sources, which derive ultimately from an eye-witness account of the campaign and most of which trace their pedigree to works of the Augustan age.

The unanimous interpretation of the sources must be set aside for two reasons. First, they misunderstand what Antony was trying to accomplish in the Near East. They assume that he was a Roman imperialist with his sights set on conquest and expansion. They ignore the regional context of his actions. We must apply a different model to Antony's actions, namely that of a Hellenistic-style dynast. Secondly, the sources are problematic because they are all tainted by Augustus' victory over Antony and the subsequent reshaping of the narrative of Antony's activities and aims in the East. The Parthian Question continued to loom large during the reign of Augustus, as can be shown by the repeated references to it in Augustan poetry and in the emperor's own self-presentation.[3] We shall return to this point at the end of the present paper to notice that Augustan policy vis-à-vis Parthia differed very little from Antony's.[4] The latter had to be misrepresented and obscured so that Augustus' achievements might stand out in higher relief.

Before we delve into these topics, it will be useful to review the events of the campaign of 36.[5] At the king of Armenia's invitation, Antony marched from Syria through Armenia and invaded neighboring Media Atropatene, where he besieged the fortress of Phraaspa, the site of the Median king's winter residence, complete with wives, children, and treasure. In his haste to get to Phraaspa, Antony had left his baggage train and siege equipment behind with a guard of two legions under the command of Oppius Statianus accompanied by the king of Armenia with a substantial force and Polemo, king of Pontus. They were attacked by a mixed force of Parthians and Medes. The king of Armenia fled, leaving the legions to be annihilated. Statianus was killed and the standards were captured along with Polemo. When the Parthian force showed up later near Phraaspa, Antony attacked and drove it off. With winter approaching, Antony withdrew from Media after making a truce with the Parthians. The Parthians nevertheless pressed him during his retreat, which was made even more difficult by bad weather, famine, and disease. Antony finally reached Armenia and proceeded through to Syria, where his army wintered. After the war the Median and Parthian kings quarreled. Fearing for his kingdom the Mede made an alliance with Antony, who began to prepare for a new campaign in the spring of 35 BCE. Ultimately, however, Antony never embarked on it; instead he occupied Armenia and deposed the king for his treachery.[6]

As noted previously, the campaign is recounted by many authors. All go back ultimately to an eye-witness account, that of Antony's lieutenant, Q. Dellius, who wrote a monograph on the subject.[7] Livy devoted book 130 of his history to the topic. The book is now lost, though an epitome survives (*Per.* 130). It is also preserved in various later and briefer works based in whole or in part on Livy, namely the work of the historian Florus (2.19–20), active during the reigns of Trajan and Hadrian; two fourth-century *Breviaria* dedicated to the emperor Valens by Eutropius (7.5–6) and Festus (18.3); and the *History* of Paullus Orosius (6.18–19), the student of St. Augustine. Other Augustan authors who treat of the campaign include Velleius Paterculus (2.78.1; 2.82) and Strabo in his *Geography* (11.13.3–4; 11.14.9; 11.14.15; 12.2.11; 16.1.28). Pompeius Trogus dealt with the campaign and his treatment survives in the epitome by Justin (42.4.7–5.5). Appian gave a full account in his lost *Parthica*, but included a few references in his history of the civil wars (*BC* 5.4–10; 5.51; 5.65; 5.75–76; 5.93–94; 5.133–136; 5.140; 5.145). Only a thumbnail sketch can be compiled from these sources. More detailed accounts are given by Plutarch in his *Life of Antony* (3, 23–26, 28, 30, 33–56, 61) and Cassius Dio in his *Roman History* (48.24–28; 48.35; 48.39–41; 48.46; 48.54; 49.17–33; 49.39–41; 49.44; 51.5.5; 51.16–18). It is precisely the richness of the detail in these two accounts that invites one to explore more deeply what is going on and ultimately to set aside the standard negative interpretation of Antony's expedition. As the old saw goes, the devil is in the details.

Before we plunge into those details, we must first identify and – it is to be hoped – exorcize our devils. We know from both Plutarch and Dio that the propaganda war between Octavian and Antony intensified in the years between Antony's expedition of 36 and the Battle of Actium in 31 BCE.[8] We also know that Antony's doings in the East were a key part of Octavian's propaganda.

The original source for our account of the campaign of 36 is Antony's lieutenant Q. Dellius, who accompanied Antony into Media and later wrote a monograph on the topic. Strabo appeals to Dellius' work by name for information about Media that he includes in his *Geography* (11.13.3). Dellius' chief contribution to the history of the age – and indeed of the world – was his introduction of Cleopatra to Antony at Tarsus in the period immediately following the triumvirs' victory over Caesar's murderers at the battle of Philippi in 42.[9] It was a service that Dellius came to regret and he defected to Octavian before Actium.[10] For both political and personal or psychological reasons, it is unlikely that Dellius' portrait of Antony would be entirely flattering and some of the criticism of Antony's handling of the campaign detailed by Plutarch must have come from him.[11] The Augustan historian Livy, who hands on Dellius' account to many – if not all – of our other authors hardly can be expected to have mitigated negative aspects of his portrayal and perhaps amplified them. Livy may have been Pompeian in his sentiments, as Augustus himself observed, but he surely was not Antonian![12]

Plutarch, whether he used Dellius directly or as mediated through Livy, also has his problems. The point of Plutarch's account of Antony's campaign, which dominates the middle part of his biography and serves as the link between Antony's earlier achievements and his disastrous mishandling of the Actian War, is to highlight one of Antony's few acknowledged virtues, namely that Antony was at his best when the going got tough.[13] It is in Plutarch's interests to focus on the hardships faced by Antony in the campaign and especially the long retreat from Media back to Armenia.[14]

Given the bias of the sources and the shadow of the ultimate Augustan victory over the telling of the history of the triumviral period, we must ask the question, before continuing, whether it is possible to say anything with certainty regarding Antony's campaign in Media. The accounts of the campaign in the ancient authors whose works are preserved make it clear that Dellius' history of the campaign was full of detail. It seems unlikely that it could all have been fabricated. Strabo and Livy both seem to have found the work dependable. In the arguments advanced in this paper, the facts as recorded in the sources will generally be trusted. The interpretation of those facts by the ancient authors will be subjected to scrutiny and often set aside.

Before turning to a detailed analysis of the campaign itself, let us address the question of its success. Though the sources uniformly present it as a disaster, many of them contain hints of its success. Florus says that after his return to Syria Antony perversely grew more confident, as if by escaping the Parthians he had been victorious.[15] Similarly, Velleius says that Antony considered his flight to be a victory because he had survived.[16]

Dio gives much greater detail. He says that the true nature of the defeat was known to some in Rome by way of rumor, though Antony's dispatches reported victories. Octavian investigated, but decided not to expose Antony's troubles. Instead he offered public sacrifices and thanksgiving. Dio says that Octavian was afraid to expose the truth because of his own difficulties with Sextus Pompeius.[17]

These three authors offer testimony to a positive interpretation of Antony's campaign of 36 and each finds a way to explain it away.[18] When these explanations are stripped away, we have the following facts: Antony reported successes in his dispatches to Rome and Octavian celebrated the good news with public sacrifices and thanksgivings.[19]

We might add three further considerations. First is the fact that the king of the Medes was so ready to switch sides after the war.[20] If Antony had made a poor showing, it is unlikely that the Median king would be inclined to throw over the victorious Parthian king, Phraates IV, in favor of the vanquished Roman. Secondly, after the campaign of 36 a pretender to the Parthian throne arose to challenge Phraates (Just. 42.5.4–9; Dio 51.18). It is hard to imagine that a king who had just achieved a signal victory over the other principal regional power would inspire an attempt to usurp his throne. Thirdly, Plutarch (*Ant.* 43.2) tells us that during Antony's retreat, his men saluted him with an imperial acclamation, an honor reserved for victorious generals.[21] When Plutarch (*Ant.* 50.1) sums up Antony's withdrawal from Media he tells us that the Romans marched for twenty-seven days, during which time they successfully engaged with the Parthians eighteen times.

The evidence is not decisive on its own, but when one considers the importance of Antony's failure in the East in Augustan propaganda, it is shocking that there is any evidence at all to the contrary. One does not want to press this too far, but at least a circumstantial case can be made that the extent of the catastrophe has been exaggerated and that at the time there was a positive assessment of Antony's achievement. There is a hint of success, even if only limited success.

There could be no success, however, if Antony's aim had been a full-scale war against Parthia. It would take a masterful spin-doctor to claim victory in such circumstances. So we must turn to the next question: What exactly was Antony claiming success for? What was he trying to accomplish through his invasion of Atropatene? We need to look at the campaign in detail, relying primarily on Plutarch and Dio, with occasional attention to the minor sources. We shall be especially interested to examine the interactions among the principal players: Antony, the Median king, the Armenian king, and Phraates. One must remember that they had motives, too, which might help us to understand what was going on.

Phraates was newly established on the throne when he first made contact with Rome through the Parthian noble Monaeses, who, fearing for his life during the purges of potential rivals that accompanied Phraates' assumption of royal office, fled to Antony (Plut., *Ant.* 37; Dio 49.23–24). Antony offered to support Monaeses' bid for the Parthian throne. Terrified, Phraates reconciled with Monaeses, who returned to Parthia. Antony was supposedly disappointed, but sent envoys with Monaeses to negotiate peace with Phraates, demanding the return of the standards captured from Crassus in 53 BCE. Plutarch and Dio inform us that this was a ruse designed to lull the Parthian while Antony prepared war.[22]

One of the most remarkable features of the story is the reconciliation between Monaeses and Phraates. One wonders what Phraates could possibly have promised to induce his potential rival to return into his murderous clutches. Nor was this merely a trick to lure him back, for we see Monaeses again later with the Parthian army in

Media, perhaps as its commander.[23] It certainly seems out of character for Phraates to be so trusting. Incredulity has led some scholars to suggest that Monaeses had been a "double agent" all along, but this merely solves the problem by adding another layer of complication.[24]

Let us look at the bare facts. Phraates was newly established on the throne. A leading noble came to Antony in Syria. Antony may have proposed backing an attempt to seize the Parthian throne. Monaeses declined and returned to Parthia, facilitating a diplomatic exchange between the triumvir and the Parthian king, during which Antony requested the return of Crassus' standards. When Augustus later requested the standards, it was intended as a goodwill gesture on Phraates' part to solidify an agreement of friendship between the two, however Augustus may have presented the exchange for domestic consumption in Rome.[25] Could he have been following in Antony's footsteps here as he did in virtually all of his other arrangements in the East? In other words, might Antony have been attempting to reach a real agreement with Phraates to be marked by the Parthian's return of the Roman standards?

There is a tantalizing piece of evidence that suggests this. Florus states that the deaths of Crassus and the Parthian prince Pacorus, who was killed by Antony's lieutenant, P. Ventidius Bassus, in 38 BCE during a Parthian invasion of Syria, gave proof of Parthian and Roman strength. After the death of Pacorus – and incidentally his father Orodes at the hands of his son and heir, Phraates – friendship was renewed and Antony concluded a treaty with the king.[26] One might be inclined to dismiss this as confusion on Florus' part. But could it possibly be true or at least have a kernel of truth? Florus goes on to state that despite the treaty Antony attacked the Parthian without cause or declaration of war. But Antony did not do so. He invaded Media Atropatene. The two sides only fought when the Parthian came to the defense of his Median ally.

It would have been a good time for an understanding between Rome and Parthia. The victory of Antony through his lieutenant, Ventidius, over the Parthians had quieted Roman demands that M. Licinius Crassus be avenged.[27] Syria had been secured by the expulsion of the Parthian forces. The frontier had been reestablished. The upheavals in the Roman world following the murder of Caesar also had died down. The death of the crown prince Pacorus had paved the way for Phraates' accession to the throne. In his request for the return of Crassus' standards, Antony might have been hoping for a settlement with Parthia. Antony was engaged in a general rearrangement of the Roman East. An agreement with Parthia would have been a key element in that. It was not to be until after Actium.

We might now turn to the events of the campaign. At the invitation of Artavasdes the king of Armenia, Antony marched into his kingdom with a large force. There he met up with his lieutenant, P. Canidius Crassus, who had spent the winter of 37/36 BCE subduing the Caucasus.[28] Artavasdes had proposed an invasion of neighboring Media Atropatene, whose king, also named Artavasdes, had been summoned to Parthia. The Armenian accompanied Antony with forces of his own. When Antony raced ahead to

Phraaspa the Armenian remained behind with the ill-fated Statianus and the baggage. He fled when the baggage was attacked.

There are many interesting features of this "Battle of the Baggage." Plutarch (*Ant.* 38) implies that it was a Parthian force that fell on the baggage; he mentions that the Parthian king arrived with an army and later refers to them as "barbarians." Dio (49.25) records that it was a mixed force of Parthians and Medes. In fact, the latter is true, for we learn later that it was Artavasdes the Mede who had captured the standards of Statianus' two legions and Polemo, the king of Pontus.[29] One might surmise from the Mede's acquisition of these plum spoils that he played a prominent role in the battle. How surprising, then, is Plutarch's failure to mention the Medes. This, however, is characteristic not only of Plutarch, but of all the sources. The king of the Medes, though it was his kingdom that was under attack, is hardly ever mentioned in the sources. In contrast, the king of Parthia is omnipresent, though Plutarch (*Ant.* 44.2) mentions on one occasion that he was never present at any of the battles.

A second interesting feature of the "Battle of the Baggage" is the unexpected nature of the attack. Antony clearly did not foresee it. Two legions is a good-sized escort to ward off brigands and minor attacks, but certainly not enough to defend against the combined forces of the Parthians and Medes. Could Antony have been that much of a fool? Even supposing he was, could the Armenian king have been? It had been his idea to invade Atropatene (Dio 49.25.1–2; *cf.* Plut., *Ant.* 39; Strabo 11.13.4). He accompanied Antony, intent no doubt on a share of the loot, until the unexpected arrival of the Parthians and Medes. Dismayed, he fled back to Armenia, later to be accused of treachery. Clearly Artavasdes was not expecting that Antony would meet such resistance. I would assume that the Armenian was more frightened by the appearance of the Parthians than the Medes. Surely Antony's forces would have been adequate to deal with the Mede alone. Judging from this it is unlikely that the Armenian viewed Antony's undertaking as a Parthian war. Rather it was a Median war.

Despite the loss of his siege equipment, Antony pressed on with the siege. Indeed, he clung tenaciously to the siege of Phraaspa. Some scholars have wondered why.[30] I assume that he wanted to capture it in order to get what was inside, namely the wives, children, and treasure of the Median king. He could have used these as leverage to force the Mede to come to terms with him and abandon his alliance with the Parthian king.

As for the battle between Antony and the Parthians, once again the narrative contains some surprising details. Plutarch (*Ant.* 39; *cf.* Dio 49.25) gives the fullest account. When he learned that the Parthians were in the neighborhood – again no mention of the Medes – Antony took ten legions and his cavalry a day's march away from Phraaspa to forage. The Parthians moved in. Antony gave the order to strike camp as though he planned to withdraw rather than fight. The Parthian cavalry arranged itself in a crescent and watched silently as Antony's forces marched by. When the Parthians were within striking distance, Antony ordered his cavalry to charge. The Parthians beat it back. Antony then ordered his infantry to charge and the Parthians retreated with minimal losses. The story is remarkable because of the passivity of the Parthians. If one did not know there was a war on, it might appear that the Parthians wanted to avoid a clash with Antony's forces. If they were not there to fight, what were they there to do? There is no suggestion that the Parthian force was trying to hinder Antony's foraging. Perhaps they were just there to project a menacing presence. They do not seem to have been there to fight.

Antony returned to the siege as winter was approaching. According to Plutarch (*Ant.* 40; *cf.* Dio 49.27) neither Roman nor Parthian could stomach the thought of wintering under canvas. Plutarch tells us that Parthian soldiers began to fraternize with Romans out on foraging detail. They approached the Romans and confided that Phraates wanted a truce so they could all go home. Of course, what the Roman soldiers did not know – but Plutarch informs us – is that it was all a trick (δόλον). Antony supposedly fell for it and sent envoys to Phraates. During the negotiations, his envoys once again requested the return of Crassus' standards. In Plutarch's account the request makes Antony look desperate, trying to salvage something from his failed campaign. But it is entirely possible that Antony was making the demand as his price for peace. If so, the Parthian refused, guaranteeing him merely a safe passage home. Antony dropped the request and struck camp. It is worth remembering that even the great Augustus had to ask Phraates twice before he got Crassus' standards back.[31]

The return to Armenia was difficult. Plutarch (*Ant.* 41–49; *cf.* Dio 49.28–33), once again, gives the fullest account. Antony set off on the wrong foot at the beginning when he opted to make his return by a route different from the one by which he had come (Plut., *Ant.* 41.1–2). He chose this route because it went by Median villages and was better stocked with supplies. He did hesitate at first to take it out of fear that he might appear to distrust the Parthians, with whom he had a truce.[32] His guide assured him that the Parthians deserved to be distrusted since the truce was all a trick to get Antony in open country where he would be vulnerable to Parthian tactics.

Antony was right to have worried that the Parthians might take it amiss that he had decided to leave Media by a different route, especially one that took him past Median villages, for a few days into their march the Romans were hindered by a flood caused by a broken dike (Plut., *Ant.* 41.3–5). Just then the Parthians descended on them to attack, but were driven off. The Parthians would continue to harass the Romans for a number of days. Gradually individual Parthians began to mingle with Roman foraging parties (Plut., *Ant.* 46.1–2). Displaying unstrung bows the Parthians declared that they were getting ready to return home, but that the Medes would continue to shadow the Romans in order to protect outlying villages. This is a significant detail; for only the second time we hear mention of the Medes. They are finally seen defending their own country, while the Parthians are backing off again. The Median desire to take care of outlying settlements is unsurprising. So, too, is Parthian ambivalence. One begins to suspect that the Parthians have not really had their heart in this war.

Antony was again inclined to trust the claims of the Parthian soldiers. At this moment Monaeses returns into the picture (Plut., *Ant.* 46.2–4). He sent an envoy named Mithridates to Antony warning him not to diverge from his present route lest he fall victim to an ambush. An ambush set by whom? We are not told. Antony stuck to his previous route until he came to a river, but when he camped at night the messenger from Monaeses returned urging Antony to make haste to cross the river (Plut., *Ant.* 48.1–2). At dawn the Romans broke camp and made for the river. The Parthians appeared for one last attack, but as the Romans reached the river the Parthians unstrung their bows and cheered the Romans on, full of praise for their valor (Plut., *Ant.* 49). One gets the sense that they were relieved that the Romans were finally gone.

What are we to make of all this? It would seem that the biggest concern of the Parthians was to keep the Romans moving. They did so by maintaining pressure on the Romans and by cutting them off from supplies. There is evidence as well that they continued to be friendly to the Romans.[33] To be sure, there is evidence of military activity, but it is hard to tell what is going on. The Medes were about and were likely to be less forgiving of the Romans. It is extremely unlikely that an army as big as Antony's could pass through enemy territory and pass by enemy villages without incident. The question that cannot be answered is: How much responsibility should be assigned to the Medes for the harassment of the Romans? Should we take at face value the Parthian soldiers' claims that they were going home and that the Medes would continue to keep watch over their outlying villages? Are Medes being turned into Parthians? But why do so? This brings us to our last point: the falling out between the Median and the Parthian kings.

Both Dio (49.33.1–2) and Plutarch (*Ant.* 52) record that a dispute arose between the kings over the division of the spoils. Plutarch adds that the Mede feared that Phraates might take his kingdom away. The Mede released Polemo to negotiate an alliance with Antony. Antony was so delighted that he bestowed Armenia Minor upon Polemo. Ultimately the Mede and Antony teamed up for a war on Armenia: sweet revenge for Antony, who had been betrayed by the Armenian king, and for the Mede, who could pay the Armenian back for setting Antony on him in the first place (Plut., *Ant.* 50.4; Dio 49.39).

Once again the details call for analysis. What spoils are we talking about? The Mede had acquired the most politically useful ones, namely Statianus' standards, which he later returned to Antony, and the client-king of Pontus. There were no other major battles whereby the Parthians and Medes might have obtained spoils. If one were to accept the reconstruction that I have presented, he might be inclined to imagine that the main bone of contention was the half-hearted commitment of the Parthians to defend Media Atropatene. They were there, but rather unenthusiastic about their role, taking care to avoid any serious conflict with the invading Romans.

It is necessary now to bring these observations together in an effort to understand Antony's policy regarding Parthia and Media Atropatene in 36. Antony may have come to the Near East in 42 BCE as a Roman imperialist, but his decade of living there and his close association with the Egyptian queen Cleopatra had its affect. At the time of his death, Caesar had been planning a Dacian War and a Parthian War. It fell to the emperor Trajan to carry out those designs, not to Antony. The triumvir's aims were more limited and yet more far-reaching. He did not set out to conquer Parthia, as perhaps, but only perhaps, Caesar would have done. Rather he sought to contain Parthia and to establish a *modus vivendi*.

We must remember the immediate context of Antony's campaign of 36. Since Crassus' death at Carrhae in 53 the initiative in Roman-Parthian relations had rested with the Parthians. Roman policy was reactive. Rome was waiting for an attack, as Cicero's letters from his governorship in Cilicia attest.[34] That attack came in the wake of Philippi when a Parthian army under the joint command of the Roman renegade Labienus and the crown prince Pacorus crossed the Euphrates and penetrated far into Syria, Judaea, and even Asia Minor. Antony's lieutenant, P. Ventidius Bassus, pushed them back, killing the two commanders in the process. Crassus was avenged and Ventidius went home to celebrate a triumph – an honor he shared with Antony, whose legate he was (Dio 49.21; Plut., *Ant.* 34.5). The defeat and death of Pacorus threw the Parthians into a turmoil that took the life of Pacorus' father King Orodes and saw Phraates succeed him.

Antony seized the initiative. He sent P. Canidius to secure the north: Armenia, Albania, and Iberia. Antony then sought to extend Roman influence into Media. The campaign of 36 did not turn out entirely as he perhaps expected. Despite Antony's attempts at negotiation with the Parthian king before setting out for Armenia, the Parthians showed up to defend Media Atropatene. A surprise attack on the baggage and siege equipment slowed down his plans. He was ultimately forced to withdraw. His losses during the withdrawal were brought on by weather and natural causes, rather than the enemy. Indeed, the Parthians were mostly non-committal after their victory over Statianus. The successes that Antony did achieve, coupled with the hesitancy of the Parthians, inspired the Median king to submit to him voluntarily. Antony then did something no other Roman could: he prepared to cement the alliance with a marriage.[35] With this Antony the dynast fully emerges.

The triumvir and consort of the queen of Egypt could interact with the eastern kings on their own terms in ways no other Roman could. The politics of the Near East were dynastic. The connections between the royal houses of Parthia, Armenia, and Media demonstrate this. Prior to Antony, Roman governors in the region had managed the kingdoms and states beyond the Roman frontier through changing or maintaining local dynasties. Antony followed this tradition before the Median War. After it, however, Antony fully entered into the dynastic politics of the region by betrothing his son by the queen of Egypt to the daughter of the king of Media. Rather than staying on the outside of the game of dynastic politics, Antony had become a player himself. At the time of Actium he had three young children, each of whom could have served dynastic purposes.[36] One can only speculate what ultimate arrangements Antony would have brought to the Near East through his participation in the region's dynastic politics, but bringing stability to Roman-Parthian relations was a first step.

That Antony's deft handling of the Parthian situation was successful finds unlikely support from Augustus himself. Antony was forced to withdraw Roman soldiers from Armenia and Media to fight the Actian War.[37] Phraates seized the opportunity to restore his influence in the two kingdoms. When Augustus came to settle things with Phraates in 20 BCE he cribbed his solution right from Antony's playbook. Tiberius was dispatched to recover Armenia and Media Atropatene, which were both entrusted to friendly kings. Augustus pressured Phraates to return the standards taken from Crassus as a sign of the Parthian's willingness to establish cordial relations between the empires. This is precisely what Antony had tried to do and might have succeeded in doing had it not been for Actium. And this is likely the reason why Augustus had to reinterpret and misrepresent Antony's aims in the East.

Notes

1. The text of the present chapter is substantially the same as that of the paper as originally read at the third meeting of the Parthia panel at the annual meeting of The American Schools of Oriental Research in November 2014. It is not meant to be an exhaustive treatment of Antony's time in the Near East nor even of Antony's Median war of 36 BCE. I have added citations to the ancient sources and some references to modern scholarship, where particularly relevant. I would like to thank Drs. Benjamin Rubin and Jason Schlude for organizing the Parthia panel at which I presented this paper and another that I did not revise for publication in the present volume. The panel provided an excellent opportunity for fruitful collaboration between students of Parthia and the Roman Near East. I would also like to thank Dr. Schlude for many long conversations, which contributed a great deal to this paper. Finally, I would like to thank Professor Erich S. Gruen for his comments on this paper when it was delivered. I have given dates using the formula "BCE" and "CE" in accordance with editorial policy rather than my own preference.
2. The principal treatments in English are Tarn 1934, 71–75; Debevoise 1938, 121–142; Syme 1939, 259–275; Huzar 1978, 169–184; Sherwin-White 1984, 307–321; Pelling 1988, 220–243; all of which adhere to the standard interpretation, though at times noting difficulties, especially Sherwin-White. The one major exception is Schieber 1979, 105–124. The author of the present paper is in substantial agreement with the conclusions reached by Schieber, though the argument here proceeds along different lines.
3. For evidence and analysis of this aspect of Augustus' program see Rose 2005, 21–75; Merriam 2005, 56–70. Well-known expressions of this theme include the depiction on the cuirass of the Prima Porta Augustus of a kneeling Parthian returning the standards taken from Crassus; the same image on an issue of *denarii* minted in 19 BCE; Augustus' own claim to have compelled the surrender of the standards on his epitaph (*RG* 29.2); and references in the poems of Horace (*e.g. Epist.* 1.12.27–28; *Carm.* 1.12.49–54; 2.13.17–18; 3.2.1–4; 3.5.2–4; 4.5.25–27; 4.15.6–8; *Carm. Saec.* 49–56) and Virgil (*e.g. Georg.* 1.509; 3.30–33; 4.312–314; *Aen.* 7.606; 12.855–859).
4. For the parallels between the Parthian policy of Augustus and Antony see Schlude 2015.
5. What follows is a composite picture of the campaign drawing on various sources. There will be more attention devoted to specific points below. The main sources for the campaign are Plut., *Ant.* 35–52 and Dio 49.24–31. Debevoise 1938, 121–142, provides a useful narrative account of the campaign.
6. Patterson 2015, 77–105, makes a very good case against the commonly supposed annexation of Armenia by Antony.

7. The citations in this paragraph are not exhaustive, but rather record the main narrative in whole or in part. For fuller citations, see Broughton 1984, 2.400; Sherwin-White 1984, 306.

8. For the propaganda war between Octavian and Antony see Scott 1933, 7–49; also Syme 1939, 270–275, who sums up well the success of Octavian's propaganda: "The version of the victors is palpably fraudulent; the truth cannot be disinterred, for it has been doubly buried, in erotic romance as well as in political mythology. Of the facts, there is and was no authentic record; even if there were, it would be necessary further to speculate upon the policy and intentions of Antonius, the domination which Cleopatra had achieved over him and the nature of her own ambitions. A fabricated concatenation of unrealized intentions may be logical, artistic and persuasive, but it is not history" (270).

9. Plut., *Ant.* 25, recounts that Dellius was aware of the effect that Cleopatra's attractions would have on Antony and encouraged her to bring her charms to bear on the susceptible triumvir.

10. Plut., *Ant.* 59.4, records that Dellius defected to Octavian when he learned that Cleopatra was plotting to kill him over a remark he had made during a dinner slighting the quality of the wine that was being served. Sen., *Suas.* 1.7, recalls that Messala Corvinus styled Dellius the "vaulter of the civil wars" (*desultorem bellorum civilium*), a reference to his deftness in deserting the losing side for the winning; he had jumped from Dolabella to Cassius, from Cassius to Antony, and from Antony to Octavian.

11. Pelling 1988, 28, ascribes some of the material in Plutarch's *Life of Antony* that is critical of Antony and especially of Cleopatra to Dellius writing after his defection. Syme 1939, 265, 484, suggests that Dellius would have been apt to exaggerate the extent of Antony's disaster. It is entirely reasonable that a man who had served Antony at such a high level would seek justification for his ultimate betrayal of his former commander and benefactor in the failings, both real and perceived – and perhaps embellished – of the triumvir. If Dellius were writing his history under Octavian, he also would have cause to tarnish the memory of the new emperor's onetime enemy in order to ingratiate himself.

12. Tac., *Ann.* 4.34: *Titus Livius, eloquentiae ac fidei praeclarus in primis, Cn. Pompeium tantis laudibus tulit, ut Pompeianum eum Augustus appellaret; neque id amicitiae eorum offecit.*

13. Plut., *Ant.* 17.3, draws attention to this virtue.

14. Pelling 1988, 221, suggests that, while Plutarch's main narrative is drawn from Dellius, the biographer himself is responsible for the emphasis placed on Antony's good generalship during the retreat. Pelling also finds numerous allusions to Xenophon's *Anabasis*, which he likewise ascribes to Plutarch's desire to embellish and shape the narrative. Plutarch (*Ant.* 45.6) himself draws attention to the similarities between the marches of Antony and Xenophon, when he records that Antony would often express his admiration for Xenophon's feat crying out, "O the Ten Thousand!" (Ὦ μύριοι).

15. Flor. 2.20.10: *tandem perfugit in Syriam, ubi incredibili quadam mentis vaecordia ferocior aliquanto factus est, quasi vicisset, quia evaserat.*

16. Vell. Pat. 2.82.3: *hanc tamen Antonius fugam suam, quia vivus exierat, victoriam vocabat.*

17. Dio 49.32.1–2: οἱ δὲ δὴ οἴκοι Ῥωμαῖοι ἠγνόουν μὲν οὐδὲν τῶν γεγονότων, οὐχ ὅτι τἀληθὲς ἐκεῖνος ἐπέστειλέ σφισι (πάντα γὰρ δὴ τὰ δυσχερῆ συνέκρυπτε, καὶ ἔστιν ἅ γε αὐτῶν καὶ ἐς τὸ ἐναντιώτατον, ὡς καὶ εὐπραγῶν, ἔγραφεν), ἀλλ᾽ ὅτι ἥ τε φήμη τὴν ἀλήθειαν ἐσήγγελλε, καὶ ὁ Καῖσαρ οἵ τε ἄλλοι οἱ συνόντες αὐτῷ καὶ ἐπολυπραγμόνουν ἀκριβῶς αὐτὰ καὶ διεθρύλουν, οὐ μέντοι καὶ ἐν τῷ κοινῷ διήλεγχον, ἀλλὰ καὶ ἐβουθύτουν καὶ ἑώρταζον· τοῦ γὰρ Καίσαρος πρὸς τὸν Σέξτον ἔτι καὶ τότε προσπταίοντος οὔτε εὐπρεπὴς οὔτε ἐπίκαιρος ὁ ἔλεγχος αὐτῶν γίγνεσθαι ἐδύνατο.

18. The justification offered by Dio for Octavian's playing along with Antony's misleading dispatches, namely that he was having his own troubles with Sextus Pompeius, can be shown to be false based on timing. Agrippa's victory over Pompeius at Naulochus occurred on September 3 of 36 BCE. Antony did not lift the siege of Phraaspa till October of that year. The only major reversal that Antony had experienced on the field of battle was the loss of two legions and the

baggage, but Antony had not been present. Other losses were suffered on the withdrawal from Media to Armenia, but those were almost entirely the result of the weather, lack of supplies, and illness.

19. Nor were these the only honors that Octavian bestowed on Antony. Dio 49.17–18 tells how Sextus Pompeius fled to Asia Minor after his defeat by Agrippa. At Lesbos he heard of Antony's expedition into Media and subsequently learned of Antony's difficulties. He was inspired to attempt a takeover of Asia. He supposedly entered into negotiations with Phraates, but was eventually captured and executed by forces loyal to Antony. In commemoration Octavian sponsored games in the Circus, set up a chariot in front of the Rostra, put statues of Antony in the Temple of Concord, and extended to Antony and his family permission to banquet in the same temple. It is true that Dio says these honors were given to Antony for his role in disposing of Sextus Pompeius, but they came right on the heels of his Median expedition. It is intriguing to speculate whether this might be further evidence of public celebration of Antony's achievements in 36, but must remain speculative. Dio ends his account by once more explaining away Octavian's public support for Antony: Octavian felt sorry for Antony and was trying to console him for his disastrous campaign against the Parthians; furthermore, Octavian was trying to prevent Antony from feeling envious of Octavian's own successes and the decrees celebrating them. The reinterpretation is not very compelling.

20. Plut., *Ant.* 52, tells the story, which we shall return to in some detail below.

21. See Pelling 1988, 232.

22. Plut., *Ant.* 37.2; Dio 49.24.5: καὶ λόγῳ μὲν τὴν εἰρήνην ἔπραττεν ἐπὶ τῷ τά τε σημεῖα καὶ τοὺς αἰχμαλώτους τοὺς ἐν τῇ τοῦ Κράσσου συμφορᾷ ἁλόντας κομίσασθαι, ἵνα ἀπαράσκευον τὸν βασιλέα διὰ τὴν τῆς σθμβάσεως ἐλπίδα λάβῃ, ἔργῳ δὲ τὰ τοῦ πολέμου πάντα ἡτοιμάζετο.

23. Plut., *Ant.* 46.4–5, makes it likely that Monaeses was involved with the Parthian opposition to Antony's Median campaign. Hor., *Carm.* 3.6.9–12, links the names of Monaeses and Pacorus to victories over Roman arms: *iam bis Monaeses et Pacori manus | non auspicatos contudit impetus | nostros et adiecisse praedam | torquibus exiguis renidet.* Pelling 1988, 221, suggests that Monaeses might have been in command at the battle in which Statianus and the baggage train were lost.

24. Monaeses as "double agent": Tarn 1934, 71; Pelling 1988, 221–222.

25. On the negotiations see Sherwin-White 1984, 322–325; see also Schlude and Rubin's contribution to the present volume, "Chapter 4. Finding Common Ground: Roman-Parthian Embassies in the Julio-Claudian Period".

26. Flor. 2.20.10: *expertis invicem Parthis atque Romanis, cum Crassus et Pacorus utrimque virium mutuarum documenta fecissent, pari rursus reverentia integrata amicitia, et quidem ab ipso foedus Antonio cum rege percussum.*

27. The passage from Florus discussed in the previous paragraph attests to this. Plut., *Ant.* 34.2, says that the Romans felt that the victory over Pacorus fully repaid the Parthians for Crassus' defeat. There was also an enduring tradition in antiquity that the defeat of Pacorus fell on the same day as had Crassus' disaster: Dio 49.21.2; Eutrop. 7.5; Fest., *Brev.* 18; Oros. 6.18.

28. The principal sources are Plut., *Ant.* 34.6; Dio 49.24.1; see Broughton 1984, 2.397, 2.401.

29. Dio 49.33.1–2 (Polemo), 44.2 (standards).

30. Sherwin-White 1984, 313–318, puzzles over Antony's strategic choice of besieging Phraaspa, but arrives at no good solution. Apart from Phraaspa being a royal residence, it is hard to see what strategic purpose the capture of Phraaspa would accomplish. If he merely sought to bring the Parthian king to battle, then why did he continue the siege after fighting the Parthian? It is even harder to imagine how capturing the town would benefit Antony in a war against the Parthian king. The aim must have been more limited to the Median context.

31. On Augustus' negotiations with Phraates IV, see Sherwin-White 1984, 322–323; see also chapter four in the present volume.

32. Antony's decision to return to Armenia by a route different from the one that had brought him to Phraaspa likely violated the truce in spirit, if not according to the letter. This requires the rather elaborate story of Parthian perfidy, to put Antony in the right as they travelled back to Armenia through territory that had not yet seen the Roman army. It was wise of Antony to return by this new route as it led past Median villages that might offer supplies to the Romans, but it is easy to see why this would be unwelcome to the king of the Medes and his ally.
33. In this connection we have to assess Monaeses' motives for helping Antony. Surely he would not have risked the displeasure of the Parthian king by reporting the king's battle-plans to Antony and allowing the Romans to escape.
34. See Sherwin-White 1984, 290–297, for an account of Cicero's governorship of Cilicia; see also Engels 2008.
35. Dio 49.44.2.
36. Indeed, Antony's daughter by Cleopatra, Cleopatra Selene, did go on to marry King Juba II of Numidia and Mauretania; their son ruled after his father until 40 CE when he was killed on the orders of his cousin Caligula. Antony's example was not followed, though after Actium the Roman world again found itself under a monarch. Augustus and his successors did not engage in such dynastic marriages outside the bounds of Roman citizenship, though they did take a great interest in the dynastic connections of kings under their authority, as for example the Herodians of Judaea and beyond.
37. Plut., *Ant.* 56.1; Dio 51.16.2; *cf.* Tac., *Ann.* 2.3.

Bibliography

Broughton, T. R. S. (1984) *The Magistrates of the Roman Republic*, vol. 1–3. Chico, California, Scholars Press.
Debevoise, N. C. (1938) *A Political History of Parthia*. Chicago, University of Chicago Press.
Engels, D. (2008) "Cicéron comme proconsul en Cilicie et la guerre contre les Parthes." *Revue belge de philologie et d'histoire* Année 86.1, 23–45.
Huzar, E. G. (1978) *Mark Antony: A Biography*. Minneapolis, University of Minnesota Press.
Merriam, C. U. (2005) "'Either with Us or against Us': The Parthian in Augustan Ideology." *Scholia: Studies in Classical Antiquity* 13, 56–70.
Patterson, L. E. (2015) "Antony and Armenia." *Transactions of the American Philological Association* 145, 77–105.
Pelling, C. B. R. (1988) *Plutarch: Life of Antony*. Cambridge, Cambridge University Press.
Rose, C. B. (2005) "The Parthians in Augustan Rome." *American Journal of Archaeology* 109.1, 21–75.
Schieber, A. S. (1979) "Antony and Parthia." *Rivista Storica dell'Antichità* 9, 105–124.
Schlude, J. M. (2015) "The Early Parthian Policy of Augustus." *Anabasis: Studia Classica et Orientalia* 6, 139–156.
Scott, K. (1933) "The Political Propaganda of 44–30 B.C." *Memoirs of the American Academy in Rome* 11, 7–49.
Sherwin-White, A. N. (1984) *Roman Foreign Policy in the East, 168 B.C. to A.D. 1*. Norman, University of Oklahoma Press.
Syme, R. (1939) *The Roman Revolution*. Oxford and New York, Oxford University Press.
Tarn, W. W. (1934) "The Invasion of Parthia." In S. A. Cook, F. E. Adcock, and M. P. Charlesworth (eds.) *The Cambridge Ancient History*, vol. 10, 71–75.

Chapter 4

Finding Common Ground: Roman-Parthian Embassies in the Julio-Claudian Period

Jason M. Schlude

and

Benjamin B. Rubin

Introduction: Defining the "Embassy" and the Problem

In our paper, we are interested in the "embassy" in the context of Roman-Parthian relations. This subject leads one to consider episodes of diplomatic exchange that happened under many different circumstances, in many different locations, and between individuals of many different ranks. Indeed, these embassies happened during times of peace, tension, and war (external and civil). They involved emperors, kings, princes, generals, statesmen, and numerous lower level envoys. The meetings took place in Rome, the Parthian empire, and in many Near Eastern locations, including Syria, Armenia, and the traditional Roman-Parthian boundary of the Euphrates river. In short, what was the significance of these embassies in Roman-Parthian history?

For many scholars, embassies in Roman-Parthian relations enjoyed little long-term impact, and what lasting impact they did have was negative. To be sure, some have rightly recognized the role of the embassy in effecting peace in certain periods.[1] Even so, many scholars characterize diplomatic exchanges as political set pieces that often encouraged hostility, conflict, and warfare. In addition, many treatments of Roman-Parthian embassies (certainly the negative, but even the more positive) underestimate their potential in cross-cultural exchange.[2] In this chapter, we aim to show how embassies, especially in the Julio-Claudian period, functioned as mechanisms for achieving peace and for more refined mutual understanding.

Previous Scholarship

Firstly, we should consider the current scholarly paradigm. For it is true that not all embassies produced lasting, happy results. From this perspective, one could look at examples from the periods in which various appointments brought Sulla, Lucullus, Pompey, Crassus, and Antony into the Near East.

As for Sulla, Plutarch tells us that while he was serving as proconsul in Cilicia and establishing Ariobarzanes as client king in Cappadocia, he was the first Roman to be approached by a Parthian embassy *c.* 96/95 BCE – and with no positive result, it seems.

> And while he [Sulla] was passing time beside the Euphrates, a Parthian by the name of Orobazos, an ambassador of king Arsaces [Mithridates II], met with him, although not yet before had the peoples had relations with one another. (But even in this respect does Sulla seem to have enjoyed great fortune: he was the first of the Romans to whom the Parthians came in their requests for alliance and friendship.) When also he is said to have put out three chairs, one for Ariobarzanes, one for Orobazos, and one for himself, sitting down in the middle he is said to have carried out negotiations with them both. For this reason the king of the Parthians later killed Orobazos, and while some approved of Sulla's mockery of the barbarians, others censured him for being crass and fond of honor at an inopportune moment.[3]

Indeed here we have an initial diplomatic engagement, which offered the possibility of collaboration via "alliance and friendship" (συμμαχία καὶ φιλίας). And while we do not hear about the ultimate decisions on such a treaty, we are led to believe that Sulla acted in an insulting manner by publically setting himself up as the powerbroker of the Near East. Many scholars in fact assume that his behavior antagonized the Parthian king Mithridates and caused him not only to execute Orobazus, but also to turn against Rome.[4]

Later embassies would only make things worse, inciting and in fact requiring acts of military conflict. Already in the midst of an invasion of the Parthian empire, Crassus found himself approached by a Parthian embassy bearing a deliberately provocative message for the general who was in Syria late in the winter of 54/53 BCE. Once again, according to Plutarch,

> while he [Crassus] was already assembling his forces from their winter quarters, envoys from Arsaces [Orodes II] arrived bearing a brief communication. For they said that if the army had been sent off by the Romans, then it meant war without truce and reconciliation. But if, as they heard, against the wishes of his country Crassus had brought arms against the Parthians and had seized their land for the sake of private gains, then Arsaces would be moderate and take pity on the old age of Crassus and set free the Roman men whom he held as prisoners more than guards. And when in response to these things Crassus boasted that he would give his answers in Seleucia, the oldest of the envoys, Vagises, laughed and pointed to the middle of the palm of his hand and said, "O Crassus, hair will spring forth from here before you will see Seleucia."[5]

In short, the Parthians hardly intended their communication to soothe Crassus. Clearly their aim was just the opposite: to antagonize. What is more, the response of Crassus in the exchange only encouraged further war, locking him into a campaign itinerary that would take him deep into the Parthian empire. Whether Seleucia-on-the-Tigris was his goal in 54 BCE, we cannot know, but it likely must have been in the campaign season of 53 BCE that followed this exchange. If he did not reach Seleucia, Crassus would lose face – something intolerable for a Roman of his caliber.[6]

As is well known, however, he never made it. In the vicinity of Carrhae, the Parthian general Surenas surrounded Crassus and his men with cavalry. They proceeded to rain arrows upon the Romans, killing many. And when the Romans attempted to flee, first to Carrhae, and then further north to the hills of northern Mesopotamia, Surenas tenaciously pursued. In the end, so the story goes, Surenas tried to gain custody of Crassus by inviting him to a treacherous parley. Whether he knew of the ambush or not (the ancient sources disagree), Crassus chose to attend. At the meeting, the Parthians attempted to spirit Crassus away, his Roman lieutenants intervened, and an ensuing scuffle left Crassus dead. As if that was not enough, Surenas had Crassus' head cut off and either filled with molten gold or shipped special delivery to Armenia, where the Parthian king Orodes was cementing his relationship with Artavasdes of Armenia by a marriage alliance between his son Pacorus and the Armenian king's sister. In the latter scenario, Crassus surprisingly made a cameo in a staging of Euripides' *Bacchae* that was part of the wedding celebration; one of the actors assumed the role of crazed Agave and held up the head of Crassus as an all-too-real stand-in for Pentheus.[7]

All this then kicked off two decades of intermittent war that left little room for constructive diplomacy. And what evidence we do have for embassies scholars have often interpreted as being rather unimportant. Consider the exchange that took place in the early 30s BCE, when Antony responded to Parthian diplomatic activity to allegedly buy time for planning his own campaign against Parthia in 36 BCE. At that time, Antony had the Parthian defector Monaeses in his control. But when Phraates IV, the Arsacid successor to Orodes, wished to reconcile with Monaeses and recalled him to the Parthian empire,

> he [Antony] sent him [Monaeses] forth on the grounds that he would win the Parthians over to himself, and sent envoys with him to Phraates. He was pretending to try to achieve peace on the condition that he receive the standards and captives taken in the disaster of Crassus. This was in order that he might catch the king unprepared on account of his hope for a settlement. But in fact, he was making all things ready for war.

In other words, like Surenas, Antony perhaps was happy to use diplomacy as part of a ruse. While his envoys were on their way to stall the Parthian king, Antony set off to prepare his troops in Armenia for the attack (which also resulted in failure, like that of Crassus). All things considered then, this kind of diplomacy was hollow – and could only serve to undermine its importance in Roman-Parthian relations.[8]

Diplomacy and Peace in the Julio-Claudian Period

Yet this picture of Roman-Parthian diplomatic exchanges is not the whole picture. Yes, certain exchanges were not entirely constructive. The meeting between Sulla and Orobazos and its consequences come to mind.[9] And other exchanges were surely detrimental, leading to violent engagements. Recall here those under Crassus. Nevertheless, amidst all this violence and the intrigue, there are still glimmers of genuine diplomatic negotiation between the Romans and the Parthians, even during the late first century BCE. There is good reason to believe, for example, that Pompey and Phraates III used diplomacy to great positive effect. As is well known, Pompey opened a line of communications with Phraates in 66 BCE that both used throughout his time in the East. Little recognized, however, is how productive it proved. A number of scholars have emphasized tension, opposition, and hostility in the diplomatic engagements between Pompey and Phraates.[10] But in fact evidence suggests that Pompey and Phraates established the first clear treaty of alliance and friendship, agreed upon the Euphrates river as a Roman-Parthian border of sorts, and, when at one time Phraates was in a territorial dispute with Tigranes the Great, decided that Roman arbitration should settle the matter.[11] These were very progressive developments.

As for Antony, while he did embark on a campaign into the Parthian empire in 36 BCE, we cannot be certain that his previous diplomatic overtures to the later king Phraates IV to return the standards lost by Crassus were only a ploy to buy time to organize this campaign. Could he not have been seriously interested in such a settlement, if it could have been arranged? Indeed, his actions in this may have appeared genuine enough to Herod the Great. Around the time that Herod saw Antony negotiating with Parthia, whose power he fully recognized back in 40 BCE, he may have used it as an opportunity to open negotiations with his eastern neighbour as well, requesting back the Jewish hostage Hyrcanus II – a serious point of tension between Herod and the Parthian king. While the Phraates IV did not return the standards at this juncture, he did opt to return Hyrcanus. In part, this was likely a diplomatic gesture with a Roman appointee, intended to be a positive step in Roman-Parthian relations. If so, it was not enough for Antony, who opted to embark on his campaign against Parthia.[12]

Leaving these exchanges behind, however, there is significant evidence for an even more constructive – and durable – diplomatic dynamic in the Augustan period. Upon the demise of Antony in 31/30 BCE, Octavian took control of Rome's eastern affairs, including Roman policy on Parthia. Looking back on the period of 54 to 31 BCE, which was punctuated with several episodes of costly bloodshed, he opted for peace with Parthia. And he pursued this interest in peace through diplomatic channels.

Of course, this was particularly challenging, considering the fact that Parthia was gripped by a civil war between 31 and 25 BCE, in which Phraates IV was struggling to retain his throne against the claimant Tiridates II. Both sides in the conflict worked to monopolize Roman support. But if Octavian had allowed that, it would have necessarily drawn the Romans into war with one powerful Parthian faction or another.

Octavian had no interest in such involvement and risk. He knew that to achieve the desired peace he had to maintain a position of neutrality in the Parthian civil war – and use diplomacy to that end. Indeed, the account of Dio suggests as much. In regards to Roman-Parthian communications at this time, he writes, "as long as the faction of Antony still resisted, even after the sea battle, not only did [Octavian] not take one of the sides of those requesting an alliance, but he did not even give an answer other than that he would think on it." Note the neutrality. While Octavian cited pressing business in Egypt as an explanation, his primary goal must have been to avoid opposition to and alienation of any Parthian faction.[13]

His policy and tactics remained the same even when the conflict spilled over into the Roman empire. When Tiridates was defeated and fled to Syria with the son of Phraates in tow as a hostage, Octavian worked to establish a good rapport with both claimants. He received the envoys of Phraates in friendly fashion. Neither did he promise Tiridates assistance, nor did he arrest and surrender him to Phraates to face a dire fate. Rather he permitted him to reside in Syria, which had some benefit for both parties. While he did not signal immediate disapproval of Tiridates by sending his hostage back to Phraates at this time, he still removed the boy from the custody of Tiridates as a favor to the king and brought him back to Rome.[14] And when an additional trust-building measure was needed for the king after Tiridates made another unsuccessful attempt on the Parthian throne *c.* 26–25 BCE,[15] leading to additional Parthian embassies (this time to the city of Rome itself), Octavian (now better called Augustus) decided to return the boy to his father Phraates – and he did so, according to Pompeius Trogus (later abbreviated by Justin), *sine pretio*, without a price.[16] In short, this was a very carefully balanced and progressive diplomatic response to what was a real crisis.

Perhaps some may protest that Augustus' diplomatic tactics were less than constructive, considering that his real goal in all this was to purposely ratchet up tensions with Parthia by securing and then manipulating Tiridates and Phraates' son as bargaining chips to influence the king.[17] But in fact, such a suggestion goes against logic and the grain of the evidence. Among other reasons, it must be recognized that to take such provocative action actually would have alienated Phraates and perhaps produced a new Parthian problem for the Romans. On the contrary, Octavian sought to diffuse tensions as much as possible and to win over Phraates. And Phraates' subsequent behavior suggests he was wholly successful in his aims. As is well known, some years later (*c.* 10 BCE) Phraates sent Augustus several other royal family members to board with him in Rome. Among others these included four sons: Seraspadanes, Rhodaspes, yet another Phraates, and Vonones.[18] Various authors suggest Phraates took this action because of internal instability and dynastic intrigue at home in Parthia – a not implausible explanation.[19] But for purposes here, we should note that this would have placed Augustus in a powerful position, being able to supply one of these royal candidates as a figurehead to a faction aligned against Phraates. Would Phraates have transferred such key figures to Augustus' custody if Augustus had used Tiridates and his other son against him in the 20s BCE? Certainly not. This is a consideration left unnoticed in scholarship. In the final analysis, we must conclude that Augustus had earned the trust of Phraates. Augustus did not use the circumstances surrounding the Parthian internal strife of 31–25 BCE as an opportunity to pressure and provoke Parthia. He aimed at fully amicable relations and used diplomacy to achieve them.

And while a challenge to this peace and use of diplomacy surfaced in 2 BCE, they ultimately carried the day once again, reinforcing the Augustan approach.[20] On the one hand, one could look at the events of that year as an aggressive shift in Augustan policy, in which war became an interest and diplomatic channels were only used to antagonize. Phraataces (=Phraates V) took over the Parthian throne after reportedly killing his father Phraates IV and decided to meddle in Armenia, then considered in the Roman sphere. As a result, Augustus mobilized Roman forces for the East under command of his grandson Gaius, suggesting (one might say) a new preference for military action. This then led to a series of diplomatic exchanges that seemed counterproductive to say the least. Phraataces demanded that Augustus hand over his brothers resident in Rome. Augustus insulted him with an address that lacked his title of king and called for him to give up the crown and Armenia. Phraataces retaliated by self-identifying as "King of Kings" and merely calling Augustus "Caesar." Ultimately, with Roman boots pounding the Near East, conflict was only avoided when Phraataces caved, pulling out of Armenia, but at least gaining Augustus' guarantee that his brothers would remain in Rome. Here diplomacy was not preferred and seemed only to further alienate both parties.

Yet one should not push these conclusions too far. It is clear that his military mobilization was not a goal in itself, but rather a means to force Phraataces to the table – which it did. In other words, it was tool of diplomacy. As for all the insults, they were more or less bluster, also designed to increase the pressure (though one should not discount the importance of a show for one's domestic audience here). At any rate, in the end diplomacy triumphed: Gaius Caesar and Phraataces convened a high-level peace summit and a settlement was reached. Velleius Paterculus, who was serving a military tribune in Syria at the time, claims to have witnessed the summit between Gaius and Phraataces first-hand. He writes:

> Gaius met with the Parthian king, a young man of exemplary character, on an island in the middle of the Euphrates, with an equal retinue on each side. At the beginning of my service as a military tribune, I witnessed this spectacle of the Roman army arrayed on one side, the Parthian on the other, while these two eminent leaders not only of their respective empires, but also of all mankind forged a pact — truly a memorable sight![21]

It is hard to imagine a scenario further removed from the failed diplomatic efforts of Sulla and Crassus a few decades earlier. There, on the Euphrates, Gaius and Phraataces met as equals, in a setting which was carefully stage-managed to generate a sense of mutual admiration and respect. The visual parity between the Roman and Parthian delegations effectively symbolizes the equivalent status of the two empires, which appear in this context to have far more in common than they do in difference. Velleius further emphasizes the similarity between the Romans and the Parthians by referring to Gaius and Phraataces as leaders not only of their respective empires, but also of "all mankind." This emphasis on their shared humanity breaks down the usual self-other dichotomy that separated Romans from "barbarians." Although Gaius may be a Roman and Phraataces a Parthian, they are both civilized men.[22] The characterization of Gaius and Phraataces as leaders of "all mankind" also implies that the Romans and Parthians together ruled over the entire *oikoumene*, a sentiment echoed by Strabo and Pompeius Trogus (the latter, once again, transmitted through Justin).[23] Ultimately, the Roman and Parthian leadership took care to arrange a spectacular diplomatic encounter that made up for the previous insults, reduced tension, and encouraged peace.

The Lasting Impact and Significance of the Embassy

It must be emphasized that the positive impact of such embassies was broad and long-lasting, often intentionally so. The gifts and cultural knowledge exchanged at these embassies formed lasting bonds that transcended the initial event. Moreover, embassies were often celebrated in official state art, on monuments like Augustus' Parthian arch, and in literature like Velleius Paterculus' *Roman History*. These re-imagined versions of the original embassies served as permanent memorials to Roman-Parthian cooperation, carefully constructed to appeal to specific audiences, both foreign and domestic. Such mechanisms for intercultural exchange were routinely entangled and intertwined in ways that make modern analysis complex, but the ancient bond strong.

To start, consider reciprocal gift-giving, which helped to foster a bond of friendship and obligation between the imperial family in Rome and the Arsacid dynasty.[24] In the case of Gaius and Phraataces, the reciprocal gift-giving took the form of ritual dining.[25] Upon concluding their pact on the Euphrates, Gaius and Phraataces entertained each other in turn on the borders of their respective empires. Although there is no record of what transpired during these dinner parties, it seems safe to assume that they were lavish affairs, which involved all sorts of appropriate princely entertainments. In addition to fine food and wine, it is not out the question to imagine Gaius and Phraataces enjoying performances by Greek-speaking poets and dramatists designed to highlight their shared love of Hellenic culture. If Phraataces had a sense of humor, he may have staged a performance of Euripides' *Bacchae*, but perhaps without using a stage prop borrowed from the person of Crassus. Whatever the precise nature of the entertainment, these dinner parties offered high-ranking Romans and Parthians an opportunity to meet and talk, and perhaps in the process even learn something about the customs of their rivals.

One of the most common gifts exchanged during high-level negotiations between Rome and Parthia were, in fact, people – and with telling consequences.[26] This included captives like the remnants of Crassus' legions, who were returned to Augustus along with the lost standards in 20 BCE.[27] As mentioned earlier in paper, Phraates IV also sent his four sons and their families to live with Augustus in Rome. Roman authors typically refer to these Parthian princes as *obsides* or "hostages," a term which implies that they were somehow imprisoned or abused. Nothing could be further from the truth. Instead, Augustus treated the Arsacid princes as distinguished guests in his house, providing them with access to books and tutors capable of teaching them about the concept of *Romanitas*.[28] The Parthian princes most likely received an education similar to that of other foreign dignitaries living in Rome around that time, such as Juba II and Cleopatra Selene, who were reputed for their impeccable knowledge of both Latin and Greek.[29] According to Suetonius, Augustus also had the Parthian princes accompany him on trips to the arena to watch spectacles, such as beast hunts and gladiatorial games.[30] If Brian Rose is correct, Augustus even had one of the Parthian princes and his mother depicted alongside the imperial family on the Ara Pacis.[31] This gives the impression that the Parthian princes were essentially *de facto* members of Augustus' own extended family. All of this was part of carefully conceived plan on the part of Augustus to produce a new generation of Arsacid rulers to place on the throne of Parthia, who would presumably be more sympathetic to the Roman cause than their central Asian kinsmen.[32] Augustus ultimately succeeded in educating Phraates' sons in proper Roman etiquette and behavior. But what is often overlooked is that the process of cultural education also worked in the other direction. After years of close contact, Augustus and his family also must have learned a great deal about Parthian culture and society from their guests, particularly Phraates and Vonones, who were already fully grown when they arrived in Rome. As adults, these men were poorly suited to accept Augustus' program of educational indoctrination. They were, however, perfectly positioned to serve as diplomats and cultural liaisons between Parthia and Rome. As conduits of cross-cultural information, the Arsacid princes in residence in Rome played an integral role in fostering peace and mutual understanding throughout the Julio-Claudian period.

And the Arsacids were the not the only ones to present "hostages" as tokens of goodwill; Augustus also reciprocated in kind. Around the time of the return of Crassus' lost standards, Augustus sent Phraates IV a beautiful Italian slave girl named Musa to serve as his concubine. According to Josephus, Phraates was enraptured by Musa's beauty, so much so that he eventually married her and named her son, Phraataces, as his heir.[33] There were likely a number of factors that motivated Phraates' marriage to Musa, infatuation perhaps being one of them. But more importantly, as a gift from Augustus, Musa represented a symbolic link to Rome. By marrying her, Phraates publicly reaffirmed his commitment to seeking a *modus vivendi* with the Julio-Claudian dynasty. An added benefit of marrying Musa was that she also served as an important conduit of intercultural communication, much like the Parthian princes living in Rome. Musa's Roman roots gave her the ability to act as a sort of cultural mediator, whose counsel was undoubtedly useful when dealing with the Romans.

In fact, the material record seems to reflect this to some degree; the coinage suggests that she was conversant with and embraced Iranian culture, but remembered and drew on her Roman background as well. After the death of Phraates IV, Musa and her son, Phraataces, promptly seized control, ruling jointly over the Parthian empire. The mother and son team celebrated their joint ascension to the throne by issuing a series of unusual double-headed drachms and tetradrachms that feature portraits of both Phraataces and Musa (Fig. 4.1).[34] The portrait of Phraataces on the obverse is rendered in traditional Arsacid style; he sports long hair and a beard and has a

Figure 4.1: Silver drachm of Phraataces and Musa. Struck 2 BCE–4CE. Ecbatana mint. Courtesy of Classical Numismatic Group.

royal diadem tied around his forehead. On the reverse, Musa is depicted wearing an elaborate three-tiered crown decorated with large gems. The standard reverse legend appearing over Musa's head reads: ΘΕΑΣ ΟΥΡΑΝΙΑΣ ΜΟΥΣΗΣ ΒΑΣΙΛΙΣΣΗΣ or "Of the Goddess Urania Musa Queen."[35] This stunning new depiction of Thea Musa represents a radical break with Arsacid tradition; never before had a Parthian queen appeared on coins.[36] Musa not only appears alongside her son on coinage, but also boasts the divine epithet Θεά Οὐρανία. There is a growing consensus that the Arsacid kings received some form of ruler cult, but it is unclear to what extent Arsacid queens were also recipients of worship.[37] Musa is the only Parthian queen known to employ the cult epithet Θεά Οὐρανία, which had traditionally been reserved for fertility goddesses like Aphrodite and Ishtar/Astarte.[38] According to Herodotus, the epithet Θεά Οὐρανία also was associated with the Iranian deity, Anahita or Anaïtis, whose cult was practiced throughout the Achaemenid empire.[39] By adopting the same cult epithet as other popular fertility goddesses, Musa effectively communicated her own divine status in a symbolic language that was easily intelligible to a wide, multi-cultural audience both inside and outside the Parthian empire.

Posing as an earthly embodiment of Aphrodite/Ishtar was entirely appropriate for a queen whose political power was predicated on her ability to produce legitimate heirs. According to Josephus, Musa was not only the mother of the reigning Arsacid king, but also his wife.[40] After poisoning her first husband, Phraates IV, in 2 BCE, Musa married her son, Phraataces, and ascended to the throne as co-ruler of the Parthian empire. Josephus and the vast majority his Graeco-Roman readers believed that close-kin marriages between mothers and sons were a taboo form of incest. As a result, Josephus presents Musa's "incestuous" marriage to Phraataces as clear evidence of her sexual licentiousness and moral depravity. What Josephus failed to recognize, however, was that Iranian peoples like the Persians and Parthians were much more open to close-kin marriages than their Graeco-Roman counterparts.[41] Iranian royalty regularly practiced close-kin marriage as a way to consolidate power within a single family, and Musa's marriage to Phraataces probably also fulfilled this function.[42] Uniting Musa's power base with her son's helped to prevent factional infighting after the death of Phraates IV. It also helped to legitimate Musa's position as co-ruler of the Parthian empire, an office never before held by an Arsacid queen. Josephus is certain that Musa and Phraataces consummated their union, which suggests that if they were able, they planned to have children.[43] Achaemenid and Sassanian kings are known to have produced legitimate heirs from consanguineous marriages.[44] The Egyptian pharaohs also successfully practiced brother-sister marriage for thousands of years, a custom which developed not only to retain power in a single family, but also to demonstrate the divine nature of the pharaohs, who married and produced heirs in the same manner as the Egyptian gods.[45] Musa and Phraataces may have hoped to send a similar message about their own divinity by practicing what could be construed as sacred incest. Regardless of their precise motivations, Musa's marriage to Phraataces placed her in the unique position of being responsible for both the present and future perpetuation of the Asracid line. Like her divine namesakes, Aphrodite, Ishtar, and Anahita, Musa's continued beauty and fecundity were now essential to the long-term well-being of the Parthian empire.

With no local Parthian precedents to follow, Musa most likely drew inspiration for her numismatic portrait from Hellenistic and Roman queens in the West. In the Mediterranean world, where Musa had grown up, the idea of depicting divine queens on coins was relatively uncontroversial. The concept was first developed in Ptolemaic Egypt during the early third century BCE. After being officially deified in 272/271 BCE, Ptolemy II began minting a series of gold mnaieia depicting the jugate busts of himself and his divine sister-wife, Arsinoe II, accompanied by the legend ΑΔΕΛΦΩΝ or "of the sibling[-lovers]" (Fig. 4.2).[46] The jugate format of the portraits emphasizes the close kinship between Ptolemy II and Arsinoe II, whose incestuous marriage mirrored that of the Greek gods and traditional Egyptian pharaohs. Arsinoe II is portrayed as a female clone of her brother with wide eyes, a prominent nose, and protruding jaw-line. She also bears a strong resemblance to contemporary Egyptian representations of goddesses like Aphrodite and Isis, with whom she was frequently compared in cultic contexts and panegyric poetry.[47] The placement of Arsinoe II's bust behind Ptolemy's in the jugate format symbolizes her relative power in relation to her brother; although an active partner in governance, Arsinoe II is still nevertheless subordinate to her male counterpart, Ptolemy. Depicted on the reverse of these coins are the matching jugate busts of Ptolemy I and his wife, Berenice I, with the legend ΘΕΩΝ ("of the gods") above. By placing his parents on the reverse, Ptolemy II draws attention to the inherited nature of his royal power and authority. His mother, Berenice I, played an integral role in passing on the mantel of divine kingship from one generation of

Figure 4.2: *Gold mnaieion of Ptolemy II and Arsinoe II. Struck c. 272–260 BCE. Alexandria mint. Courtesy of Classical Numismatic Group.*

Ptolemies to the next and, in return, is posthumously honored by having her image placed on coins alongside the male founder of the Ptolemaic dynasty.

The coins of the early Ptolemaic queens created a new paradigm of numismatic representation that was widely emulated by later Hellenistic and Roman rulers.[48] Musa was probably most familiar with coins of divine queens produced in her own lifetime like those of Cleopatra VII of Egypt.[49] In 32 BCE, Mark Antony and Cleopatra issued a famous series of double-headed denarii that circulated throughout the Roman Republic (Fig. 4.3).[50] On the obverse is a draped and diademed bust of Cleopatra, whose prominent nose and strong jaw-line bear an unmistakable resemblance to the portraits of her Ptolemaic ancestors. The Latin legend above reads CLEOPATRA REGINAE REGVM FILIORVM REGVM or "Of Cleopatra, Queen of Kings and of the Children of Kings." The phrase *Filiorum Regum* is somewhat ambiguous and could also be understood to mean "whose children are kings." This ambiguity was likely intentional because it allowed Cleopatra to simultaneously tout her illustrious heritage, while also highlighting the fact that she had given birth to children with two of Rome's most powerful generals, Julius Caesar and Mark Antony. On the reverse is a bare-headed portrait of Mark Antony, *de facto* king of the eastern Roman provinces. The iconography of Antony's portrait is strikingly similar to that of Cleopatra's; he shares the same hooked nose and projecting chin characteristic of the Ptolemaic dynasty.[51] By subtly adjusting his portrait features to fit Ptolemaic norms, Antony casts himself as a legitimate heir to the throne of Egypt. The visual parity between their two portraits also suggests that Antony and Cleopatra share a close political kingship equivalent to the sibling marriages of earlier Ptolemaic rulers. Above Antony's portrait is the legend ANTONI ARMENIA DEVICTA or "Of Antony, who conquered Armenia." A small Armenian tiara

Figure 4.3: Silver denarius of Cleopatra VII and Mark Antony. Struck c. 32 BCE. Unknown eastern mint. Courtesy of Classical Numismatic Group.

located behind Antony's head visually references his victory. The conquest of the Armenians was ideologically significant to the Roman people because it demonstrated Antony's ability to maintain control over lands once conquered and controlled by the Romans under Lucullus and Pompey the Great. Through a skillful combination of text and imagery, Antony and Cleopatra created a coin that simultaneously presented them as divine monarchs in the Ptolemaic mold, while also appealing to the ideological and cultural yearnings of the Roman people.

The double-headed denarii of Antony and Cleopatra represent a close historical parallel to the jointly minted coins of Musa and Phraataces. This is likely no coincidence given Musa's cultural origins in the western Mediterranean. When faced with the difficult task of legitimating her new position as co-ruler of the Parthian empire, Musa looked to familiar *exempla* for guidance. No Hellenistic queen was more famous (or infamous) than Cleopatra VII. Even decades after her death, Roman writers continued to remember Cleopatra as one of the most beautiful and accomplished women in the Hellenistic world.[52] Cleopatra was a natural role model for Musa for a variety of reasons. Not only was Cleopatra famous, but she also shared power with a string of male co-rulers, beginning with her brother Ptolemy XIII, all of whom threatened to overshadow her authority and subsume her identity. Nevertheless, Cleopatra always found a way to pursue her own ideological goals and assert her authority as a co-equal, if not dominant partner with her male counterparts. Nowhere is this better illustrated than on the double-headed denarii that she minted with Mark Antony, where Antony's portrait features are assimilated with hers. Much like Musa, Cleopatra also found herself in the difficult position of acting as a cultural and political mediator between her own kingdom and Rome. Cleopatra used her inside knowledge of Greek, Roman, and Egyptian culture to forge an ideological program that resonated across cultural and geographical boundaries. This made Cleopatra an ideal source for emulation for Musa when she was developing her own numismatic imagery.

In addition to Cleopatra VII, Musa probably also drew inspiration from numismatic portraits of contemporary female members of the Roman imperial family, such as Livia and Julia.[53] The Emperor Augustus' wife, Livia, never appeared on official imperial coinage produced at the central mint in Rome. Why Livia was omitted from central mint issues during Augustus' lifetime is not entirely clear. Scholars have often postulated that Augustus wanted to avoid the accusation that he was setting up a Hellenistic-style monarchy in Rome.[54] If that was the case, however, it is difficult to explain why Augustus *did* mint coins featuring the portrait of his daughter, Julia. For example, in 13 BCE, Augustus minted a denarius with a portrait of Julia on the reverse, flanked by the busts of her two sons, Gaius and Lucius (Fig. 4.4).[55] The dynastic overtones of such an image are difficult to miss; Julia deserves special honor for giving birth to the next generations of Caesars, who Augustus hopes will one day replace him. The image of Julia flanked by her two god-like children also recalls similar pairings in Ptolemaic art from Berenice I with Ptolemy II and Arsinoe II to Cleopatra VII with Alexander Helios and Cleopatra Selene II.[56] If Augustus wished to avoid comparisons with Hellenistic kings, this was not the way to accomplish it. Moreover, Livia and Julia were both regularly depicted on provincial bronze coins, especially those minted in the Greek-speaking cities of the eastern Mediterranean.[57] When appearing on Greek provincial issues, Livia is typically identified as a goddess, often with the title ΘΕΑ ΛΙΒΙΑ or "the Goddess Livia."[58] The city of Clazomenae in Asia Minor, for instance, minted a double-headed bronze denomination featuring Augustus' portrait on the

Figure 4.4: Silver denarius of Augustus and Julia. Gaius Marius moneyer. Struck 13 BCE. Rome mint. Courtesy of Classical Numismatic Group.

Figure 4.5: Provincial bronze of Augustus and Livia. Struck 27 BCE–14 CE. Clazomenae mint. Courtesy of Mediterranean Coins.

obverse and Livia's on reverse, accompanied by the legend ΘΕΑ ΛΙΒΙΑ (Fig. 4.5).[59] This obverse-reverse pairing of the Roman emperor and empress closely mirrors the format of earlier Ptolemaic and Seleucid coins, as well as the silver drachms issued by Musa and Phraataces. It is particularly striking that Musa adopts the same title as Livia, who is also addressed on coins as "Thea." By adopting the same visual format commonly employed to depict Augustus and Livia on provincial coinage, Musa and Phraataces implicitly likened their power to that of the Roman imperial family. This message would have resonated particularly well with traders, diplomats, and other people living on the border between Parthian and Roman empires, who were presumably familiar with both sets of coinage. If imitation is the sincerest form of flattery, Musa's decision to model her numismatic persona, at least in part, on Livia's demonstrates a clear willingness to engage in cultural exchange with the Roman imperial family. Musa and Phraataces sought to conduct this exchange as co-equal partners with their Romans counterparts, which helps to explain the persistent emphasis on parity both in their coinage and in the staging of Phraataces' embassy with Gaius.

Unfortunately, given the paucity of our sources, it is difficult to gauge how different constituencies within the Parthian empire responded to Musa's numismatic portrait. Publically styling oneself as a Parthian version of Cleopatra or Livia was a controversial move, which had the potential to anger some of the more traditionally-minded Parthian nobles who made up Musa and her son's power base. If Musa turned off this key contingency, it may help to explain why she and her son were abruptly removed from power in 4 CE. At any rate, after six years of rule (2 BCE–4 CE), Musa and Phraataces were deposed and replaced by Orodes III.[60] As we know from our own day, foreign policies of politicians that encourage peace with neighboring states are not always met with enthusiasm by all their domestic constituents – but this is an issue for another paper. What should be emphasized here is how this material program reflected a process of cultural exchange and gift-giving that fostered intercultural communication and peaceful foreign relations between Rome and Parthia.

To remain on the subject of material culture, it is also important to note that the emperor Augustus created his own complex program of imperial art and ideology designed to legitimate his policy of peaceful coexistence with the Parthians. After Phraates returned Crassus' lost standards in 20 BCE, whether on his own initiative or at the prompting of Augustus,[61] Augustus commissioned a series of monuments across the empire celebrating his diplomatic victory.[62] Among them was a triple-bayed triumphal arch erected next to the Temple of the Divus Iulius in Rome. The arch itself has not survived, but it is represented on contemporary coins, probably most accurately on the denarii of L. Vinicius from 17/16 BCE (Fig. 4.6).[63] From the coins, it is possible to reconstruct the basic appearance of the monument. On top of the central arch bay was a statue of Augustus in a four-horse chariot, holding a scepter in his right hand. While we know from literary sources that Augustus did not in fact celebrate a full triumph, but rather a lesser *ovatio*, evidenced by the fact that he entered Rome on horseback, not in a triumphal chariot,[64] the chariot and scepter of the arch nevertheless conjure the image of Augustus as a victorious general celebrating a triumph. The rest of the monument, however, is much more in line with the reality of this event: rather than beating the Parthians into submission, Augustus had achieved a lasting peace without shedding a drop of blood. The peaceful nature of Augustus' victory is conveyed through the iconography of the two Parthian soldiers who stand flanking Augustus on the lateral arch bays. Each soldier holds a

Figure 4.6: Silver denarius depicting the Parthian arch of Augustus. L. Vinicius moneyer. Struck 16 BCE. Rome mint. Courtesy of Ars Numismatica Classica.

Figure 4.7: Augustus of Primaporta. Marble copy of an original from c. 20 BCE. Courtesy of Francesco Bini.

bow in one hand and a Roman battle standard in the other, which he voluntarily offers up to Augustus. These armed, upright statues of Parthian soldiers stand in stark contrast to traditional representations of conquered barbarians on Roman triumphal monuments, which were typically bound, beaten captives tied to trophies.[65] Breaking with tradition, Augustus depicts his Parthian rivals as powerful, active, if somewhat subordinate partners in peace.

We see a similar presentation of the Parthians on the breastplate of the famous Primaporta statue of Augustus (Fig. 4.7). Originally displayed in Livia's villa outside Rome, the Primaporta statue depicts Augustus as a heroic general, addressing his troops with his arm upraised in a gesture of *ad locutio*. Augustus wears a traditional Roman cuirass decorated with a variety of mythological and allegorical figures arranged into three distinct registers. The Upper Register is filled with celestial deities like Sol and Luna, who symbolically chase each other across the sky, symbolizing the timelessness of the Augustan regime. By contrast, the Lower Register is populated with gods more closely associated with terrestrial realm, including Diana and Apollo, who Augustus credited with helping him to win the battle of Actium.[66] At the center of the composition is a scene celebrating the return of Crassus' lost standards, with bearded male personification of Parthia[67] handing over a composite standard with eagle and phalerae to a representative of the Roman people.[68] Of the two figures, the Parthian is clearly the more eye-catching. He wears baggy trousers and V-neck tunic, clearly identifying him to Roman viewers as an eastern barbarian.[69] But there is no prostration here. The personification of Parthia stands upright, in a posture that actually echoes the body position of Augustus. This parity is emphasized by the fact that the Parthian representative is male, in contrast to the mourning female personifications of Gaul and Spain framing the scene. Once again Parthia is represented as an active partner in peace. And one cannot help but think of the later accord reached on the Euphrates by Gaius and Phraataces. Of course, all of these monuments have a glow of military victory about them – a clear fiction, since diplomacy produced the peace. But Augustus understood his domestic audience better than Musa and Phraataces it seems. Diplomacy brings dialogue and peace, and art should speak to and encourage it, but it must be carefully modulated for those at home to be a complete success.

And this diplomatic approach by Augustus was a success, to be sure. To fully understand the scope of this accomplishment, one need only look beyond his death and notice how these policies instructed the actions of later Julio-Claudian emperors. The continued importance of diplomacy as a tool of peace is perhaps best exemplified during the reigns of Nero (r. 54–68 CE) and Vologaeses I (r. 51/52–78/79 CE). At that time, Romans and Parthians were again at odds over control of Armenia, with Vologaeses attempting to install a Parthian vassal by the name of Tiridates on the Armenian throne.[70] The Roman response was the same as before: the mobilization of military forces on the eastern border, now under the leadership of the generals Corbulo and Paetus. Yet in this case there would be episodes of direct military engagement – in 58/59 CE, 61 CE, and 62 CE.[71] But surely more remarkable in the sources are the numerous back-and-forth diplomatic exchanges between Vologaeses and Tiridates on the one hand and Nero (in Rome) and Corbulo and other generals (in the Roman East) on the other.[72] More than ever, diplomacy was an important mechanism of intercultural communication.

Its primacy becomes all the more clear when one considers its relationship vis-à-vis war at this time. In short, war was a tool of diplomacy. Already in 58 CE Nero seemed content with a compromise solution: that he would approve a Parthian nominee for the Armenian throne.[73] But sufficient disruption in Roman-Parthian relations had taken place by this point that both sides needed to demonstrate strength to their respective domestic constituencies. As a result, to ensure the success of a diplomatic solution both sides needed military victories (or at least actions resembling them) so as to present the desired compromise as a settlement dictated by their own leaders. By 61 CE Vologases had exhibited enough aggressive behavior, including the limited siege of the Armenian capital Tigranocerta which then Roman troops garrisoned, to be ready to adopt the compromise.[74] But it took Nero a bit longer, especially due to an unexpected defeat and surrender of Paetus in 62–63 CE.[75] His more reliable general Corbulo corrected the problem by invading Armenia again and advancing against forces of Vologases and Tiridates.[76] War then had served its purpose. The two parties met, a settlement was fixed, and it was carried out in grand fashion. It was agreed that Tiridates would remove his diadem and place it at the feet of a statue of Nero in the presence of the Roman and Parthian armies in the East. He would then travel to Rome to pay homage to Nero and receive the diadem by the Roman emperor's hand.[77] And so it happened, the visit to Rome taking place in 66 CE. Tiridates, other Arsacid family members, and 3,000 members of the famed Parthian cavalry travelled to Rome, where Nero crowned Tiridates immediately before his Roman subjects.[78] What we would emphasize is that throughout this war, while military engagements there were, they routinely and purposely were restrained and mainly served as a mechanism to put pressure on the opponent and prepare one's own domestic constituency for compromise and peace. In other words, little had changed from the time of Augustus. Diplomacy remained a preferred and effective instrument of peace under Nero.[79]

Conclusion

To conclude, the embassy in Roman-Parthian history was significant, and not because it most often led to alienation and conflict between Rome and Parthia. On the contrary, though this did happen upon occasion, as in the course of Crassus' Parthian campaign in 54–53 BCE, diplomacy in the time of Augustus and the Julio-Claudian dynasty nicely demonstrated the positive potential of the embassy in intercultural communication. Romans and Parthians both used embassies to discuss matters of shared significance, facilitate negotiations, and ultimately shape collaborations that helped to establish lengthy periods of peace between Rome and Parthia. What is more, such accomplishments were reinforced by various forms of gift-exchange and were enshrined in inscriptions, in literature, and on monuments that collectively had an impact on all Romans. To be sure these other forms of cultural communication served several complex purposes, including the projection of images of strength vis-à-vis Parthia, but the maintenance of peace remained a priority.

Notes

1. Consider, for example, Campbell 1993, 213–240. See also Schlude 2013, 163–181.
2. Examples abound for this view of Roman-Parthian embassies. See discussion below for embassies during the times of Sulla and Mithridates II (in the 90s BCE), Pompey and Phraates III (in the 60s BCE), Crassus and Orodes II (in the 50s BCE), Antony and Orodes II (in the 30s BCE), and Augustus and Phraates IV and Phraataces (=Phraates V) (from 31/30 BCE to 2 CE).
3. Plut., *Sull.* 5.4–5: διατρίβοντι δὲ αὐτῷ παρὰ τὸν Εὐφράτην ἐντυγχάνει Πάρθος Ὀρόβαζος, Ἀρσάκου βασιλέως πρεσβευτής, οὔπω πρότερον ἀλλήλοις ἐπιμεμιγμένων τῶν γενῶν· ἀλλὰ καὶ τοῦτο τῆς μεγάλης δοκεῖ Σύλλα τύχης γενέσθαι, τὸ πρώτῳ Ῥωμαίων ἐκείνῳ Πάρθους συμμαχίας καὶ φιλίας δεομένους διὰ λόγων ἐλθεῖν. ὅτε καὶ λέγεται τρεῖς δίφρους προθέμενος, τὸν μὲν Ἀριοβαρζάνῃ, τὸν δὲ Ὀροβάζῳ, τὸν δὲ αὑτῷ, μέσος ἀμφοῖν καθεζόμενος χρηματίζειν. ἐφ' ᾧ τὸν μὲν Ὀρόβαζον ὕστερον ὁ τῶν Πάρθων βασιλεὺς ἀπέκτεινε, τὸν δὲ Σύλλαν οἱ μὲν ἐπήνεσαν ἐντρυφήσαντα τοῖς βαρβάροις, οἱ δὲ ὡς φορτικὸν ᾐτιάσαντο καὶ ἀκαίρως φιλότιμον.
4. Debevoise 1938, 46–47; Sherwin-White 1984, 219–220; Sullivan 1990, 118–119; Osgood 2006, 184; Sampson 2008, 52 and 86–87. *Cf.* Keaveney 1981, 195–212, who sees the provocative character of Sulla's behavior, but avoids reading the subsequent behavior of Mithridates as directly oppositional to Rome.

5. Plut., *Crass.* 18.1–2: ἤδη δὲ τὰς δυνάμεις ἐκ τῶν χειμαδίων συναθροίζοντος αὐτοῦ πρέσβεις ἀφίκοντο παρ᾽ Ἀρσάκου βραχύν τινα λόγον κομίζοντες, ἔφασαν γάρ, εἰ μὲν ὑπὸ Ῥωμαίων ὁ στρατὸς ἀπέσταλται, πόλεμον ἄσπονδον εἶναι καὶ ἀδιάλλακτον, εἰ δὲ τῆς πατρίδος ἀκούσης, ὡς πυνθάνονται, Κράσσος ἰδίων ἕνεκα κερδῶν ὅπλα Πάρθοις ἐπενήνοχε καὶ χώραν κατείληφε, μετριάζειν Ἀρσάκην καὶ τὸ μὲν Κράσσου γῆρας οἰκτείρειν, ἀφιέναι δὲ Ῥωμαίοις τοὺς ἄνδρας, οὓς ἔχει φρουρουμένους μᾶλλον ἢ φρουροῦντας· πρὸς ταῦτα Κράσσου κομπάσαντος ὡς ἐν Σελευκείᾳ δώσει τὰς ἀποκρίσεις, γελάσας ὁ πρεσβύτατος τῶν πρέσβεων Οὐαγίσης καὶ τῆς χειρὸς ὑπτίας δείξας τὸ μέσον "ἐντεῦθεν," εἶπεν, "ὦ Κράσσε, φύσονται τρίχες πρότερον ἢ σὺ ὄψει Σελεύκειαν." Cf. Dio 40.16.1–3.
6. Such readings are common in the scholarship. See, for example, the analysis of Debevoise 1938, 81–84; Colledge 1967, 38–39; Sheldon 2010, 32–35. See also Sampson 2008, 106–107, who accepts the veracity of Plutarch's account when it comes to Crassus' comment, but not the personal insults dealt by the Parthians.
7. The most important ancient accounts of the battle and its immediate results are Plut., *Crass.* 14–33 and Dio 39.33.2, 40.12.1–28.2. Modern discussions include: Rawlinson 1873, 150–181; Debevoise 1938, 78–95; Tarn 1951, 604–612; Ziegler 1964, 32–33; Bivar 1983, 48–56; Sherwin-White 1984, 279–290; Sullivan 1990, 306–309; Wolski 1993, 128–133; Farrokh 2007, 135–140; Sampson 2008, especially 94–147; Sheldon 2010, 29–49; Traina 2011; Weggen 2011; Schlude 2012, 11–23. Plut., *Crass.* 30.1–33.4 suggests that Crassus knew of the Parthian treachery in the diplomatic meeting and that his head was used as a stage prop in the *Bacchae*. See also Polyaenus, *Strat.* 7.41. Dio 40.26.1–27.4 recounts that Crassus was fooled and that his thirst was quenched with molten gold. See also Flor. 1.46.9–10; Fest., *Brev.* 17.
8. The quote is from Dio 49.24.5. See also Plut., *Ant.* 37.1–3. Many assume that this analysis of Dio and Plutarch is accurate: *e.g.* Sherwin-White 1984, 308–309; Sullivan 1990, 313; Sheldon 2010, 65. For the campaign of 36 BCE and its results, the two primary accounts are Plut., *Ant.* 37–51 and Dio 49.24.2–31.4. For discussion and bibliography, see Holmes 1928, 123–128; Debevoise 1938, 121–132; Ziegler 1964, 35–36; Bucheim 1960, 77–79, 82–83; Colledge 1967, 44–45; Bengtson 1974; Schieber 1979, 107–114; Bivar 1983, 58–64; Dąbrowa 1983, 37–38; Sherwin-White 1984, 307–321; Wolski 1993, 141–145; Pelling 1996, 30–34; Dąbrowa 2006, 343–352; Osgood 2006, 303–306.
9. It should be noted, however, that Mithridates' killed his envoy surely as a public display for his domestic audience – not Rome. In this way, we should not read too much into the event when it comes to its practical significance for Roman-Parthian relations.
10. *E.g.* Debevoise 1938, 73–75; Ziegler 1964, 30–31; Colledge 1967, 36–37; Keaveney 1981, 202–208; Dąbrowa 1983, 26–33, n. 64; Sherwin-White 1984, 213, 222–226; Sullivan 1990, 302–303; Butcher 2003, 22; Sampson 2008, 89–90; Shayegan 2011, 323–329.
11. See again Schlude 2013, 163–181.
12. For a full discussion of Herod and the Parthians, see chapter five by Schlude and Overman, "Herod the Great: A Near Eastern Case Study in Roman-Parthian Politics."
13. For these events, see Dio 51.18.2: στασιασάντων γὰρ αὐτῶν καί τινος Τιριδάτου τῷ Φραάτῃ ἐπαναστάντος, πρότερον μέν, καὶ ἕως ἔτι τὰ τοῦ Ἀντωνίου καὶ μετὰ τὴν ναυμαχίαν ἀνθειστήκει, οὐχ ὅσον οὐ προσέθετό τῳ αὐτῶν συμμαχίαν αἰτησάντων, ἀλλ᾽ οὐδ᾽ ἀπεκρίνατο ἄλλο οὐδὲν ἢ ὅτι βουλεύσεται, πρόφασιν μὲν ὡς καὶ περὶ τὴν Αἴγυπτον ἀσχολίαν ἔχων, ἔργῳ δὲ ἵν᾽ ἐκτρυχωθεῖεν ἐν τούτῳ μαχόμενοι πρὸς ἀλλήλους. Interestingly, Dio concludes these comments with the suggestion that Octavian pursued this neutrality "in order that [Phraates and Tiridates] might be exhausted at the time by fighting against one another." While this is merely the analysis of Dio, it is conceivable that this may have been considered an additional benefit when it came to the security of the eastern Roman empire.
14. Dio 51.18.3: τότε δὲ ἐπειδὴ ὅ τε Ἀντώνιος ἐτελεύτησε, καὶ ἐκείνων ὁ μὲν Τιριδάτης ἡττηθεὶς ἐς τὴν Συρίαν κατέφυγεν, ὁ δὲ Φραάτης κρατήσας πρέσβεις ἔπεμψε, τούτοις τε φιλικῶς ἐχρημάτισε, καὶ τῷ Τιριδάτῃ βοηθήσειν μὲν οὐχ ὑπέσχετο διαιτᾶσθαι δὲ ἐν τῇ Συρίᾳ ἐπέτρεψεν, υἱόν τέ τινα

τοῦ Φραάτου ἐν εὐεργεσίας μέρει παρ' αὐτοῦ λαβὼν ἔς τε τὴν Ῥώμην ἀνήγαγε καὶ ἐν ὁμηρείᾳ ἐποιήσατο.

15. Isid. Char. 1; Dio 53.33.1–2. Numismatic evidence puts Tiridates in some control of Seleucia-on-the-Tigris in 26-25 BCE; see McDowell 1935, 185, 222; *cf.* Debevoise 1938, 137–138. More recent is de Callataÿ 1994, 42–47, 55–57, who explicitly suggests that Tiridates enjoyed Roman assistance in this venture, presumably based on the title of ΦΙΛΟΡΩΜΑΙΟΥ that Tiridates adopted on his coins in 26 BCE. But while this is clearly a striking and unprecedented title on a Parthian coin, it remains speculative to conclude that substantial Roman support motivated its adoption. Phraates clearly did not consider it significant when he sent his royal family members to stay with Augustus at Rome fifteen years later (see discussion below). As for the title's intended meaning, it could have signalled one's status as a Roman client king in a Roman context. So Timpe 1975, 157, understands it. In a Parthian context, however, such ethnic terminology might have offered the illusion of power over some Roman constituency. Tiridates perhaps considered both interpretations advantageous, since they had the potential to inspire support among different groups. For an alternative explanation of this title, see Gaslain and Maleuvre 2006, 182–183, who follow others in assuming Roman support (they explicitly mention financial and military support), but seem to suggest the possibility that actually Augustus and Phraates were conspiring together in this event, setting Tiridates up for a fall! The suggestion is extremely intriguing, though ultimately unlikely.
16. Just. 42.5.9.
17. Debevoise 1938, 136–137; Campbell 1993, 222; Seager 1972, 17; Dąbrowa 1983, 40–41; Sherwin-White 1984, 322–324; Levick 1999, 25; Gaslain and Maleuvre 2006, 169–194; Farrokh 2007, 146–147; Lerouge 2007, 103–104; Linz 2009, 57–60; Sheldon 2010, 76, 81–85.
18. Strab. 16.1.28; *cf.* Strab. 6.4.2; *Mon. Anc.* 32.2; Vell. Pat. 2.94.4; Joseph., *AJ* 18.42; Tac., *Ann.* 2.1; Suet., *Aug.* 21.3; Eutrop. 7.9; Oros. 6.21.29. It may even be that Parthian hostages entered Roman hands in 20 BCE along with the Roman standards and captives (see Gruen 1996, 159–160).
19. See Strab. 16.1.28; Tac., *Ann.* 2.1; Joseph., *AJ* 18.39–43, providing juicy details.
20. See Dio 55.10 and Joseph., *AJ* 18.39–43 for what follows.
21. Vell. Pat. 2.101.1–3.
22. Recent scholarship has cautioned against oversimplified conceptions of the "Other" when discussing identity construction in antiquity. See Gruen 2005 and 2011. For specific treatment of Roman views of Persians and Parthians, see Schlude, "Cyrus the Great and Roman Views of Ancient Iran," forthcoming in R. Shayegan (ed.), *Cyrus the Great: Life and Lore* (Boston and Washington, DC: Ilex Foundation and Center for Hellenic Studies).
23. Strab. 16.1.28: "The Euphrates and the land beyond it are the border of the Parthian empire. Those parts on this side, however, are held by the Romans and the tribal leaders of the Arabians up to Babylonia, some paying court more to the Parthians, others to the Romans, whose neighbors they are." Just. 41.1.1: "At this time power over the East belongs to the Parthians, as it were, since a division of the world has been made [by them] with the Romans."
24. There is extensive anthropological literature on the importance of reciprocal gift-giving as a tool of diplomacy. See *e.g.* Malinowski 1922; Mauss 1954; Thomas 1991; Avruch 2002, 158f. In the case of the Romans and Parthians, their interactions were dictated specifically by the rules of *xenia* or guest-friendship, a Greek concept that called for the reciprocal exchange of gifts between guest and host. The mutual practice of *xenia* helped the Romans and Arsacids to forge bonds of mutual friendship and respect. It should be noted that the diplomacy practiced by the Romans and Arsacids also established an important precedent for later diplomatic embassies held between the Byzantines, Arabs, and Sassanian Persians. See Cutler 2001.
25. The symposium ritual was a common feature of elite culture throughout the Hellenistic world. It provided elites from a variety of different cultural and ethnic backgrounds with a shared ritual framework for interaction and networking. The Romans and Parthians both practiced

their own form of ritualized elite dining based on the Hellenistic symposium. There are abundant material and literary sources on the elite Roman *convivium*, and the dining customs of the imperial family in particular. See Vössing 2004 and 2015; Dunbabin 2004. We are less well informed, however, about the Parthian equivalent. Our best evidence of Arsacid dining rituals outside of our Graeco-Roman literary sources comes from the excavations at Old Nisa, where the Italian excavators have uncovered a Square Hall with couches similar to triclinia used for ritual dining. See Invernizzi 2001, 298–300.

26. Since the early Republic, the Romans had practiced hostage-taking as a means of maintaining loyalty among their subjects and allies. Often these hostages were the children of well-connected elites, like Polybius, who wrote his history of Rome while technically under the forced supervision of the Scipio family. More often than not, these hostages were eventually returned to their families, having internalized many of the same values as the Roman people. The Romans often described the transfer of hostages using the language of guest-friendship. When conceived in the terms of *xenia*, hostages were part of an elaborate system of reciprocal gift-gifting, which bound guest to host in a sacred bond of friendship. See Allen 2006, especially 67–94. The Parthians also had a long and complex history of taking and sending hostages. See the discussion of Nabel in chapter two of this volume.

27. See Dio 53.33.2, 54.8.1.

28. The imperial family dedicated significant resources to educating provincial elites and foreign princes in Rome. Woolf 1998, especially 54–76, and Woolf 2001 have argued convincingly that this was part of a conscious policy to create a shared Roman imperial culture (or "*humanitas*") based on common virtues. How successful this initiative was is a matter for debate.

29. On the education of Juba II and Cleopatra Selene in Rome, see *e.g.* Plut., *Caes.* 55.1–2: "Then he celebrated Egyptian, Pontic, and Libyan triumphs, the Libyan being not for a victory over Scipio, but supposedly for his victory over Juba the king. At this time also Juba, the son of that [king], was led in triumph while in his infancy. As a captive, he was the most fortunate taken; he went from being a barbarian and Numidian to entering the ranks of the most learned historians of Greece."

30. Suet., *Aug.* 43.3.

31. Rose 2005, 39–45.

32. This is not to say that Augustus did not have other goals in mind, too, when it came to hosting these Arsacid princes. Once again, see chapter two of this volume, in which Nabel emphasizes that Augustus used these Parthians as tangible reminders for his domestic (Roman) audience of Roman power over the Parthians.

33. Joseph., *AJ* 18.2.4.

34. On the coinage of Phraataces and Musa, see Bigwood 2004, especially 37–38; Pasmans 2005; Strugnell 2008, 286–287; Sinsi 2012, 286. The coins of Phraataces and Musa are probably mentioned in the Chinese *Hanshu*, the annals of the Western Han dynasty, written in the second half of the first century CE. See Wang 2007, 94–95.

35. See Sellwood 1980, types 58.8–10 and 58.12; Shore 1993, 324.

36. The only other Parthian coins to depict the King and Queen together were minted under Artabanus II (10/11–38 CE), likely in imitation of the coinage of Phraataces and Musa. The queen depicted on the reverse of Artabanus II's chalkoi is not named. It is possible that this woman is no queen at all, but rather a goddess like Tyche. See Sellwood 1980, no. 63.20; Shore 1993, no. 324, 5.

37. On the Arsacid ruler cult, see Invernizzi 2007; Dąbrowa 2011.

38. Zahn 1923; Bigwood 2004, 52; Strugnell 2008, 287.

39. Hdt. 1.133f. Strugnell 2008, 286–287, suggests that Musa probably did not wish to be associated with an Achaemenid deity like Anahita. It is important to note, however, that Anahita continued to be worshipped long after the collapse of the Achaemenid empire not only in the Iranian

heartland, but also in cities as far west as Sardis and Hierocaesarea in Asia Minor where the cult of Artemis Anaïtis (or "Persian Artemis") flourished well into the third century CE. See Boyce and Grenet 1991; Harland 2014, 147; Paus. 5.27.5. Such an association could potentially prove advantageous for Musa in areas where Anahita's cult was still practiced.

40. For this and what follows, see Joseph., *AJ* 18.2.4.

41. On Parthian and Persian close-kin marriage, see Lee 1988; Frandsen 2009.

42. Lewy 1944, 211, n.132; Bigwood 2004, 46; Strugnell 2008, 297.

43. Musa's age when she married Phraataces is uncertain. We know that Musa was given to Phraates IV as a concubine in 20 BCE. If she was in her mid- to late teens when that occurred, Musa would have been in her thirties when she married Phraataces and most likely still capable of bearing children.

44. The Achaemenid kings frequently married and produced children with their sisters, daughters, and cousins. Darius III, for example, was the product of a brother-sister marriage between Arsanes and Sisygambis. See Wiesehöfer 2001, 84; Briant 2002, 772. Our primary sources regarding Achaemenid close-kin marriage were primarily written by Greek and Roman historians, such as Herodotus and Ctesias. Brosius 1996 and Bigwood 2009 reject the reliability of Graceo-Roman authors regarding Achaemenid marriage customs. Our Graeco-Roman sources were clearly biased against the Persians. Nevertheless, it seems highly unlikely that they completely manufactured the tradition of Achaemenid close-kin marriage. Close-kin marriage is well-documented by indigenous sources in later periods of Iranian history (Lee 1988; Frandsen 2009). By the Sassanian period, close-kin marriage was practiced by all levels Iranian society and encouraged by Zoroastrian teaching. So it seems more likely than not that there were Achaemenid period precursors, particularly given the unanimous testimony of our Graeco-Roman sources.

45. Middleton 1962; Shaw 1992; Ager 2005 and 2006. Tax documents from Roman Egypt suggest that brother-sister marriage was also practiced among the general population. See Remijsen and Clarysse 2008; Frandsen 2009.

46. The precise dating of these coins is uncertain. Most scholars favor an early date for their production, *c.* 272/271 BCE, coinciding with the deification of Ptolemy II and Arsinoe II. It is possible, however, that they were not issued until after Arsinoe II's death in 270 BCE. See Von Reden 2009, 51–52; Lorber 2012, 215. Ptolemy II also issued a series of silver decadrachms and later gold mnaieia depicting an individual portrait of Arsinoe II. The reverse image of these coins is a double cornucopia, symbolizing royal tryphé and the fertility of the Ptolemaic queens. See Hölbl 2001, 92; Ager 2005, 23–27; Von Reden 2009, 52; Lorber 2012, 215.

47. Hölbl 2001, 101–104.

48. On the coinage of later Ptolemaic and Seleucid queens, see Macurdy 1932; Von Reden 2009; Lorber 2012. On the numismatic portraits of the first Roman empresses, see Kleiner 1996, especially 56–60 and 64–67; Kleiner 2005, 230–250.

49. Strugnell 2008, 287, suggests that Musa's "idealized" portrait features were modelled on Arsinoe II and Cleopatra Thea. It is certainly possible that Musa had access to Ptolemaic and Seleucid heirloom coins to use as models. The emperor Augustus is reported to have collected ancient Greek coins himself, which he passed out to his friends as party favors (Suet., *Aug.* 75). There was no need, however, for Musa to look into the distant past for inspiration when there were numerous coins minted in her own lifetime featuring divine queens. Musa's coin portrait may have elicited comparisons to Arsinoe II or Cleopatra Thea in the minds of some viewers, but most of her audience probably associated Musa with more contemporary figures like Cleopatra VII and Livia, whose portraits were presumably much more familiar to them. See discussion below.

50. The denarii of Antony and Cleopatra (RRC 543) were minted on the traditional Roman standard, which allowed them to circulate across the empire. Antony and Cleopatra also issued

double-headed coins meant for circulation in the East, including double-headed tetradrachms and chalkoi (*e.g.* BMC Berytus 14: 217). On the tetradrachms, Cleopatra is identified as "Cleopatra Thea II." The date and place of production of these coins is uncertain. For discussion, see Meadows 2001, 233–235; Kleiner 2005, 144–145; Lorber 2012, 228–229.

51. Williams 2001, 237.

52. On Cleopatra's legacy in the Rome, see Kleiner 2005, 157–178.

53. Portraits of powerful Roman women first began to appear on coins during the imperatorial period. Mark Antony minted a variety of different denominations featuring images of his first wife, Fulvia, and second wife, Octavia. This paved the way for later Roman emperors to place their sisters, daughters, and wives on official imperial coinage. See Kleiner 1996, 56–60; Williams 2001, 238–239; Kleiner 2005, 230–241.

54. See *e.g.* Hekster 2015, 119.

55. RIC I 405. A portrait of Julia in the guise of Diana also appears on another denarius minted under the auspices of Augustus in 13 BCE (RIC I 403). Greek provincial coinage echoes the central mint issues, depicting Julia both as a mother and a goddess in her own right. For discussion of Julia's coins, see Kleiner 1996, 57–58; Kleiner 2005, 239–241; Pollini 2012, 77–79; Hekster 2015, 118–119.

56. Kleiner 2005, 240, suggests that the image of Julia with her sons may have been modelled on Cleopatra VII and Caesarion. A more likely source of inspiration, however, is Cleopatra VII's two children with Mark Antony, Alexander Helius and Cleopatra Selene. After his victory in Armenia, Antony organized a public ceremony in which he awarded his son and daughter control over much of southwestern and central Asia, including the kingdom of Parthia, which was by no means in Antony's control. Through this grand gesture, Antony publically dubbed his children with Cleopatra as the heirs to his eastern empire. Kleiner and Buxton (2011) have argued that the visual and rhetorical representations of Antony and his Egyptian family later influenced the presentation of the imperial family on the Ara Pacis in Rome.

57. Hekster 2015, 118–120.

58. Severy 2004, 115; Hekster 2015, 119.

59. BMC Ionia no. 118.

60. Joseph., *AJ* 18.2.4.

61. See Schlude 2015, especially 150–153.

62. For a thorough discussion of all the monuments celebrating Augustus' victory over Parthia, see Rose 2005.

63. Kleiner 1985; Rose 2005, 31–33; Pollini 2012, 82–83.

64. Dio 54.8.3.

65. Rose 2005, 33f. On Roman triumphal art in the early Republic, see Holliday 1997 and 2002, especially 23–121; Östenberg 2009, especially 189–261.

66. On Apollo in Augustan Rome, see Zanker 1988, 85–91; Galinsky 1996, 213–224; Miller 2009, especially 54–94.

67. Schneider 2007, 54. It also has sometimes been suggested that this figure is meant to represent a specific Parthian like Phraates IV or Mithridates I, which is not outside the realm of possibility and may have been true at least in the minds of some viewers.

68. The identity of the figure receiving the lost standards from Parthia is highly controversial. Scholars have proposed a variety of identifications, including Roma, Augustus-Aeneas, Romulus, Mars, Tiberius, and a personification of the Roman army, all of which have some merit. Given the polyvalent nature of Augustan art, it is also possible that the figure's identity was left intentionally ambiguous. This would allow viewers to supply their own meaning to the scene. For further discussion, see Kleiner 1992, 67; Rose 2005, 26–28.

69. On the iconography of Parthians in Roman art, see Ferris 2000, Rose 2005, Schneider 1986 and 2007.

70. Tac., *Ann.* 12.50–51.

71. 58/59 CE: Tac., *Ann.* 13.34, 13.40; 61 CE: Tac., *Ann.* 15.4–5; Dio 62.20.2–3; 62 CE: Tac., *Ann.* 15.7–17; Dio 62.21–22.
72. *E.g.* Tac., *Ann.* 13.9, 13.37, 13.38, 15.5, 15.13, 15.14, 15.17, 15.24, 15.27, 15.28–30, 15.31; Dio 62.20.4, 62.21.2–3, 62.22.3, 62.23.1–4.
73. Tac., *Ann.* 13.34, 13.37.
74. Tac., *Ann.* 15.4–5; Dio 62.20.2–3.
75. Tac., *Ann.* 15.7–17; Dio 62.21–22.
76. Tac., *Ann.* 15.25–27; Dio 62.22.4–23.1.
77. Tac., *Ann.* 15.28–31; Dio 62.23.2–3.
78. Dio 62.23.3, 63.1–7; Suet., *Ner.* 13.
79. One also may note that these continuities extended to their material culture programs. While Nero sought a real *modus vivendi* with Parthia, like Augustus before him, he wished to maintain an aggressive image of Rome as fighting and defeating Parthia, too. Thus he raised yet another celebratory Parthian arch in Rome, images of which survive in coinage. Located on the Capitoline, this arch was topped by Nero in his own four-horse chariot accompanied by Peace and Victory. He projected then the image of himself as the dominant conqueror of Parthia, even if the reality was far more complex. As we have seen, this tactic was also part of the Augustan formula for Roman-Parthian relations. For a full discussion of this arch, see Kleiner 1985.

Bibliography

Ager, S. L. (2005) "Familiarity Breeds: Incest and the Ptolemaic Dynasty." *Journal of Hellenic Studies* 125, 1–34.

Ager, S. L. (2006) "The Power of Excess: Royal Incest and the Ptolemaic Dynasty." *Anthropologica* 48, 165–186.

Allen, J. (2006) *Hostages and Hostage-Taking in the Roman Empire.* Cambridge, Cambridge University Press.

Avruch, K. (2002) "Reciprocity, Anxiety and Status Equality in the Amarna Letters." In R. Cohen and R. Westbrook (eds.) *Amarna Diplomacy: The Beginnings of International Relations*, 154–164. Baltimore, Johns Hopkins University Press.

Bengtson, H. (1974) *Zum Partherfeldzug des Antonius.* Munich, Bayerische Akademie der Wissenschaften.

Bigwood, J. M. (2004) "Queen Mousa. Mother and Wife (?) of King Phraatakes of Parthia: A Re-evaluation of the Evidence." *Mouseion*, ser. 3, 4.1, 35–70.

Bigwood, J. M. (2009) "Incestuous Marriage in Achaemenid Iran: Myths and Realties." *Klio* 91, 311–341.

Bivar, A. (1983) "The Political History of Iran under the Arsacids." In E. Yarshater (ed.) *The Cambridge History of Iran, Volume 3 (1): The Seleucid, Parthian and Sasanian Periods*, 21–99. Cambridge, Cambridge University Press.

Boyce, M. and Grenet, F. (1991) *A History of Zoroastrianism: Zoroastrianism under Macedonian and Roman Rule.* Leiden, Brill.

Brosius, M. (1996) *Women in Ancient Persia.* Oxford, Clarendon Press.

Briant, P. (2002) *From Cyrus to Alexander: A History of the Persian Empire.* Translated by P. Daniels. Winona Lake, Eisenbrauns.

Bucheim, H. (1960) *Die Orientpolitik des Triumvirn M. Antonius.* Heidelberg, Carl Winter Universitätsverlag.

Butcher, K. (2003) *Roman Syria and the Near East.* Los Angeles, J. Paul Getty Museum.

Campbell, B. (1993) "War and Diplomacy: Rome and Parthia, 31 BC–AD 235." In J. W. Rich and G. Shipley (eds.) *War and Society in the Roman World*, 213–240. New York, Routledge, 1993.

Colledge, M. A. R. (1967) *The Parthians.* New York, Frederick A. Praeger Publishers.

Cutler, A. (2001) "Gifts and gift exchange as aspects of Byzantine, Arab and related economies." *Dumbarton Oak Papers* 55, 247–278.

Dąbrowa, E. (1983) *La politique de l'état parthe à l'égard de Rome - d'Artaban II à Vologèse I (ca 11-ca 79 de n.e.) et les facteurs qui la conditionnaient.* Kraków, W Drukarni Uniwersytetu Jagiellońskiego.

Dąbrowa E. (2006) "Marc Antoine, les Parthes et l'Armenie." In G. Traina (ed.) *Studi sull'età di Marco Antonio,* 343–352. Galatina, Congedo.

Dąbrowa, E. (2011) "ΑΡΣΑΚΝΣ ΘΕΟΣ. Observations on the Nature of the Parthian Ruler Cult." In C. Lippolis and S. De Martino (eds.) *Un impaziente desiderio di scorrere il Mondo. Studi in onore di Antonio Invernizzi per il suo settantesimo compleanno,* 247–254. Firenza, Le Lettere.

Debevoise, N. C. (1938) *A Political History of Parthia.* Chicago, The University of Chicago Press.

de Callataÿ, F. (1994) *Les tétradrachmes d'Orodès II et de Phraate IV: Étude du rythme de leur production monétaire à la lumière d'une grande trouvaille.* Paris, Association pour l'avancement des études iraniennes.

Dunbabin, K. (2004) *The Roman Banquet: Images of Conviviality.* Cambridge, Cambridge University Press.

Farrokh, K. (2007) *Shadows in the Desert: Ancient Persia at War.* Oxford, Osprey Publishing.

Ferris, I. M. (2000) *Enemies of Rome. Barbarians through Roman Eyes.* Stroud, The History Press.

Frandsen, P. (2009) *Close-Kin Marriage in Egypt and Persia. An Examination of the Evidence.* Copenhagen, Museum Tusculanum Press.

Galinsky, K. (1996) *Augustan Culture: An Interpretive Introduction.* Princeton, Princeton University Press.

Gaslain, J. and Maleuvre, J. "Auguste et les Arsacides, ou le prix des enseignes," *Parthica* 8, 169–194.

Gruen, E. S. (1996) "The Expansion of the Empire under Augustus." In A. K. Bowman, E. Champlin, and A. Lintott (eds.) *The Cambridge Ancient History, Volume X: The Augustan Empire, 43 B.C.-A.D. 69,* 147–197. Cambridge, Cambridge University Press.

Gruen, E. S. (ed.) (2005) *Cultural Borrowings and Ethnic Appropriations in Antiquity.* Stuttgart, Franz Steiner Verlag.

Gruen, E. S. (2011) *Rethinking the Other in Antiquity.* Princeton, Princeton University Press.

Harland, P. (2014) *Greco-Roman Associations: Text, Translations and Commentary. II North Coast of the Black Sea, Asia Minor.* Berlin, De Gruyter.

Hekster, O. (2015) *Emperors and Ancestors: Roman Rulers and the Constraints of Tradition.* Oxford, Oxford University Press.

Hölbl, G. (2001) *A History of the Ptolemaic Empire.* Translated by T. Saavedra. London, Routledge.

Holliday, P. (1997) "Roman Triumphal Painting: Its Function, Development and Reception." *Art Bulletin* 79, 130–147.

Holliday, P. (2002) *The Origins of Roman Historical Commemoration in the Visual Arts.* Cambridge, Cambridge University Press.

Holmes, T. R. (1928) *The Architect of the Roman Empire.* Oxford, Clarendon Press.

Invernizzi, A. (2000) "The Square House at Old Nisa." *Parthica* 2, 13–53.

Invernizzi, A. (2007) "Royal Cult in Arsakid Parthia." In P. P. Iossif, A. S. Chankowski, and C. C. Lorber (eds.) *More than Men, Less than Gods: Studies on Royal Cult and Imperial Worship, Proceedings of the International Colloquium organized by the Belgian School at Athens (November 1-2, 2007),* 651–690. Leuven, Peeters.

Keaveney, A. (1981) "Roman Treaties with Parthia circa 95 – circa 94 B.C." *American Journal of Philology* 102, 195–212.

Kleiner, F. (1985) *The Arch of Nero in Rome. A Study of the Roman Honorary Arch before and under Nero.* Rome, Giorgio Bretschneider.

Kleiner, D. E. E. (1992) *Roman Sculpture.* New Haven, Yale University Press.

Kleiner, D. E. E. (2005) *Cleopatra and Rome.* Cambridge, Harvard University Press.

Kleiner, D. E. E. and Buxton, B. (2011) "Pledges of Empire: the Ara Pacis and the Donations of Rome." *American Journal of Archaeology* 112.1, 57–89.

Kleiner, F. (1996) "Women on the Coin of the Realm." In D. E. E. Kleiner and S. B. Matheson (eds.) *I, Claudia: Women in Ancient Rome,* 56–60, 64–67, 70, 76–81, 86–89. Austin, University of Texas Press.

Lewy, H. (1944) "The Genesis of Faulty Persian Chronology." *Journal of the American Oriental Society* 64.4, 197–214.

Lee, A. D. (1988) "Close-Kin Marriage in Late Antique Mesopotamia." *Greek, Roman and Byzantine Studies* 29, 403–413.

Lerouge, C. (2007) *L'image des Parthes dans le monde gréco-romain: Du début du Ier siècle av. J.-C. jusqu'à la fin du Haut-Empire romain*. Stuttgart, Franz Steiner Verlag.

Levick, B. (1999) *Tiberius the Politician*. New York, Routledge.

Linz, O. (2009) *Studien zur römischen Ostpolitik im Principat*. Hamburg, Verlag Dr. Kovač.

Lorber, C. (2012) "Coinage of the Ptolemies." In W. E. Metcalf (ed.) *The Oxford Handbook of Greek and Roman Coinage*, 211–234. Oxford, Oxford University Press.

Macurdy, G. H. (1932) *Hellenistic Queens: A Study of Woman-Power in Macedonia, Seleucid Syria, and Ptolemaic Egypt*. Chicago Ridge, Ares Publishing.

Malinowski, B. (1922) *Argonauts of the Western Pacific*. London, George Routledge and Sons.

Mauss, M. (1954) *The Gift: Forms and Functions of Exchange in Archaic Societies*. Translated by I. Cunnison. London, Cohen and West.

McDowell, R. H. (1935) *Coins from Seleucia on the Tigris*. Ann Arbor, University of Michigan Press.

Meadows, A. (2001) "Coinage and the administration of Antony's empire." In S. Walker and P. Higgs (eds.) *Cleopatra of Egypt: from History to Myth*, 233–235. London, British Museum Press.

Middleton, R. (1962) "Brother-Sister and Father-Daughter Marriage in Ancient Egypt." *American Sociological Review* 27.5, 603–611.

Miller, J. (2009) *Apollo, Augustus and the Poets*. Cambridge, Harvard University Press.

Osgood, J. (2006) *Caesar's Legacy: Civil War and the Emergence of the Roman Empire*. Cambridge, Cambridge University Press, 2006.

Östenberg, I. (2009) *Staging the World. Spoils, Captives, and Representations in Roman Triumphal Processions*. Oxford, Oxford University Press.

Pasmans, P. (2005) "De Munten van de Parthische Koningin Musa." *De Muntklapper, Europees Genootschap voor Munt-en Penningkunde* 45, 1–5.

Pelling, C. (1996) "The Triumviral Period." In A. K. Bowman, E. Champlin, and A. Lintott (eds.) *The Cambridge Ancient History, Volume X: The Augustan Empire, 43 B.C.–A.D. 69*. Cambridge, Cambridge University Press, 1–69.

Pollini, J. (2012) *From Republic to Empire: Rhetoric, Religion and Power in the Visual Culture of Ancient Rome*. Norman, University of Oklahoma Press.

Rawlinson, G. (1873) *The Sixth Great Oriental Monarchy: Geography, History, and Antiquities of Parthia*. London, Longmans, Green, and Co.

Remijsen, S. and Clarysse, W. (2008) "Incest of Adoption? Brother-Sister Marriage in Egypt Revisited." *Journal of Roman Studies* 98, 53–61.

Rose, C. B. (2005) "The Parthians in Augustan Rome." *American Journal of Archaeology* 109, 21–75.

Sampson, G. C. (2008) *The Defeat of Rome: Crassus, Carrhae, and the Invasion of the East*. Barnsley, Pen & Sword Military.

Schieber, A. S. (1979) "Antony and Parthia." *Rivista Storica dell'Antichità* 9, 105–124.

Schlude, J. M. (2012) "The Parthian Response to the Campaign of Crassus." *Latomus* 71, 11–23.

Schlude, J. M. (2013) "Pompey and the Parthians." *Athenaeum* 101.1, 163–181.

Schlude, J. M. (2015) "The Early Parthian Policy of Augustus." *Anabasis: Studia Classica et Orientalia* 6, 139–156.

Schlude, J. M. (forthcoming) "Cyrus the Great and Roman Views of Ancient Iran." In R. Shayegan (ed.) *Cyrus the Great: Life and Lore*. Boston and Washington, DC, Ilex Foundation and Center for Hellenic Studies.

Schneider, R. M. (1986) *Bunte Barbaren: Orientalstatuen aus farbigen Marmor in der römischen Repräsentationskunst*. Worms, Wernershe Verlagsgesellschaft.

Schneider, R. M. (2007) "Friend *and* Foe: the Orient in Rome." In V. S. Curtis and S. Stewart (eds.) *The Age of the Parthians, The Idea of Iran*, vol. 2, 50–86. London, I. B. Tauris Publishers.

Seager, R. (1972) *Tiberius*. London, Eyre Methuen Ltd.

Sellwood, D. G. (1980) *An Introduction to Parthian Coinage*. London, Spink & Son.

Severy, B. (2004) *Augustus and the Family at the Birth of the Roman Empire*. London, Routledge.

Shaw, B. (1992) "Explaining Incest: Brother-Sister Marriage in Graeco-Roman Egypt." *Man* 27, 267–299.

Shayegan, M. R. (2011) *Arsacids and Sasanians: Political Ideology in Post-Hellenistic and Late Antique Persia*. Cambridge, Cambridge University Press.

Sheldon, R. (2010) *Rome's War in Parthia: Blood in the Sand*. London, Vellentine Mitchell.

Sherwin-White, A. N. (1984) *Roman Foreign Policy in the East, 168 B.C. to A.D. 1*. London, Duckworth.

Shore, F. B. (1993) *Parthian Coins and History: Ten Dragons against Rome*. Quarryville, PA, CNG.

Sinisi, F. (2012) "The Coinage of the Parthians." In W. E. Metcalf (ed.) *The Oxford Handbook of Greek and Roman Coinage*, 275–296. Oxford, Oxford University Press.

Strugnell, E. (2008) "Thea Musa, Roman Queen of Parthia." *Iranica Antiqua* 43, 275–298.

Sullivan, R. D. (1990) *Near Eastern Royalty and Rome, 100–30 BC*. Toronto, University of Toronto Press.

Tarn, W. (1951) "Parthia." In S. Cook *et al.* (eds.) *The Cambridge Ancient History, Volume IX: The Roman Republic, 133–44 B.C.*, 574–613. Cambridge, Cambridge University Press.

Thomas, N. (1991) *Entangled Objects: Exchange, Material Culture and Colonialism in the Pacific*. Cambridge, Harvard University Press.

Timpe, D. (1975) "Zur augusteischen Partherpolitik zwischen 30 und 20 v. Chr." *Würzburger Jahrbücher für die Altertumswissenschaft*, 155–169.

Traina, G. (2011) *Carrhes, 9 juin 53 av. J.-C.: Anatomie d'une défaite*. Paris, Les Belles Lettres.

Von Reden, S. (2009) *Money in Ptolemaic Egypt: from the Macedonian Conquest to the End of the Third Century BCE*. Cambridge, Cambridge University Press.

Vössing, K. (2004) *Mensa Regia: das Bankett beim hellenistischen König und beim römischen Kaiser*. Munich, K. G. Saur Verlag.

Vössing, K. (2015) "Royal Feasting." In J. Wilkins and R. Nadeau (eds.) *A Companion to Food in the Ancient World*. Chicester, West Sussex, Wiley-Blackwell.

Wang, T. (2007) "Parthia in China: A Re-Examination of the Historical Records." In V. S. Curtis and S. Stewart (eds.) *The Age of the Parthians, The Idea of Iran*, vol. 2, 87–104. London, I. B. Tauris Publishers.

Weggen, K. (2011) *Der lange Schatten von Carrhae: Studien zu M. Licinius Crassus*. Hamburg, Verlag Dr. Kovač.

Wiesehöfer, J. (2001) *Ancient Persia from 550 BC to 650 AD*. London, I. B. Tauris Publishers.

Williams, J. H. C. (2001) "Antony, descendant of Herakles." In S. Walker and P. Higgs (eds.) *Cleopatra of Egypt: from History to Myth*, 237. London, British Museum Press.

Williams, J. H. C. (2001) "Antony, godlike ruler of the East." In S. Walker and P. Higgs (eds.) *Cleopatra of Egypt: from History to Myth*, 238. London, British Museum Press.

Williams, J. H. C. (2001) "The dynasty and legacy of Antony." In S. Walker and P. Higgs (eds.) *Cleopatra of Egypt: from History to Myth*, 237. London, British Museum Press.

Wolski, J. (1993) *L'empire des Arsacides*. Leuven, E. Peeters.

Woolf, G. (1998) *Becoming Roman. The Origins of Provincial Civilization in Gaul*. Cambridge, Cambridge University Press.

Woolf, G. (2001) "The Roman Cultural Revolution." In S. Keay and N. Terrenato (eds.) *Italy and the West: Comparative Issues in Romanization*, 173–186. Oxford, Oxford University Press.

Zahn, R. (1923) "Ein Kleines Historisches Monument." In W. H. Buckler and W. M. Calder (eds.) *Anatolian Studies Presented to Sir William Mitchell Ramsey*. Manchester, University of Manchester.

Zanker, P. (1988) *The Power of Images in the Age of Augustus*. Translated by A. Shapiro. Ann Arbor, University of Michigan Press.

Ziegler, K. H. (1964) *Die Beziehungen zwischen Rom und den Partherreich: ein Beitrag zur Geschichte de Völkerrechts*. Wiesbaden, Franz Steiner Verlag.

Chapter 5

Herod the Great: A Near Eastern Case Study in Roman-Parthian Politics

Jason M. Schlude

and

J. Andrew Overman

Introduction

In the history of the ancient Near East, Pompey's decision to make Syria a Roman province in 64 BCE was a significant moment.[1] While Rome had been active militarily on the eastern Mediterranean seaboard for more than a century previous to this point, this event involved an entrenchment of Roman power in the region, giving Rome control over the heart of the once-great Seleucid empire. Now Rome directly administered a territory on the other side of the Amanus mountains that extended east to the Euphrates river and south to the territories of the Jewish people. The importance of this new province was clear. Rome equipped it with two legions and used it as a military base that provided access to Mesopotamia and territories as far south as Egypt. Indeed, Rome launched attacks from this base many times over the following centuries.

One of the most famous instances involved Marcus Licinius Crassus who set off from Rome in 55 BCE to serve as governor of Syria. When he arrived in Syria, he arrived with no shortage of ambition. Although the Romans and their eastern neighbors the Parthians were at peace from the time of their first known contact *c.* 96/95 BCE down to his own time, Crassus led an army of perhaps seven legions across the Euphrates river into the Parthian empire, which by this time was rebounding in power following its brief eclipse by the Armenian empire of Tigranes the Great (r. 95–55 BCE).[2] The result was disaster for the Romans. To be sure, Crassus embarked on an initial campaign season in 54 BCE just east of the Euphrates that met with moderate success. He took control of several cities, including Zenodotia where his soldiers hailed him *imperator*. But afterwards he returned to Syria to winter and earned the ill repute of locals by looting the temple in Jerusalem.[3] The impious act foreshadows disaster for Rome. Crassus renewed his efforts across the Euphrates in the spring of 53 BCE and found himself confronted by a formidable cavalry force of mounted bowmen led by Surenas, a powerful local aristocrat loyal to the Parthian king Orodes II (r. 58–38 BCE). Far more mobile than the Roman infantry troops, these horsemen avoided direct engagement and instead devastated the invaders with volley after volley of arrows. Crassus was forced to retreat to the nearby town of Carrhae, but the Parthians pursued and continued to exert pressure. In addition to the Romans they took as captives, the Parthians managed to secure a number of their military standards – something always considered a major dishonor to the Roman people. Crassus ultimately tried to negotiate his way out of the conflict in a diplomatic parley that turned to violence and produced his death. What Romans survived hastened to Syria in flight. Led by the Roman General Cassius the surviving Romans went into Syria and "took possession of it," according to Josephus. They arrived at Tyre on the coast and then fell back all the way to the Sea of Galilee and the Hellenistic city of Taricheae.[4] Cassius took the city, enslaved many of the inhabitants, and was drawn into a Judean civil dispute by Antipater, father of famed Herod the Great.

Leaving aside the setback of 53 BCE, however, a longer view of Roman-Parthian history may suggest that the Romans prevailed in their struggle with Parthia in the Near East. While the Parthians occasionally crossed the Euphrates into Syria and its environs, the Romans ultimately maintained control of the area from the time of Crassus to the end of Parthian empire in the late 220s BCE. In addition, it is important to note that Crassus was only the first of several Romans to campaign aggressively within the Parthian empire. Other such efforts were conducted under the triumvir Mark Antony in 36–35 BCE and emperors Trajan in 114–117 CE, Marcus Aurelius and Lucius Verus in 163–166 CE, Septimius Severus in 195–199 CE, and Caracalla in 215–217 CE.[5] From this angle, the Romans maintained a powerful presence in the Near East for almost 250 years, holding on to their territory west of the Euphrates and repeatedly attacking and showing the vulnerabilities of the Parthian empire to their east. In all of this, Syria was a Roman powerbase, which underscores the significance of its provincialization.

Yet such a compressed narrative has its dangers. A product of hindsight, it first of all exaggerates the control that the Roman state enjoyed on the Near Eastern frontier that served as its border with the Parthian empire. The narrative evokes too much of the inevitable. It is worth considering to what extent Parthia exercised more potency even west of the Euphrates, whether it was a potency real or perceived. Indeed, even perceived power can have very tangible consequences. Secondly, this sort of storyline almost leaves the impression that the Near Eastern border was devoid of any populations and local elites interested and capable of playing an active role in the negotiation of power in the region. In other words, while it stands to reason that the Romans and Arsacids had tremendous influence in the Near East, locals may not have been their passive playthings in every instance. Neglect of their perspective results in oversimplification. It is entirely possible that local peoples and elites acted as agents in what is often viewed only as *Roman-Parthian* politics.

We seek to explore these possibilities to shed additional light on the political dynamic of the Near East during the period in which the Roman and Parthian empires loomed so large in its history. The challenge, of course, is identifying a coherent data set to test the hypotheses. If evidence for Roman–Parthian relations is thin, then evidence for local perspectives in their negotiation is frustratingly sparse. Still evidence for the latter does exist – and it merits consideration. One good example is that of the Jewish people in Palestine and their (eventual) king: Herod the Great (r. 40–44 BCE). Scholarly treatments of the Jews in this region, and especially of Herod the Great, tend to emphasize the influence of Rome,[6] sometimes with the result of diminishing local agency in politics. But is this assessment sound? We intend to argue that it is in need of some revision. In fact, a consideration of Herod the Great in the context of Roman–Parthian politics reveals that both Romans and Arsacids exerted strong gravitational pulls in the Near East, and that local figures like Herod actively involved themselves in Roman-Parthian politics and manipulated them to achieve their own aims. To be sure, not only did Herod adroitly straddle these political realities and personalities in the Near East, he raised this skill to an art form. He has very few equals in this regard. Herod's political life and skill provide us with perhaps an unequalled case study of a deft client lord balancing and manipulating the pressure and threat of two great imperial powers: Parthia and Rome.

The Complexity of Herod the Great

Herod emerges from our sources as a complex figure. In fact, a wealth of scholarship has demonstrated how liminal he was. Much of this attention, however, has been given to his Jewishness and to what degree he belonged to a Jewish vs. non-Jewish world.[7] On the one hand, for example, his father was an Idumaean, which may speak for his Jewishness. In the late second century BCE John Hyrcanus theoretically converted the resident population of Idumaea, only allowing those to remain in the territory who agreed to circumcision and to follow Jewish laws.[8] In this regard then, perhaps he was an "authentic" Jew. We know that Herod declined to permit the marriage of his sister Salome to the Nabataean Syllaeus because the latter refused to adopt Jewish customs (certainly including circumcision).[9] And we may consider the quip by the late source Macrobius that it was better to be Herod's pig than his son, which, if true, may suggest Herod kept kosher.[10] In addition, Herod's expansion and elaboration of the Jewish temple in Jerusalem, one of his greatest building projects, may further speak to his dedication to Judaism.[11] Perhaps the tendency of Herod most often to avoid figural art in wall paintings, mosaics, and coins should be read similarly.[12] Such behavior would seem to speak to his general observance of Jewish customs.

Yet this was not the whole picture. Idumaea was also the land of Edom. In terms of Herod's temple project, we must bear in mind that Herod was the figure who endorsed the placement of an eagle sculpture above the great gate of the Jewish temple – a controversial decision for some Jews, viewed perhaps as a violation of the second commandment.[13] And of course we are well aware of the *three* Roman imperial cult temples that Herod built at Samaria Sebaste, Caesarea Maritima, and in the region of Banias![14] These acts fit less comfortably into a Jewish world as traditionally understood. They make Herod a more liminal figure. Indeed, these three temples celebrating Augustus were themselves liminal. They were in settings where Jews and traditional Greco-Romans lived together or near one another. They were mixed places and populations. Where did Herod's cultural loyalties lie then? It is clear even from this selective review that Herod lived along and probably on both sides of religious and cultural borders in and around his realm.

Herod's extensive and well-documented building program is itself an enduring expression of the loyalties and boundaries he had to constantly balance. For these projects, Herod would need tacit and often explicit approval from Roman administrators, if not Caesar himself. Yet local sensibilities and traditions had to be balanced with the imperial favor Herod curried. Josephus captures this hard reality when he concludes his discussion of the third Augusteum built by Herod to honor Caesar.

> Also at this time he [Herod] remitted a third of the taxes to those in his kingdom, the pretext being that they might recover from the dearth of crops. But rather he was trying to win over those ill-disposed to him. For when it came to his completion of such endeavors, they were stomaching it with difficulty since their religion was being undone and their customs were changing for the worse.[15]

Yet nowhere among Herod's building projects is the need to balance broader Roman support with local reactions and sentiment more apparent than in the case of building of the temple in Jerusalem. In Herod's speech to his people announcing this unparalleled project, he makes clear two things. First, this is a project motivated by piety. "I was given this kingdom so that I may render a perfect piety unto God." And second, by the way, this can happen in large measure because "the Romans, who are the rulers of all men, so to speak, are my loyal friends."[16] He always had to strike a balance between his allegiances to Rome and his endorsement and support of Jewish piety.[17]

In what follows we are most interested in the political borderlines Herod negotiated and balanced. His political career was that of a deft, liminal, eastern client who contended with a wide range of competing forces, pressures, and claims. Over the years, scholars have explored what kind of king Herod was and have gone far to highlight the range of the political interests and roles that he had to balance. Most of this discussion has centered on his responsibilities as a Roman client-king. Appointed by Rome in 40 BCE, Herod was sensitive to that relationship and cultivated it with care ever after. Yet he was also a king of the Jews and ruled with an eye to their interests (though some may question to what precise degree). And certain scholars have considered Herod as a Hellenistic king, a model that better helps to explain his many benefactions, not only at home, but also abroad – in Syria, Phoenicia, Asia Minor, Aegean islands, and Greece. From these various perspectives, we have come to appreciate the many political roles negotiated by Herod: Roman client, Jewish king, and Hellenistic ruler.[18]

But his political complexity ran deeper still. There is no doubt that Rome played a key role in Herod's rise to prominence and kingship, and Herod lived within the confines of territory dominated by Rome most of the time. We say "most" since this was not *always* the case. For a crucial window of time between 40 and 39 BCE Judaea and its environs actually fell into the empire of Parthia, when its prince Pacorus led a force west of the Euphrates that conquered the Roman east, from Idumaea to Caria in Asia Minor. This is just the most striking example of how the geopolitical world of the Near East was more than the playground of Rome. Herod was not only in the orbit of Rome, but also in that of Parthia.[19] In the first century BCE, Roman and Parthian efforts resulted in an evolving imperial boundary and dynamic to which those in the Near East had to respond. As the following will show, Herod adeptly positioned himself between Rome and Parthia, sometimes embracing one while rejecting the other, sometimes extending his hand to each where possible, with the result that it would not be inappropriate for us to consider Herod the friend of the Romans and the Parthians, if only for a time.

The Model of Antipater

It is not surprising that Herod approached politics open to some collaboration with the Parthians. His father Antipater shaped many of his inclinations. Antipater was a powerful Idumaean who supported the rights of the Hasmonean Hyrcanus II over his brother Aristobulus II. He was also a figure who consistently displayed international interests in his political behavior – interests that were by no means one-dimensional. Little argument is necessary to convince one that Antipater linked himself to the most powerful Romans of the day. This process began in 64/63 BCE with Pompey's entrance into the region and would continue thereafter for the rest of Antipater's career (lasting to 43 BCE), as well as, of course, his son Herod's career. It is more important here for us to notice how he took care to make friends in many places besides so as to strengthen his own security. As Josephus emphasizes, "He had won the support of powerful men everywhere through kindnesses and hospitality."[20] Antipater had many accomplishments in his relations with Roman leaders and eastern dynasts alike.

Consider first of all the relationship that he developed with the Nabataeans. Antipater married Cypros, Herod's mother, who was "Arabian" and connected to the Nabataean royal family. This permitted him to establish a friendship with the Nabataean king Aretas III, to whom he subsequently entrusted his children during one episode of his on-again, off-again conflict with Aristobulus.[21] In fact, this relationship was strong enough by *c.* 65 BCE that Antipater was able to arrange actual Nabataean military assistance for Hyrcanus.[22] And not long after, in 63/62 BCE, when Pompey's subordinate officer Scaurus besieged Aretas, Antipater even played a key role in securing a settlement between Scaurus and Aretas.[23] While Josephus indicates that

Antipater supported Roman interests in this instance, especially in the *War*, there is little doubt that he also was doing a favor to the Nabataeans (and he certainly spun it that way, too). Through his efforts, the Romans ultimately raised the siege for a sum of 300 talents – an amount for which Antipater, according to the *Antiquities*, actually served as surety.

One could read other international efforts of Antipater similarly. In 55 BCE he brought aid to Gabinius when he was in the process of restoring Ptolemy XII Auletes to the throne of Egypt. In addition, he at this time engaged in negotiations with various Jewish Egyptians to smooth the army's advance.[24] And Antipater also assisted Caesar in Egypt in 48–47 BCE, when to support him he joined the army of Mithridates of Pergamon and secured the help of the "Arabians" and others prominent in the region, *e.g.* a certain Ptolemy and Jamblichus, as well as more Jewish Egyptians.[25] Obviously such actions directly assisted the Romans – and Antipater was handsomely rewarded. Thus, Caesar conferred upon him Roman citizenship, tax exemption, and official guardianship of Judaea.[26] Yet Antipater surely had other motivations beyond cultivating a relationship with the Romans. He would have enjoyed the opportunity to broaden his circle of friends to include the Ptolemaic rulers whose position in Egypt he helped to solidify, as well as other bigwigs in the region. Antipater advanced his own prominence, influence, and power through developing relations with Romans, but also with Nabataeans, Egyptians, and even others. He worked the west and the east.

But what about the Parthians? The fact is that we have no explicit evidence documenting relations between Antipater and the Parthians. Yet his Nabataean ties make it likely that he had contact and exchange with them. Nabataea was very much in the sphere of the Arsacid empire. We can bring much evidence to bear on this point. For example, it is notable that when Herod turned to the Nabataean king Malchus for assistance during the Parthian invasion of 40 BCE, the king turned Herod away in accordance with orders from the Parthians.[27] Such a historical detail highlights the close relationship between the Nabataeans and Arsacids.

And so also does another anecdote, this time related by the Roman historian Tacitus. Between the years 18 and 19 CE, Tiberius' adopted son Germanicus and the appointed Syria governor C. Calpurnius Piso were at odds in the administration of the Roman East. Of republican orientation and temperament, Piso resented the sweeping authority of Germanicus, who had been granted *maius imperium* ("greater power") over the eastern provinces. The resentment surfaced in several public events, one in fact being at the Nabataean court. There the Nabataean king hosted a banquet for the Roman brass, including Germanicus and Piso. When he bestowed honorary crowns upon the Romans, and particularly big ones on Germanicus and his wife Agrippina, Piso publically – and bitingly – remarked that such a practice was fit more for the son of Parthian king than the son of a Roman emperor. He capped off his comment by dashing his own crown to the ground. Germanicus ignored the comment and act, no doubt to avoid drawing further attention to such a diplomatic debacle.[28] The incident is interesting from several angles. For purposes here it clearly illustrates the close link between the Nabataeans and Parthians. While mocking and rejecting gifts in this context is the most obvious insult to the Nabataeans, Piso's comments likely also called into question the loyalty of the Nabataeans. At a meeting intended to strengthen Rome's relationship with Nabataea, Piso hinted at the latter's loyalty to the Arsacid king instead![29]

Nabataean material culture also indicates a close Nabataean-Parthian association. Andreas Kropp has recently highlighted the Parthian imagery and dress among Nabataean Kings. The coins of Aretas IV (9–40 CE), Malikhos II (40–70 CE) and Rabbel II (70–106 CE) depict these rulers in Parthian royal costume. This includes a Parthian tunic and pearls. This, along with some of the hairstyles, show a Nabataea with decided eastern and Parthian leanings.[30]

With this in mind, we see that Antipater's balancing of relations with Rome and Nabataea was no small feat. And Parthian influence and Parthian sympathies in the Nabataean realm must have contributed substantially to the complexity. But we also find circumstantial evidence in the Nabataean-Parthian association to believe that Antipater likely also had relations with the Parthians.

It stands to reason that Herod would have been informed by this political approach at a critical stage of his development. Antipater prepared and paved the way for him. He put him in touch with a world bigger than Rome – and Herod saw some of its security benefits firsthand. In the end, Herod would demonstrate a facility and skill in diplomacy and *realpolitik* that matched that of his father, and through it all a keen interest in Parthia on the part of Herod would have been natural.

Herod and Parthia

What is more, such an interest in Parthia was necessary, considering the geopolitical power struggles of his day. As we have mentioned already, Roman and Parthian interests in the Near East brought Roman statesmen in contact with the Arsacid kings of Parthia in the mid-90s BCE. After they maintained peace for several decades, even settling on the Euphrates river as a working border of their respective empires under Pompey and Phraates III in the mid-60s BCE,[31] Crassus ended that more cooperative legacy with his disastrous campaign in 54–53 BCE. Indeed, it was an unqualified defeat for the Romans. Yet this was not Rome's only black eye; matters worsened for them in subsequent years. In 40 BCE Orodes commissioned his son Pacorus to carry out a major invasion of the Roman east.[32] Pacorus crossed the Euphrates and exerted Parthian control over a territory extending from Idumaea through Caria. An effective Roman response came not too long thereafter; Mark Antony's subordinate Ventidius pushed the Parthians out and renewed Rome's presence in the Near East in 39–38 BCE. But the damage had been done. The Parthians proved to locals in the Near East that Roman invincibility was a fiction and that Parthia was also a significant player in the region. They could not ignore the power and long reach of the Parthians.

Such recognition had important consequences for Herod. In this context, local dynasts and elites must have felt compelled to make connections with Rome and Parthia, when possible. Their survival demanded it. While hindsight tells us that Rome would remain dominant west of the Euphrates, they could not assume that. Many might have thought events were trending in another direction. They also recognized the advantage of their position on the Roman–Parthian border: they could use the climate of Roman–Parthian distrust and conflict when negotiating with either side. With all this in mind, we see that there was incentive to take action. The tense circumstances afforded them some agency and the opportunity to manipulate their relations with Rome and Parthia to advance their own positions. To return to Herod specifically, while the evidence is not as full as we may like, there is certainly enough to demonstrate that Herod's rise to power in Judaea and its environs is only fully understandable if we appreciate that Herod was in an area where the orbits of Rome and Parthia overlapped. In this situation, he took advantage of the Roman–Parthian power struggle and tried to work with each side, at key points and when possible, to enhance and shore up his position.

A couple examples illustrate this process. First, consider the reasons for Herod's elevation as King in 40 BCE. This resulted not only from Herod's ability in general. It was largely a reaction to Herod's specific use of the Parthian invasion of 40 BCE to gain the throne. In this invasion, the Parthians installed Aristobulus' son Antigonus as their vassal king in Judaea. In addition, they arrested Hyrcanus, brought him back to Parthia, and chased out Herod.[33] Interestingly, Herod's first instinct was to approach the Nabataean king Malchus and try to utilize his family's connections to his court to secure funding for negotiation with the Parthians. Josephus indicates that he wished to ransom his brother Phasael, whom the Parthians had arrested along with Hyrcanus – and who, unbeknownst to Herod, had perished by suicide or foul play by this point. Yet one also wonders whether Herod hoped to secure enough cash to persuade the Parthians to come to terms as well; Josephus mentions Herod's interest in 300 talents, the same price that Antipater convinced the previous Nabataean king Aretas to pay to have Scaurus lift a Roman siege. At any rate, at the order of the Parthians, the Nabataean king Malchus refused assistance.[34] So the Nabataean option was closed to Herod.

As a result, Herod finally decided to go to Rome for support. There he informed Antony of everything, emphasizing the Parthian aggression and threat, and angled for kingship and Roman assistance.[35] To be sure, it is well known that Josephus, our primary source for all this, at one point remarks that Herod actually went to Rome to secure the royal rights of his brother-in-law Aristobulus III.[36] But as has been rightly recognized by a number of scholars, this was clearly a later attempt by Herod to rewrite history for a domestic audience.[37] In reality, it was not unreasonable for Herod to think that he had a shot at the kingship. Cassius had promised it in 43 BCE,[38] Antony not long after made Herod a "tetrarch" in 42/41 BCE,[39] and Herod was betrothed to a member of the royal Hasmonean family.[40] Furthermore, Josephus makes clear that he was after the throne when he notes that Herod, in Rome in 40 BCE, offered Antony a bribe contingent upon his kingship.[41] In the end, Herod's efforts paid off; he was presented favorably to the Roman senate and achieved his goal. As Josephus describes,

> When Messala and Atratinus after him assembled the Senate, they produced Herod, reviewed the benefactions of his father, and recalled the good will, which he himself had for the Romans. And they at once leveled charges against Antigonus and proved him hostile, not only because of his first quarrel with them, but because he received his royal power from the Parthians and thereby had slighted the Romans. And when the Senate had been stirred by these things, Antony came forward and instructed them that it was also advantageous for the war against the Parthians that Herod be king. And since this seemed good to all, they voted to approve it.[42]

Parthia then was a major factor in Herod's promotion to king of Judaea, as commonly recognized by scholars.[43] Fundamentally, it was Roman outrage over the Parthian installment of a vassal king in Judaea that led the senate to appoint its own man, Herod, king of the territory. But Herod's active role in this deserves emphasis. In the midst of the Parthian invasion of 40 BCE, he first considered and moved toward negotiation with the Parthians, but then changed tactics and appealed to Rome, where he deftly manipulated Roman concerns about the Parthian threat to secure a crown. The creation and negotiation of the Roman–Parthian border was a complex process involving the active participation of multiple parties: Roman statesmen, Parthian royals, and the many elites and dynasts living between the Mediterranean seaboard and the Euphrates river. Standing on that border, Herod used it for his own benefit.

The second example of such borderline activity involves an attested direct diplomatic exchange between Herod and the Parthian king Phraates IV in 36 BCE. As remarked upon earlier, after his arrest Hyrcanus was brought back into the Parthian empire in 40 BCE, no doubt as a partial check on Antigonus, the new Parthian vassal. And he remained there for several years as a newly crowned Herod returned to the Near East in 39 BCE as part of the Roman effort to recover lost territory. Incidentally, they were able to complete this process by 37 BCE. Ventidius defeated the Parthians, and Herod tenaciously eliminated resistance from Antigonus' supporters. Eventually, he took Jerusalem, Antigonus surrendered to the Romans, and Mark Antony had him executed.[44] It was after all this that Herod initiated a diplomatic exchange with the Parthians, in which Phraates granted permission for Hyrcanus to return to Judaea in 36 BCE. According to Josephus,

> Herod wrote and called on him [Hyrcanus] to ask Phraates and the Jews there to not refuse this opportunity for him to share the kingship with Herod. For it was just the right time for Herod to repay and Hyrcanus to be rewarded for the good deeds that he enjoyed when he had been supported and saved by him. While writing these things to Hyrcanus, Herod also sent Saramalla as an envoy and a great number of gifts to Phraates, asking that he not prevent Herod from showing his favor to the benefactor who similarly treated him so well. But that was not the reason for his eagerness. Rather, on account of the fact that he himself was not worthy to rule, he feared the changes that might come for good reason.

> And he hastened to get Hyrcanus into his own hands or even to completely put him out of the way. For this he did later.[45]

As mentioned, Phraates agreed, and Hyrcanus returned. For our purposes, we would emphasize how Herod here carried out a productive and direct diplomatic exchange with the Parthian king Phraates. This is an exchange that many scholars neglect to highlight. As for why he initiated it then, two factors are key. First, the Parthian vassal Antigonus was no longer a complicating factor. And second, it came right after an important shift in the Parthian kingship. Just before, in 37 BCE, Orodes had died. It was under his auspices in 40 BCE that the Parthian invasion and installation of Antigonus as king took place. But now that Orodes was out of the way, and a new king Phraates reigned, there was the chance for some diplomatic negotiation.

It is no coincidence that Antony at this time also opened up diplomatic channels with Parthia. As Cassius Dio tells us, in winter/spring of 36 BCE, after allowing a Parthian refugee named Monaeses to return to the Parthian empire, Antony also sent envoys to Phraates in peace, to negotiate for the return of the standards and prisoners-of-war once lost by Crassus in 53 BCE.[46] Dio would have us believe that this was all part of a ruse to throw Phraates off, while Antony was preparing war.

> Accordingly, he [Antony] sent him [Monaeses] forth on the ground that he would win the Parthians over to himself, and sent envoys with him to Phraates. He was pretending to try to achieve peace on the condition that he receive the standards and captives taken in the disaster of Crassus. This was in order that he might catch the king unprepared on account of his hope for a settlement. But in fact he was making all things ready for war.[47]

Dio then clearly suggests that Antony was not single-minded in his tactics. And perhaps some of that hypothesizing is true. But there is no reason to think that Antony could not have been somewhat optimistic that he could score the standards and captives through diplomatic means at this time of political change in Parthia.

More to our point, it is interesting to consider whether Herod or Antony contacted the Parthian king first. Unfortunately, the sources themselves do not give us a lock on the relative chronology. In fact, with the ambiguity that exists, one may even ask if the two collaborated on a joint diplomatic effort. Such questions are important; answers to them have bearing on our understanding of Herod's role in the negotiation of the Roman-Parthian border. Was Herod a passive figure, who absolutely took his lead and operated inseparably from Rome, or was he more of an agent who reached out to Phraates on his own, whether without Roman foreknowledge or after some prior justification of the action (perhaps in light of Antony's interest in warming Roman–Parthian relations)? This is a many-sided question, not every part of which can be surely answered. What evidence we do have, however, at least suggests that this was an independent action by Herod. As we have seen, neither Dio nor Josephus connect these two diplomatic efforts, much less suggest that there was a common embassy of any sort. And this is particularly notable in the case of Josephus, whose account routinely highlights the Herodian family's collaborative efforts with Romans.

Herod then seems to have sent an embassy in his own name – and no doubt with multiple aims. As Josephus points out, it was an opportunity to take possession of the ranking member of the Hasmonean royal family from the Parthians, who were still clearly a threat. Only a few years before, they controlled the Near East. Perhaps they could do it again. But in addition, Herod certainly also used it as a chance to build up a rapport with the new Parthian king in the same dicey geopolitical context. Herod had real reason to be in the good graces of Parthia, too. As with Antipater, he was not a passive one-dimensional figure. In a world dominated and divided by Rome and Parthia, Herod also actively worked the west and east.

Herod's Tactics After 31/30 BCE

This brings us back to the beginning. Based on these observations, we would say that we can properly understand the Near East in the first century BCE through early third century CE only if we fully appreciate the influence of the Arsacids and the potentially active role of local peoples and elites in regional politics. Even if a Roman-appointed king, Herod secured that position by using the threatening power of Parthia. And in the years soon thereafter, while the evidence is thin (as often), we can see that Herod worked to improve his standing with Parthia, too. He engaged productively with both of the states seeking hegemony in the Near East – at least through the mid-30s BCE.

After 31/30 BCE, however, Herod's circumstances changed. Following the battle of Actium, in which Octavian fought and defeated Antony, who then went on to commit suicide, Octavian became the Roman in charge in the Near East. And Herod now feared for his own position, due to his alignment with Antony against Octavian and the fact that Hyrcanus was still alive. Might Octavian not dispense with him and crown Hyrcanus as king? Perhaps. He was the last surviving Hasmonean heir. But to guard against this possibility, Herod now eliminated Hyrcanus, an act that was vicious but effective. Limited in his choices, Octavian maintained Herod as king.[48]

Scholars also have noted this act, but have not recognized its significance with regard to Parthia. Recall that Phraates returned Hyrcanus on the understanding that he was to be honored back in Judaea. One in fact wonders whether Josephus' language that Hyrcanus was "to share the kingship with Herod" was at least in part a reflection of the way in which Phraates publically presented Hyrcanus' return. Phraates might have given some within his empire the impression that he was effectively installing a Parthian vassal. As a result, the fact that Herod now killed him (to serve his more immediate needs) likely would have caused significant tension between Herod and Phraates. The problem would not have been Phraates' personal concern for Hyrcanus and his ethical orientation in general. We have to remember that Phraates was a political realist and had a brutal streak as well. In fact, he may have come to power in 37 BCE through the murder of Orodes, his own father, and thereafter he killed his brothers and perhaps even a son to make his grip on the throne absolutely secure.[49] More likely, Herod's decision to eliminate Hyrcanus caused problems in public policy and reputation. Indeed, this hardly would have looked good for Phraates in the Parthian empire. The Babylonian Jewry, an important constituency that honored Hyrcanus, would have been displeased and could have viewed Phraates as complicit in the act. Alternatively, it might have reflected poorly on Phraates by highlighting weakness of judgment or power. In 31/30 BCE Herod then must have compromised to some degree the relationship he had developed with this Parthian king. From then on, Herod was even more fully dependent on Rome – much more a Roman client-king as normally defined, but again after 31/30 BCE.

This public tension between Herod and Phraates may even be visible in some unexpected places. For example, the story of Matthew 2.1–12 comes to mind. In this story, "magi from the east" (μάγοι ἀπὸ ἀνατολῶν) come to Jerusalem to find "the one who was born king of the Jews" (ὁ τεχθεὶς βασιλεὺς τῶν Ἰουδαίων). First, Herod points them in the direction of Bethlehem, and then a star takes them the rest of the way, stopping at the dwelling of the infant Jesus. There they kneel and offer gifts before returning to the east "by another road" (δι' ἄλλης ὁδοῦ) – a quick decision made out of fear of Herod. What is interesting is that the story plays with the revered institution of embassy between eastern royals. Here we have Zoroastrian priests from the Parthian empire going to Judaea. But when they arrive, they rebuff Herod and proceed to flee from him. The storyline is full of Christian legend – and Herodian–Parthian tension. It reflects the later troubled public relationship between Herod and the Arsacid king.

This change, however, does not mean that Herod completely cut off all connections to Parthia, as some have pointed out.[50] It may be that Herod continued to be in contact with the Arsacid administration. One could imagine, for example, that Herod might have played some part in the Parthian return of the lost standards and captives in 20 BCE. In this scenario, when Augustus (the proper designation for Octavian after 27 BCE) travelled to Syria in the late 20s BCE, it was Herod who put him in contact with the Parthian envoys whom he then used to request back the standards and captives. And when Augustus met with success in this effort, Herod escorted him back to the Mediterranean and then proceeded to erect a Roman temple in celebration of the achievement – a temple possibly excavated at the site Omrit on the outskirts of Banias/Caesarea Philippi. Such a reconstruction is plausible and, if true, would speak to Herod's continued contact with the court of the Parthian king Phraates.

Yet the evidence still may confirm that not everything was business as usual for Herod and Phraates after 31/30 BCE. The fact is that no ancient source credits Herod with the facilitation of this productive Roman-Parthian exchange, not even Josephus.[51] Obviously, this need not mean that Herod played no such role. It was not unheard of for Roman client-kings to help facilitate Rome's relationship with neighboring dynasts. In fact, the record documents Herod's offspring played precisely such a role with Parthia later on![52] Still, if true, the silence is peculiar, particularly in Josephus. Yet it would be explicable in light of the limited role that Herod perhaps played, as well as the special circumstances surrounding this episode. As for Herod's role, it would have had to be low profile, considering once again his decision to kill Hyrcanus. Phraates likely could not afford to work too publically with Herod, a lightning-rod figure for him. And this only would have been more the case for the diplomatic engagement of 20 BCE, since it led Phraates to send Parthian notables (as "hostages") to Rome at this time.⁵³ Neither side would have had interest in putting a spotlight on Herod in that exchange; he had killed an important person secured through diplomacy with Parthia.

While one could protest that this may seem too cloak-and-dagger, there are other attested instances of clandestine exchanges with Arsacid kings. To stay in the realm of Jewish affairs, we might recall the brothers Asinaios and Anilaios, particularly effective Jewish gangsters in Mesopotamia. According to Josephus, after summoning and meeting with the brothers under a pledge to do them no harm, the Parthian king Artabanus III (r. 10/11–38 CE) encouraged his military commander Abdagases to attack and dispatch them on their return trip home, without the king's official knowledge. But then Artabanus sent secretly to Asinaios to warn him of the impending attack – a warning that allowed him to expedite his return and avoid the ambush. This complex exchange resulted from the king's desire to maintain the safety and support of the brothers as a counterweight to his rebellious Parthian satraps and from his simultaneous need to appear to be opposed to the Jewish brothers. All this required secret coordination with these Jewish notables.⁵⁴ With this in mind, if Herod participated in a low-profile exchange in 20 BCE, it certainly was not the only time that a Parthian king had to be diplomatically discrete.

As for the special circumstances, it has been well demonstrated how important this diplomatic accomplishment was for Augustus. He presented it in Rome as a military victory, and it became a cornerstone of his self-image.⁵⁵ Perhaps Herod understood the significance of this event for Augustus and gave him credit and a monopoly on its benefits. To the extent that this is true, it is reasonable to conclude that Herod maintained some contact with the Parthian court, though it was necessarily less public.

Conclusion

The Romans dominated the Near East – but they did not do so alone. The Arsacids also exercised extensive influence there as well. Yet even with the appreciation of this fact, our picture of political dynamics in the Near East remains incomplete unless we recognize that local figures also played an active role in Roman–Parthian politics. Herod the Great was one such elite. He was a borderline figure in many ways, including the political. While he negotiated his responsibilities to Rome on one hand and the Jewish people on the other, another major borderline with which he contended was that between the Roman and Parthian empires. It is most useful to conceive of Herod's behavior in this regard as part of a multiparty and dynamic process in which Romans, Parthians, and Near Eastern elites all took part in the definition and manipulation of the Roman–Parthian border. As we have seen, always to the end of maintaining and enhancing his own position, Herod tried to work with the Romans and the Parthians, when possible, sometimes with the result of making their border more hostile, other times with the result of encouraging their peace. In the end, Herod helped to shape the character of Roman–Parthian relations – and always to his own advantage.[56]

Notes

1. For discussion with treatment of Pompey's motivations, see Dobiáš 1931, 244–256, who explains it as part of Pompey's efforts to eliminate piracy in the eastern Mediterranean; Mommsen 1857, who argues it was a response to the potential aggression of the Parthian empire, followed by Sherwin-White 1983, 206–213, 225–226, and Butcher 2003, 19–23; see also Sartre 2005, 37–40, who provides a balanced assessment of these and other reasons, noting also Pompey's interest in elevating his self-image as much as possible; Schlude 2013, 170–171, 178–180, who suggests that Pompey made the move to fill the power vacuum left by the fall of the Armenian empire, but that Pompey looked not to oppose, but in fact to coordinate with the Arsacids in this effort.
2. The principal sources for the Crassan campaign include: Plut., *Crass.* 14–33 and Dio 39.33.2, 40.12–28. For discussion see Debevoise 1938, 78–95; Tarn 1951, 604–612; Ziegler 1964, 32–34; Bivar 1983, 48–56; Sherwin-White 1984, 279–290; Sullivan 1990, 306–309; Wolski 1993, 128–133; Sampson 2008; Traina 2010.
3. Joseph., *BJ* 1.179; *AJ* 14.105. Plut., *Crass.* 17 indicates that Crassus' avarice led him to confiscate the wealth of other temples and cities as well, including Hierapolis.
4. For a full report on the recent excavations of the site, see De Lucca 2009, 343–562.
5. For surveys of these campaigns, see Debevoise 1938, 121–132, 218–239, 245–254, 256–266; Sheldon 2010, 65–74, 125–143, 157–173.
6. See the recent publication of Jacobson and Kokkinos 2009, an excellent volume that focuses on Herod's relationship with Augustan Rome. It should be noted that certain articles within it slightly broaden the volume's scope, *e.g.* Gruen 2009, 13–27 (see below).
7. A topic discussed in some form in any comprehensive treatment of Herod. See, for example, Richardson 1999, who deals with the issue from several different angles in chapters on Herod's family (33–51), building program (174–215), and religious orientation (240–261).
8. Joseph., *AJ* 13.257–258.
9. Joseph., *AJ* 16.220–225; *BJ* 1.401.
10. Macrob., *Sat.* 2.4.11.
11. Joseph., *Ant.* 15.380–425; see also *BJ* 1.401 and 5.184–226. See Jacobson 2007, 145–176, who reviews the monument's architectural details and Herod's motivations. Jacobson, however, explains the project less as an issue of personal Jewish piety and more in the context of Hellenistic and Roman patronage and style. For the architecture, see also Netzer 2006, 137–178.
12. For this issue and what follows, see Japp 2007, 227–246, especially 242–244. This remains the case even in Herodium where spectacular, resplendent wall paintings have recently been found in Herod's "royal box" above the theater. There is one small fragment from Herodium that seems to depict two men crowned with ivy wreaths reclining on a couch at a symposium. See Rosenberg 2013, 189.
13. Joseph., *AJ* 17.149–167; *BJ* 1.648–655.
14. Joseph., *BJ* 1.403–414; *AJ* 15.331–341. Netzer 2006 provides a convenient and streamlined review of the archaeological evidence, with reference to key bibliography: 85–89 (Samaria Sebaste), 103–106 (Caesarea Maritima), and 218–222 (Banias). The location of the Augusteum at Banias has proven a point of debate. Excavations since 1999 at the site Omrit, just south of Banias, have produced a good candidate: the temple identified as "Temple One" at Omrit. For a final report on its architecture, see Nelson 2015. Overman and Schowalter 2011 provides additional interpretive discussion. See also the review of the latter volume by Berlin 2013, 244–247, who

suggests alternative explanations for this and another Omrit temple (called "Temple Two"). While Netzer 2006 was less inclined to accept the identification (222), other excavators at Banias have received it with more favor, *e.g.* Wilson and Tzaferis 2007, 141; *cf.* Wilson 2004, 16. See below for further discussion.

15. Joseph., *AJ* 15.365.
16. Joseph., *AJ* 15.387.
17. Richardson 1999, 249, is right in emphasizing that Herod required both the approval of Roman authorities and at the least domestic acquiescence, if not support. This necessarily "required masterful negotiations, both inside and outside the country." As he says, "The project avoided the Scylla of internal unhappiness and the Charybdis of external opposition ... This balancing act was a major coup, a masterful piece of religious diplomacy."
18. For a number of excellent studies that explore these roles of Herod, see Jacobson and Kokkinos 2009. Again, the focus of this corpus is Herod's relationship with Augustan Rome. But sensitivity is shown to elements of his behavior best explained in reference to the culture of Hellenistic kingship. See, for example, Gruen 2009, 13–27, who investigates the image that Herod projected of himself for various audiences as a "partner" of Rome, "benefactor of the multi-ethnic peoples of Palestine," and Hellenistic king.
19. Significant considerations of Herod in the context of Roman-Parthian relations include: Overman 2009, 279–299; Kasher 2011, 227–245. A range of other scholars, however, also acknowledge the significance of Parthia for Herod: *e.g.* Braund 1984, 24–25; Rappaport 1989, 374–375; Sullivan 1990, 222–225; Roller 1998, 14–15, 69; Richardson 1999, 119–121, 124–130, 153–157, 161–162. Despite this attention, no scholar has addressed all Herod's decisions and actions potentially bearing on his relationship with Parthia. This paper attempts to treat them all.
20. Joseph., *BJ* 1.181.
21. Joseph., *BJ* 1.181; *AJ* 14.121–122.
22. Joseph., *BJ* 1.123–129; *AJ* 14.14–33.
23. Joseph., *BJ* 1.159; *AJ* 14.80–81.
24. Joseph., *BJ* 1.175; *AJ* 14.100.
25. Joseph., *BJ* 1.187–193; *AJ* 14.127–136.
26. Joseph., *BJ* 194–200; *AJ* 14.137–143.
27. See discussion below.
28. For Piso's behavior, see Tac., *Ann.* 2.55 and 2.57, the latter recounting the Nabataean banquet scene. For further discussion of Piso's relationship with Germanicus, see Seager 1972, 98–102, 105–106; Marsh 1931, 88–96. For an alternative understanding of their relationship, see Rapke 1982, 61–69. See also the response by Bird 1987, 72–75.
29. For another reading of this incident and how it may have caused Germanicus to avoid a meeting with the Arsacid king Artabanus at the Euphrates river, see Schlude, "Rome and Parthia in the Late Republic and Early Empire," forthcoming in P. Edwell (ed.), *Blackwell Companion to Rome and Persia* (Oxford: Wiley-Blackwell).
30. Kropp 2013, 67. Kropp here is building off of the earlier examination by Seyrig 1937, 31–53.
31. See Schlude 2013, 163–181.
32. For this invasion in the context of Parthian activities after the Crassan campaign, see Schlude 2012, 11–23.
33. Joseph., *BJ* 1.248–273; *AJ* 14.330–369.
34. Joseph., *BJ* 1.274–276; *AJ* 14.370–373. It is notable that Iturea also fell under the influence of Parthians. A smaller and less well-known region located in modern day N.E. Upper Galilee and southern Lebanon, Iturea was ruled by Lysanias in 40 BCE. Since he allied himself with Parthians at this time, Mark Antony had him beheaded when he assumed control of the region in 36 BCE. Augustus ultimately gave the Iturean kingdom to Herod in 20 BCE to control and to cleanse of anti-Roman influences. For discussion, see Jones 1931, 265–275; Overman 2004, 287–298.

35. See in general Joseph., *AJ* 14.3.74–89, which is fuller than *BJ* 14.277–285.
36. Joseph., *AJ* 14.386–387.
37. See recently Kasher 2011, 239–240.
38. Joseph., *BJ* 1.225; *AJ* 14.280.
39. Joseph., *BJ* 1.244; *AJ* 14.326.
40. Joseph., *BJ* 1.241; *AJ* 14.300.
41. Joseph., *AJ* 14.382.
42. Joseph., *AJ* 14.384–385; *cf. BJ* 1.284.
43. *E.g.* Rappaport 1989, 375; Sullivan 1990, 222; Roller 1998, 14–15, 69; Richardson 1999, 127–128; Kasher 2011, 239–240.
44. Joseph., *BJ* 1.286–357; *AJ* 14.390–491.
45. Joseph., *AJ* 15.18–19; *cf. BJ* 1.434, which is condensed.
46. Dio 49.24.
47. Dio 49.24.5.
48. Joseph., *AJ* 15.161–178.
49. Dio 49.23.3–4; Just. 42.4.14–42.5.2; Plut., *Crass.* 33.5.
50. For what follows, see Overman 2011, 12–15; *cf.* Overman, Olive, and Nelson 2007, 177–195; Overman 2009, 290–297.
51. The key sources for the return of the standards include: Dio 54.7–9; Augustus, *RG* 29; Strab. 16.1.28; Vell. Pat. 2.91.1; Suet., *Aug.* 21.3.
52. Herod Antipas, for example, played a role in the diplomatic efforts to attain a Roman-Parthian peace and settlement during the negotiations of the Parthian king Artabanus III and Roman general Vitellius in 37/38 CE on the banks of the Euphrates river. Antipas hosted a celebratory feast in the middle of the Euphrates. See Joseph., *AJ* 18.101–105.
53. Suet., *Aug.* 21.3; Eutr. 7.9; Oros. 6.21.29.
54. Joseph., *AJ* 18.325–339. For further discussion of this episode and other references in Josephus to Parthian affairs, see Rajak 1998. For a collection of articles discussing Jewish engagement with other peoples and cultures in Sasanian Iran in the context of the Babylonian Talmud, see Bakhos and Shayegan 2010.
55. Much work has been done on this issue. See for example the excellent piece by Rose 2005, 21–75, with comprehensive bibliography.
56. We wish to acknowledge with appreciation the appearance of an earlier version of this article in the *University of Toronto Journal of Jewish Thought* 5 (2015): 9–21. This version has been expanded, including discussion of additional significant evidence.

Bibliography

Bakhos, C. and Shayegan, M. (eds.) (2010) *Talmud in its Iranian Context.* Tübingen, Mohr Siebeck.
Berlin, A. (2013) Review of Overman, J. A. and Schowalter, D. N. (eds.) (2011) *The Roman Temple Complex at Horvat Omrit: An interim report.* Oxford, BAR International Series. *BASOR* 369, 244–247.
Bird, H. W. (1987) "Tiberius, Piso, and Germanicus: Further Considerations." *Acta Classica* 72–75.
Bivar, A. (1983) "The Political History of Iran under the Arsacids." In E. Yarshater (ed.) *The Cambridge History of Iran, Volume 3 (1): The Seleucid, Parthian and Sasanian Periods*, 21–99. Cambridge, Cambridge University Press.
Braund, D. (1984) *Rome and the Friendly King.* London, Croon Helm.
Butcher, K. (2003) *Roman Syria and the Near East.* Los Angeles, J. Paul Getty Museum.
Debevoise, N. (1938) *A Political History of Parthia.* Chicago, University of Chicago.
De Lucca, S. (2009) "La città ellenistico-romana di Magdala/Taricheae. Gli scavi del Magdala Project 2007–2008." *Liber Annus* 59, 343–562.

Dobiáš, J. (1931) "Les Premiers Rapports des Romains avec les Parthes et l'Occupation de la Syrie." *Archiv Orientální* 3, 215–256.

Gruen, E. (2009) "Herod, Rome, and the Diaspora." In D. Jacobson and N. Kokkinos (eds.) *Herod and Augustus*, 13–27. Leiden, Brill.

Jacobson, D. (2007) "The Jerusalem Temple of Herod the Great." In N. Kokkinos (ed.) *The World of the Herods*, 145–176. Stuttgart, Franz Steiner Verlag.

Jacobson, D. and Kokkinos, N. (eds.) (2009) *Herod and Augustus*. Leiden, Brill.

Japp, S. (2007) "Public and Private Decorative Art in the Time of Herod the Great." In N. Kokkinos (ed.) *The World of the Herods*, 227–246. Stuttgart, Franz Steiner Verlag.

Jones, A. H. M. (1931) "The Urbanization of the Iturean Principality." *Journal of Roman Studies* 21, 265–275.

Kasher, A. (2011) "Josephus on Herod's spring from the shadows of the Parthian invasion." In J. Pastor (ed.), *Flavius Josephus: Interpretation and History*, 227–245. Leiden, Brill.

Kokkinos, N. (ed.) (2007) *The World of the Herods*. Stuttgart, Franz Steiner Verlag.

Kropp, A. J. M. (2013) *Images and Monuments of Near Eastern Dynasts, 100 BC–AD 100*. Oxford, Oxford University Press.

Marsh, F. B. (1931) *The Reign of Tiberius*. London, Oxford University Press.

Mommsen, T. (1857) *Römische Geschichte: Von Sullas Tode bis zur Schlacht von Thapsus*. Berlin, Weidmannsche Buchhandlung.

Nelson, M. (2015) *The Temple Complex at Horvat Omrit: Volume 1: The Architecture*. Leiden, Brill.

Netzer, E. (2006) *The Architecture of Herod the Great Builder*. Michigan, Baker.

Overman, J. A. (2009) "Between Rome and Parthia: Galilee and the Implications of Empire." In Z. Rodgers, M. Daly-Denton, and A. Fitzpatrick McKinley (eds.) *A Wandering Galilean: Essay in Honour of Seán Freyne*, 279–299. Leiden, Brill.

Overman, J. A. (2011) "Omrit as Part of the Roman East." In J. A. Overman and D. N. Schowalter (eds.) *The Roman Temple Complex at Horvat Omrit: An interim report*, 7–17. Oxford, BAR International Series.

Overman, J. A. (2004) "The Importance of the Iturean Principality According to Josephus and His Contemporaries." In A. Avery-Peck (ed.) *When Judaism and Christianity Began: Essays in Memory of Anthony J. Saldarini*, vol. 1, 287–298. Leiden, Brill.

Overman, J. A., Olive, J. and Nelson, M. (2007) "A Newly Discovered Herodian Temple at Khirbet Omrit in Northern Israel." In N. Kokkinos (ed.) *The World of the Herods*, 177–195. Stuttgart: Franz Steiner Verlag.

Overman, J. A. and Schowalter, D. N. (eds.) (2011) *The Roman Temple Complex at Horvat Omrit: An interim report*. Oxford, BAR International Series.

Rajak, T. (1998) "The Parthians in Josephus." In J. Wiesehöfer (ed.) *Das Partherreich und seine Zeugnisse*, 309–324. Stuttgart, Franz Steiner.

Rapke, T. T. (1982) "Tiberius, Piso, and Germanicus." *Acta Classica* 61–69.

Rappaport, U. (1989) "The Jews between Rome and Parthia." In D. French and C. Lightfoot (eds.) *The Eastern Frontier of the Roman Empire*, 373–381. Oxford, BAR International Series.

Richardson, P. (1999) *Herod: King of the Jews and Friend of the Romans*. Minneapolis, Fortress Press.

Roller, D. (1998) *The Building Program of Herod the Great*. Berkeley, University of California.

Rose, C. (2005) "The Parthians in Augustan Rome." *American Journal of Archaelogy* 109, 21–75.

Rosenberg, S. (2013) "Interior Decoration in Herod's Palaces." In S. Rosenberg and D. Mevorah (eds.) *Herod the Great: The King's Final Journey*, 167–223. Jerusalem, The Israel Museum.

Sampson, G. (2008) *The Defeat of Rome: Crassus, Carrhae, and the Invasion of the East*. Barnsley, Pen and Sword.

Sartre, M. (2005) *The Middle East under Rome*. Translated by C. Porter *et al.* Cambridge, Harvard University Press.

Schlude, J. (2013) "Pompey and the Parthians." *Athenaeum* 101.1, 163–181.

Schlude, J. (forthcoming) "Rome and Parthia in the Late Republic and Early Empire." In P. Edwell (ed.) *A Companion to Rome and Persia*. Oxford, Wiley–Blackwell.

Schlude, J. (2012) "The Parthian Response to the Campaign of Crassus." *Latomus* 71, 11–23.

Seager, R. (1972) *Tiberius*. London, Eyre Methuen Ltd.

Seyrig, H. (1937) "Sur quelques sculptures palmyréniennes (*antiquités syriennes* 21)." *Syria* 18, 31–53.

Sheldon, R. (2010) *Rome's War in Parthia: Blood in the Sand*. London, Vellentine Mitchell.

Sherwin-White, A. (1984) *Roman Foreign Policy in the East, 168 B.C. to A.D. 1*. Norman, University of Oklahoma Press.

Sullivan, R. (1990) *Near Eastern Royalty and Rome, 100–30 BC*. Toronto, University of Toronto Press.

Tarn, W. (1951) "Parthia." In S. Cook *et al.* (eds.) *The Cambridge Ancient History, Volume IX: The Roman Republic, 133–44 B.C.*, 574–613. Cambridge, Cambridge University Press.

Traina, G. (2010) *Carrhae, 9 juin 53 av. J.-C.: Anatomie d'une défaite*. Paris, Belles Lettres.

Wilson, J. (2004) *Caesarea Philippi: Banias, The Lost City of Pan*. London, I. B. Tauris.

Wilson, J. and Tzaferis, V. (2007) "An Herodian Capital in the North: Caesarea Philippi (Panias)." In N. Kokkinos (ed.) *The World of the Herods*, 131–143. Stuttgart, Franz Steiner Verlag.

Wolski, J. (1993) *L'Empire des Arsacides*. Peeters, Acta Iranica.

Ziegler, K. (1964) *Die Beziehungen zwischen Rom und den Partherreich: ein Beitrag zur Geschichte de Völkerrechts*. Wiesbaden, Franz Steiner Verlag.

Chapter 6

Osrhoene and Mesopotamia between Rome and Arsacid Parthia

Peter Edwell

The Parthian wars of the emperor Trajan represent an obvious milestone in relations between Rome and Parthia. Roman provincial administration was established, albeit briefly, as far as southern Iraq, and a Roman army marched all the way to the Persian Gulf. Future Roman emperors would consciously emulate Trajan's military actions, and Parthian rulers were on notice as to long-term Roman imperial intentions. Importantly, the ramifications of Rome's ongoing tensions with Parthia were felt directly for the first time in regional communities east of the Euphrates. In northern Mesopotamia, the rulers of regional kingdoms and principalities experienced the full force of the Roman military and the ramifications of a Roman Emperor's displeasure. Rome's imperial power had steadily grown in the eastern provinces since the arrival of Lucullus and Pompey despite some notable setbacks on occasion, especially at Carrhae. Importantly, Roman economic power became an increasing factor from the first century BCE to the reign of Trajan with the growing wealth especially of the cities of the empire resulting in an exponential increase in trade originating in and passing through the whole of the Near East and Arabia. Evidence from Dura Europos, for example, a city provably under Parthian control during this whole period, suggests stronger economic connections with the Roman world than with Parthia.

Trajan's military and administrative activity from 114 to 117 placed a new emphasis on competition between Rome and Parthia especially in northern Mesopotamia. Since the decline of the Seleucids and the rise of the Parthian Empire in the mid-second century BCE, kingdoms and principalities based on the cities of Edessa, Carrhae, Nisibis, and Singara and their surrounding territory had been strongly within the orbit of Parthia. This was true in military, political, and especially cultural terms. The combination of growth in Roman economic and military power in the east resulted in a marked change in the politics and culture of these entities in northern Mesopotamia across the second and early third centuries. This became especially evident during and after the Parthian war of Lucius Verus in the mid-160s and also as a result of the conflicts between Rome and Parthia under the Severans. Trajan's successes against the Parthians and subsequent territorial organization signalled to the ruling elites of northern Mesopotamia that theirs was now disputed territory in imperial terms. This potentially gave local ruling elites leverage and when Roman imperial power arrived east of the Euphrates permanently from the 160s, some were able to take advantage. When opportunities arose, though, some of these rulers would assert greater independence. Significantly, Rome's extension of power east of the Euphrates was also to have cultural ramifications, especially with regard to Hellenism.

Trajan's Campaigns Against Parthia

While Dio emphasized Trajan's desire for glory as the motive for the emperor's eastern campaign, the Armenian king, Parthamasires, appears to have been courting Parthian favor, which provided Trajan with a more immediate motive for war.[1] Trajan arrived in Antioch early in 114 and when the campaigning season began it did not take long for the Romans to assert control over Parthamasires' kingdom. Rulers of other principalities quickly submitted to the emperor, which likely is reflected in the representation of three rulers standing before the emperor having their kingdoms reassigned to them (Fig. 6.1).[2] Trajan's success in Armenia also saw embassies from various kings along the east coast of the Black Sea and in the Caucasus confirming

Figure 6.1: Sestertius of Trajan depicting three rulers before the emperor and the reverse legend REGNA ADSIGNATA. Struck 115–116 CE. BMCRE 1043; RIC II 666. Rome Mint. Courtesy of the Classical Numismatic Group.

themselves as clients of Rome, further strengthening Rome's hand in the region and recalling the days of Lucullus' and Pompey's invasions over 150 years earlier.[3]

Having met with limited resistance in Armenia and developing an increasing understanding of problems within the Arsacid royal succession at the time, Trajan turned his mind to the broader possibility of an invasion of northern and southern Mesopotamia.[4] At some stage before arriving in Mesopotamia, Trajan gave the rulers of the various northern Mesopotamian principalities the opportunity of an audience essentially to establish friendship, but there had been particular reluctance to do so by Abgar of Edessa, Mannos of Arabia, and Sporakes the ruler of Anthemusia.[5] Soon after his departure from Antioch in 115, Trajan crossed the Euphrates and captured Anthemusia/Batnae followed by Nisibis, for which he was granted the title "Parthicus."[6] Following the capture of Batnae to the west of Edessa and Nisibis to its east Trajan turned back to Edessa, essentially isolating the city beforehand. Abgar of Edessa was finally forced to present himself to Trajan on learning that the emperor was making his way to the city. Friendship was established between the two rulers before Trajan continued on to Adiabene. Broadly contemporary with these events, Lusius Quietus, one of Trajan's most dependable generals, defeated the king of Adiabene, Mebarsapes.[7] Soon afterwards he occupied the strategically important city of Singara at the foot of Jebel Sinjar in modern northern Iraq. Trajan set out in the spring of 116 for the Tigris with the aim of again subduing Adiabene whose king had re-asserted authority during the winter.[8] The army was divided and part of it captured the key Adiabenian cities of Nineveh, Arbela, and Gaugamela, after which the province of Assyria was formed.[9] The other section of the army made its way south and captured Babylon while Trajan himself seems to have doubled back to the Euphrates in order to lead a force downriver as part of attacking Seleucia-Ctesiphon.[10] It was perhaps at this time that Roman troops occupied Dura-Europos on the Middle Euphrates and the triumphal arch dedicated to Trajan was constructed outside it.[11] On arriving at the point where the Euphrates and Tigris flow closest to each other in the vicinity of the blocked up Naarmalcha canal, Trajan ordered his ships hauled across the land in between before crossing the Tigris to Ctesiphon and capturing the city with virtually no resistance.[12] The emperor sailed down the Tigris to the Persian Gulf and won over Athambelus who was king of Mesene and also controlled Spasinou Charax at the river's mouth.[13] Both Mesene and especially Spasinou Charax were closely connected to Palmyra through trade at this time.

On returning to Babylon, Trajan learned that much of the captured Parthian territory was in open rebellion. The emperor appointed and crowned a Parthian client-king, Parthamaspates, in the wake of the rebellions (Fig. 6.2), and on the way back to Antioch he besieged the desert city of Hatra in what proved to be an unsuccessful attempt to punish the city's disloyalty.[14] Arriving in Antioch soon afterwards, and suffering increasingly from ill health, Trajan departed for Rome, but died at the port of Selinus in Cilicia on 8 August, 117.[15] Hadrian soon gave up all of Trajan's gains beyond the Euphrates, reverting to the Augustan policy of keeping the empire within its natural boundaries.[16]

Figure 6.2: Sestertius of Trajan depicting REX PARTHIS DATUS (Parthamaspates). RIC II 667. Struck 116–117 CE. Rome Mint. Courtesy of the Classical Numismatic Group.

The rebellion had included the various principalities and kingdoms of northern Mesopotamia, Nisibis, and Edessa among them. Lucius Quietus apparently captured and burned the latter.[17] It is possible that Edessa was the subject of Roman military occupation under Lucius Quietus for approximately two years, signaling that Abgar had been dethroned. Trajan's nominee to the Parthian throne, Parthamaspates, was possibly transferred to Edessa as a satrap after the withdrawal under Hadrian for a period just short of five years.[18] He was then succeeded in 121/122 by Ma'nu the son of Izates who had links with the rulers of Adiabene.

The overall suggestion by Ross is that due to this activity in Edessa before and after the Roman withdrawal, pro-Roman sentiment developed in the Osrhoenian kingdom and the cities of northern Mesopotamia to the east, which saw pro-Roman factions emerge as features of their politics.[19] This remained until the invasions of Lucius Verus approximately 50 years later and played a role in Verus' success in establishing Roman hegemony over kingdoms and principalities that had long been part of the Parthian sphere. While this might be an appealing proposition, the term "pro-Roman" in fact may be misleading. Trajan's invasions and the territorial reorganization that followed was very short-lived, making any long-term impact on factionalism in civic politics of the region somewhat unlikely. Trajan's invasions signaled to civic elites, however, that there was a potential future alternative to Parthian hegemony. This could present opportunities in terms of playing off competing Parthian and Roman imperial interests. This was already the case in Armenia, and it was an increasing factor there in the second and third centuries. Rome's economic influence east of the Euphrates also was growing in the years before Trajan's invasions and continued to be an important factor in northern Mesopotamia after Hadrian's abandonment of Trajan's territorial organization.

Northern Mesopotamia from Trajan to Lucius Verus

Contemporary evidence from Nisibis, Carrhae, and Edessa in the period *c.* 115–160 which might shed light on the longer-term impact of Trajan's invasions and territorial organization in the second century is virtually non-existent. However, evidence from Dura Europos during this period may help to illuminate the nature of Roman occupation of cities in northern Mesopotamia and what Parthian control looked like from Hadrian to Lucius Verus.

Dura Europos came under some form of Roman control as a result of Trajan's Parthian campaign in either 115 or 116. The fragmentary remains of a Roman victory arch dedicated to Trajan outside the city in 116 are clear evidence of the Roman presence at the city.[20] The numbers of Roman denarii from Trajan's reign discovered in excavations at the site and which did not form parts of hoards were the highest of any Roman emperor before that of Septimius Severus by which time the city had been under Roman control for approximately 30 years.[21] In addition to this, an inscription dated year 428 of the Seleucid Era (116/117 CE), later reused in the Roman-period Mithraeum, dedicated the renovation and enlargement of a shrine that included the replacement of doors to the *naos* that the Romans had taken with them when they left the city.[22] There is some conjecture as to whether the inscription is confirmatory of the general Roman withdrawal from Mesopotamia under Hadrian or that the Roman occupation of Dura was only in the immediate period around the city's capture in 116 and thus relatively transitory.[23] The Seleucid year 428 ended in October 117, some two months after the death of Trajan, making it possible that the doors of the shrine were taken by the Romans as part of a general withdrawal from the territories organized by Trajan. If it is indicative of this, the Roman withdrawal was somewhat hasty.

Papyrological evidence from Dura may go some way towards understanding the situation at Dura and more broadly in northern Mesopotamia between the beginning of Hadrian's reign and the Parthian invasions of Lucius Verus. Millar discusses a group of ten Greek parchments discovered at Dura during the Yale excavations of the 1920s and 30s that date from 87 CE to 159/160 and how they might assist in developing a better understanding of Parthian administration in Dura and Parapotamia, the administrative unit of the Parthian Empire in which Dura was located.[24] One of the important points to note about these documents, all of which record private financial transactions, is that they strongly indicate Parthian administrative processes and ongoing institutions of imperial control in Dura and Parapotamia before, during, and after the Roman capture of and withdrawal from the city. There is nothing in these documents to indicate any lasting or even transitory Roman impact on administration and organization at Dura Europos as a result of the Trajanic invasions. Indeed, the distinct impression we are left with, whatever the motivating factor for the Roman withdrawal, is that the Romans departed as quickly as they arrived. Any occupation and organisation of the city and the territory of Parapotamia was, therefore, transitory. In broader terms, however, Trajan's invasions had exposed the military weakness of the Parthian rulership and demonstrated the might of the Roman military machine. Although transitory, Roman administration had made a brief appearance and the impact of the Roman economy, especially the economic power of cities such as Antioch and Palmyra, continued to be felt east of the Euphrates.[25] The various rulers of the principalities of northern Mesopotamia, including Osrhoene, had been forced into acknowledging Roman hegemony, albeit briefly, and despite their rebellion against Trajan, the memory of Roman military successes would remain. When Rome and Parthia went to war almost 50 years later, Trajan's shadow and the continued growth of Rome's economic and military power in the interim would play their part in the loyalties of the principalities and kingdoms of northern Mesopotamia.

Lucius Verus' Parthian War

Lucius Verus' Parthian War resulted from developments in Armenia just as Trajan's war had. In 161, the Parthian king, Vologases IV, contravened the long-standing agreement between Rome and Parthia over Armenia by placing a member of his own family on the throne without the agreement of Rome.[26] Roman and Parthian forces clashed on the upper Euphrates and the province of Syria came under threat. The Parthians gained the initial advantage with the destruction of a Roman legion and the death of the governor of Cappadocia.[27] The Roman military response was under the command of Lucius Verus, but Dio consistently claims this was nominal, pointing instead to Avidius Cassius, legatus of Legio III Gallica, as the actual field commander. The Romans made substantial gains against the Parthians throughout 163, and by 165 Armenia was ruled by a Roman nominee, the Parthians had been ejected from northern Mesopotamia, and the key city of Nisibis was under the control of Roman troops. The kingdom of Osrhoene, which occupied the western portion of northern Mesopotamia, was a dependent kingdom of Rome, and control of the Euphrates River was considerably extended.[28]

The Parthian war of Lucius Verus marked an important change to the nature of Parthian and Roman imperial control and influence in northern Mesopotamia. Rome was now considerably stronger in Armenia, and Osrhoene was a dependent kingdom.[29] Roman power also extended further along the middle Euphrates to Dura Europos and beyond, making Seleucia-Ctesiphon more vulnerable, and the desert kingdom of Hatra was now potentially closer to the Roman orbit of power. Closely connected with this is the increase in Roman power on the Khabur in the direction of Nisibis. While the extent and nature of the Roman military presence in Mesopotamia before the reign of Septimius Severus is not entirely clear, Roman control of the middle Euphrates and the lower Khabur River came to play an important role in strengthening and supporting Roman power in Mesopotamia in the third century CE. The Khabur was also the means by which northern Mesopotamia and Syria were connected, and this becomes more evident following the formation of the Roman province of Mesopotamia under Septimius Severus.

Osrhoene and Edessa

Developments in the territory of Osrhoene as a consequence of Lucius Verus' war against the Arsacids were among the most important in the longer term and the evidence is most plentiful for them. From this point, Osrhoene was more firmly within the Roman orbit, and by the Severan period much of the kingdom had been converted into a Roman province and the city of Edessa itself was a client-kingdom of Rome. There is some evidence of Roman and Parthian competition at Edessa in the context of the Romano-Parthian wars of the 160s and the most revealing is of a numismatic nature. Up to the 160s, there is no evidence for minting of coins at Edessa under the Abgarids. Indeed, the minting of coins at Edessa from the 160s may in itself be evidence of greater Roman influence on the city. In the years 163–165, three crude bronze coin-types were minted at Edessa that name a king Wael in Syriac. One was either contemporary with or preceded by a coin (tetrachalkon) with Vologases IV on the obverse and a distinctive symbol dominating the reverse field accompanied by the legend "Vologases king of kings" in Syriac (Fig. 6.3).

The other two types depict and name Wael in Syriac on their obverses along with a temple on their reverses.[30] This material is likely indicative of the installation of Wael as king of Edessa and Osrhoene at the behest of Vologases IV following the deposition of the Ma'nu VIII who was supportive of Rome in or about 163. It is possible that this also was linked with Vologases' installation of Pacorus on the Armenian throne in contravention of the long-standing agreement between Rome and Parthia over the selection and investiture of the Armenian king that was initially the key factor in the Roman conflict with the Arsacid ruler. Epigraphic evidence from Sumatar Harabesi, some 30 km to the east of ancient Edessa, some of which dates to the mid-160s, may also

Figure 6.3: Bronze tetrachalkon of Vologases IV. Struck c. 163 CE. Edessa Mint. BMC Parthia, p. 236, 96 (Vologases III). Courtesy of the Classical Numismatic Group.

be reflective of competition between pro-Roman and pro-Parthian elements at Edessa and the territory under the city's control at the time of Rome's war with Parthia in the mid-160s.[31] The victories of Lucius Verus over the Parthians in 165 saw the return of Ma'nu VIII to the throne of Edessa. Ma'nu had been forced to flee to the Romans after his deposition at the hands of Vologases in 163. It is possible that Ma'nu's reinstatement is indicated by the minting of a bronze issue that depicts Ma'nu on the obverse and a reverse entirely in Syriac script that describes Ma'nu as *Philoromaios* (Fig. 6.4).

Ma'nu VIII originally came to power at Edessa on the death of his father, Ma'nu VII, in 139.[32] His deposition by the Parthian king in 163 and subsequent flight to the Romans is clearly indicative of his sympathies towards Parthia's imperial enemy. There is no indication as to when in his long reign Ma'nu adopted this position but it was enough of a problem by the early 160s for the Parthian king to depose him. Ma'nu's pro-Roman stance was a gamble based on a perception of where future power lay, and it paid off for Ma'nu with his reinstatement as King of Edessa by Lucius Verus in 165.

A series of unpublished silver drachms have been attributed to an imperial mint operating in Mesopotamia in the wake of the Roman victory over the Parthians thought to be at either Edessa or Carrhae. The coins are temporarily catalogued at present in volume 4 of the Roman Provincial Coinage project of the Ashmolean Museum at Oxford. These coins initially were attributed to Carrhae by Babelon, but the opinion that they were minted at Edessa as expressed by Hill in BMC Arabia 28 has prevailed.[33] The coins contain Greek legends and are minted in the names of Marcus Aurelius and Lucius Verus and their wives Faustina and Lucilla, respectively. Most of the male obverse portraits are laureate with some bare-headed while some of the female obverse portraits depict pearl braids and earrings or are bare-headed with hair tied back. The obverse legends

Figure 6.4: Bronze of Lucius Verus with Ma'nu VIII Philoromaios. Struck c. 165 CE. Edessa Mint. RPC online 6485; cf. BMC 28, p. 92, no. 4 for similar bust type. Courtesy of the Classical Numismatic Group.

simply name the emperor or empress (*e.g.*, Faustina Sebaste (4.3498), Autokrator Markos Aurelios Antonin (4.6496), Loukilla Sebaste (4.6502), Autokrator Lukios Aurelios Veros Sebastos (4.8034)). The reverse legends follow a relatively uniform formula of ΥΠΕΡ ΝΙΚΗϹ ΡΟΜΑΙΩΝ/ΡΟΜΑΙ and ΥΠΕΡ ΝΙΚΗϹ ΤΩΝ ΚΥΡΙΩΝ ϹΕΒΑϹ(ΤΩΝ), indicative of the victory over the Parthians in the war of the mid-160s. This legend is important in attributing the coins to an imperial mint different from Rome and to suggesting that they were minted at one specific mint (Fig. 6.5 and 6.6).

Figure 6.5: Silver drachm of Lucius Verus. Struck c. 165–169 CE. Reverse legend: ΥΠΕΡ ΝΙΚΗϹ ΤΩΝ ΚΥΡΙΩΝ ϹΕΒΑϹ(ΤΩΝ). Edessa Mint. See RPC online 8028 for similar reverse. Courtesy of the Classical Numismatic Group.

Figure 6.6: Silver drachm of Marcus Aurelius. Struck c. 165–180 CE. Reverse legend: ΥΠΕΡ ΝΙΚΗϹ ΡΟΜΑΙΩΝ. Edessa Mint. See RPC online 9578 for obverse. Courtesy of the Classical Numismatic Group.

Figure 6.7: Silver drachm of empress Faustina. Struck c. 165–175 CE. Edessa Mint. See RPC online 4398 for reverse depicting the imperial twins Commodus and Antoninus. Courtesy of the Classical Numismatic Group.

A range of reverse illustrations accompany the obverse portraits of the emperors and empresses, including the imperial twins, Commodus and Antoninus (4.3498) (Fig. 6.7), Nike (4.6494, 4.8034), female deities (likely Athena, Venus, Ceres) holding items such as a globe/apple and patera (4.6496, 4.6498, 4.6499, 4.6500, 4.6502, 4.8030, 4.8032), and depictions of a seated Armenia who is named in the exergue (ARMEN) (4.6495, 4.8031, 4.8035).

The depictions of Armenia are references to Lucius Verus' victory in Armenia over the Parthians and represent an imperial claim to have subdued Armenia. The personification of Armenia is seated with a shield and standard lying next to her. Two of these coin-types depict and name Marcus Aurelius on their obverses (4.6495, 4.8035), and the other depicts Lucius Verus (4.8031). The coins that depict Marcus Aurelius on the obverse and Armenia seated with headdress and shield and military standard on the reverses also display close similarities to denarii minted at Rome under Marcus Aurelius (Fig. 6.8).[34]

An important set of silver drachms, which appears to provide the most secure basis for attributing all of the coins under current discussion to the mint at Edessa, depicts Faustina and Lucilla as empresses on their obverses with Juno/Demeter on the reverses accompanied by the inscription *Basileus Mannos Philor* (4.6487), *Basileus Mannos Philoroma* (4.6488) and *Basileus Mannos Philoromai* [sic] (4.6489) (Fig. 6.9). The obverse and reverse portraits bear striking iconographic similarities to those appearing on the other coins. The denarii are strongly indicative of the impact on Edessa of Rome's victory over the Parthians and the reinstatement of Ma'nu VIII in the mid-160s. The likely operation of an imperial mint at the city suggests that Roman administration was present there in some form and that Edessa, and the surrounding territory of Osrhoene of which Edessa had acted as a capital, was bound closely to Rome as a client-kingdom.

Figure 6.8: Silver denarius of Marcus Aurelius. Struck 164 CE. Rome mint. RIC III 78; epiction of Armenia on reverse similar to RPC online 6495, 8031, 8035. Courtesy of the Classical Numismatic Group.

Figure 6.9: Silver drachm of Lucilla with Ma'nu VIII Philoromaios. Struck c. 167–169 CE. Salus seated left, feeding from patera serpent arising from altar and holding cornucopia. Edessa Mint. Courtesy of the Classical Numismatic Group.

Ma'nu VIII's second reign, which began on his reinstatement in 165, lasted another fourteen years until his death in 179. His son, Abgar VIII (later known as the Great), ruled until 214, and during this period bronze coins were minted at Edessa depicting Abgar on the obverse with Commodus and Septimius Severus, respectively, on their reverses (Fig. 6.10).[35] Indeed, some of these coins name Abgar as Lucius Aelius Septimius Abgaros and Aelius Aurelius Septimius Abgaros, conflations of the

Figure 6.10: Bronze of Commodus with Abgar VIII. Struck 177–192 CE. Edessa Mint. BMC 28 Arabia 12. Courtesy Classical Numismatic Group.

imperial titulature of Commodus and Septimius Severus. Bronze coins bearing the same reverse inscription, *Uper Nike Romewn*, as the silver coins of the Aurelius/Verus joint reign were minted under Commodus and also are thought to have come from Edessa or Carrhae (4.8046, 4.8047, 4.10746). If this distinctive reverse legend is the key to attributing the silver coins to Edessa then the bronzes also should be attributed to the city. A key distinction between the silver and bronze coins is that the bronzes, of which there are only three known types, portray Tyche veiled, draped, and wearing a mural crown, giving them a resemblance to the provincial bronze issues of the northern Mesopotamian mints in the third century.

The coins of Edessa minted under Ma'nu VIII and Abgar VIII, together with the imperial silver in the names of Marcus Aurelius, Lucius Verus, and their wives, suggest that Rome's defeat of the Parthians in the mid-160s was decisive in swaying Edessa and the kingdom of Osrhoene away from its traditional leanings toward Parthia. Given the decisive nature of the Roman victory over the Parthians in the 160s and the long-term effects this had on Edessa and Osrhoene and northern Mesopotamia more broadly, there was little choice for local rulers and elites other than to accept the status quo. When civil war began to brew in the Roman Empire in the early 190s, however, some of these rulers attempted to take advantage, some even attempting to go back to the Parthian fold. Roman power had been expressed clearly in Edessa and Osrhoene since the 160s, and this included the backing of client-kings. Despite this, as is discussed further below, the loyalty of these rulers was not guaranteed.

Carrhae

At Carrhae, bronze coins were also minted bearing the bust of Marcus Aurelius on their obverses with reverse legends proclaiming KAPHNWNPHILPWM (Fig. 6.11).[36] In

Figure 6.11: Bronze of Marcus Aurelius. Struck c. 165 CE. Carrhae mint. BMC Arabia 1. Courtesy of the Classical Numismatic Group.

contrast with Edessa, there is no depiction of a local ruler accompanying the reverse legend, suggesting that the city itself was a "friend of the Romans" during the reign of Marcus Aurelius. It is likely that this was retained during the reign of Commodus.

The relationship between Edessa and Carrhae before the third century CE is not easy to establish in exact terms. The ancient city of Carrhae is located approximately 40 km southeast of ancient Edessa (modern Sanliurfa), and there is little doubt that both cities had an impact on each other, especially Edessa on Carrhae given the city's relative size and regional significance. Pliny the Elder includes both Edessa and Carrhae in the area of Osrhoenian Arabia in the first century CE, but appears only vaguely informed about the nature of Osrhoenian territorial control across northern Mesopotamia.[37] The extent of Edessene authority over Osrhoene is not any clearer in the written sources in the second century in the wake of Trajan's short-lived provincial organization in northern Mesopotamia in the early second century. As Ross points out, Carrhae, along with Batnae/Anthemusia, Callinicum, and Edessa, were part of the province of Osrhoene during Justinian's reign, and this is likely reflective of the civic composition of the kingdom before it was provincialized in the third century.[38] A cautionary note should, of course, be sounded in extrapolating this situation back to the latter part of the second century CE when the Abgarids ruled at Edessa.

Ross also points to epigraphic evidence originating in the Tur Abdin and dating to the 160s that indicates that Edessa's territorial authority stretched as far as Constantia, approximately 40 km due east from the city, similar to the distance Carrhae was from Edessa to the southeast.[39] The exact nature of Carrhae's relationship with Edessa in terms of Abgarid monarchical authority is beyond us without further evidence, but it is reasonable to assume that Carrhae was within the monarchical authority of the kings of Edessa at this time. The bronze coins depicting Marcus Aurelius that proclaim Carrhae as Philoromaios are likely to be part of the same numismatic program that produced the coins minted in Edessa displaying the same epithet.

With regard to the minting of coins, the situation in what would become the Roman province of Mesopotamia from the Severan period up to the death of Julian provides an interesting contrast with Osrhoene. The more specific territory under consideration here is the eastern portion of northern Mesopotamia stretching from the Tur Abdin in the north to Jebel Sinjar in the south, the Tigris to the east and northeast and the Khabur river in the west. The most important cities in this territory were Nisibis, Rhesaena, and Singara, and it was these cities that were of central importance to the urban and military fabric of the Roman province of Mesopotamia from Septimius Severus to Julian. In contrast to Edessa and Carrhae from the 160s onwards, there is no evidence for minting of coins at Nisibis until the reign of Macrinus (218), Rhesaena until Caracalla (212–218) and Singara until Gordian III (238–244), by which time all three cities had long been within Provincia Mesopotamiae. Is the lack of coinage from these cities in the second half of the second century CE an indication of less Roman influence over their administration? In other words, was the minting of civic coinage a marker of the extent of Roman administrative, political, and military influence at this time?

Dura Europos and the Middle Euphrates in the Second Half of the Second Century CE

It is possible that the situation in Osrhoene and northern Mesopotamia from Lucius Verus to Septimius Severus was similar to that at Dura Europos and Palmyra during the same period. It has long been accepted that Dura came under Roman control as a result of Lucius Verus' successful campaign against the Parthians, and there is epigraphic evidence from Dura to support this assumption.[40] The most important evidence from this category is represented in two dated tauroctony reliefs re-used in a Severan-period Mithraeum that contain dedications by a troop of Palmyrene archers in 168 and 170/171 CE.[41] The archers appear to have been the key element in the Dura garrison from the mid-160s until their formal organization as an auxiliary cohort, cohors XX Palmyrenorum, by the early 190s and probably earlier.

Evidence from other sites on the Euphrates, especially Anatha and Gamla which lie approximately 100 km downstream from Dura, demonstrates the extent to which the Palmyrenes controlled parts of the lower Euphrates during much of the second century. A dedicatory inscription from an altar at Palmyra refers to a Palmyrene cavalryman who was in camp at Anatha in 132 CE, thus providing clear evidence of a Palmyrene military presence on the island.[42] Gawlikowski proposes that the Palmyrene control of Anatha also extended to the smaller fortified sites of Bijan and Gamla, further down the river.[43] In turn, because Palmyra was strongly within the Roman orbit in the second century it can be argued that the Roman Empire indirectly controlled this section of the river. Approximately one hundred kilometers upstream at Dura Europos, however, the Parthians were in control until Lucius Verus' Parthian war in the 160s. In the aftermath of Lucius Verus' Parthian war, Roman power and influence increased significantly in the Euphrates valley and the situation appears to have been similar in northern Mesopotamia. The reign of Septimius Severus saw substantial provincial reorganization throughout Syria and Mesopotamia that is reflected in the written sources and archaeology.

Roman Military Presence in Northern Mesopotamia after the Parthian War of Lucius Verus

While Roman political power across the Euphrates in Osrhoene and northern Mesopotamia during the 170s and 180s was increasingly strengthened, there is no direct evidence for a Roman military presence there during this period. Dillemann suggested, therefore, that the Romans exercised "occupation sans annexion".[44] There is, however, indirect evidence that may point to a build-up in the Roman military presence in the 180s. Firstly, Dio indicates that the Osrhoeni and Adiabeni had attacked Nisibis prior to the civil war between Severus and Niger in 193, suggesting that Nisibis had received a Roman garrison before that date.[45] Dio also reports that after Niger's death at Byzantium in 195, the Osrhoeni and Adiabeni attempted to negotiate with Severus and justified their attack on Nisibis by claiming that this was part of undermining Niger. Importantly, in their attempts to negotiate, the Osrhoeni and Adiabeni refused to hand over forts they had captured while also demanding the removal of Roman garrisons which were still there. On the evidence of Dio, then, Roman forts and garrisons existed across the Euphrates, including Nisibis itself, prior to the beginning of the civil war between Severus and Niger. There is no evidence, however, for when they were established or what units comprised these garrisons. While conjectural, it seems reasonable to conclude that these forts and garrisons had their origins at least in the reign of Commodus or perhaps even earlier.

Of particular interest in Dio's account of this military activity is the report of Osrhoene and Adiabene attacking Roman forts and demanding the removal of Roman garrisons. The attack on Nisibis specifically took place before the civil war between Severus and Niger and in negotiations with Severus in 195, the two principalities, in concert, felt strong enough to demand the removal of Roman garrisons in northern Mesopotamia. The late reign of Commodus and the period of civil war soon after his death in 192 saw upheaval for Roman imperial leadership that had not been experienced since the end of the Julio-Claudian period. The Osrhoeni, along with their allies in Adiabene, took clear advantage demonstrating that despite the reinstatement of Ma'nu VIII with Roman support and a seemingly close relationship between Roman and Osrhoenian rulers in the decades that followed, they were prepared to take quick advantage of instability in Roman imperial rulership. The Parthians faced similar problems at this time, which perhaps further emboldened both the Osrhoeni and Adiabeni. Political independence from the Roman and Parthian Empires was perhaps always an aspiration, although rarely a realistic one. When the chance came, the Osrhoeni and their emboldened neighbours took it. When Septimius Severus finally emerged from the war with Niger and established his rule securely, northern Mesopotamia and especially the Osrhoeni would be dealt with.

The Severan Wars with Parthia and Territorial Outcomes

Following Pescennius Niger's self-proclamation as Imperator at Antioch in 193, Septimius Severus confronted and defeated him the following year.[46] Osrhoene's treachery before and during the civil war, in alliance with Adiabene and possibly Hatra, resulted in the conversion of much of the kingdom into a Roman province under the governorship of a procurator in 195.[47] The city of Edessa itself was established as a client-kingdom with Abgar VIII confirmed as king. It is likely that the province of Mesopotamia also was established at this time, although it is possible it was formed a few years later in 198.[48] The role of the Parthians in the actions of Osrhoene and other northern Mesopotamia principalities is unclear and may only have been nominal due to revolts in Seleucia-Ctesiphon and eastern Iran at this time.[49] Towards the end of summer 197, following the successful elimination of the usurper Albinus in Rome, Severus turned east again and this time dealt directly with the Parthians. The three important written sources on the Parthian campaigns of Septimius Severus are Dio, Herodian, and the Historia Augusta (HA).[50] There are clear inconsistencies between the three accounts with Herodian's seemingly the most troublesome and Dio's the most reliable. Severus' motives for the war against the Parthians were both defensive and glory-seeking. Herodian and the HA emphasise glory as the key motivation while Dio suggests a Parthian attack on Mesopotamia, especially Nisibis, as Severus' main reason for the invasion.[51] Herodian proposed alternatively that Severus used his desire to exact revenge on Hatra as retribution for its support of Niger during the civil war of 193 as a prelude to mounting a full-scale attack on Armenia and then the Parthian Empire.[52]

On relieving Nisibis, Severus proceeded down the Euphrates with a fleet of boats with the aim of attacking Ctesiphon. An un-named brother of Vologases V accompanied the Romans, clearly indicating how fractured the Parthian royal dynasty was at this stage.[53] A further indication of the difficulties faced by the Parthians was that Severus captured Seleucia and Babylon, which had both been abandoned, and Ctesiphon appears to have been captured easily. Severus was not interested in remaining in southern Mesopotamia for long and quickly withdrew after plundering Ctesiphon. It was at this point, likely in early 199, that the first and brief siege of Hatra took place.[54] Realising the difficulties in besieging such an imposing fortress, Severus withdrew and returned the following year to prosecute a lengthier and better-prepared siege.[55]

Despite more extensive preparations for the second siege of Hatra, probably in 200 CE, Severus was unable to capture the city.[56] The fortress of Hatra had developed a more formidable reputation as a result, having held out against Trajan in 116 CE and now repulsing the forces of Septimius Severus twice. It would also hold out against the Sasanians in 230 CE before finally falling to the new Persian regime in 241. It is unclear if Severus' attempts to capture Hatra were due to its earlier support for Niger (Herodian, above) or its likely support of the Parthians in their attack on Mesopotamia in 197. Dio simply states that Severus wished to capture Hatra because it alone had withstood his forces during the military actions against Parthia in 198/199.[57] It is possible that the emperor was concerned about potential threats from Hatra to the newly formed province of Mesopotamia, as the city was clearly a powerful presence in the northern Mesopotamian landscape.

Septimius Severus journeyed to Antioch before returning to Rome at the end of 202 via Egypt where he had visited Pompey's tomb and made a sacrifice.[58] Severus celebrated his decennalia in lavish style in Rome with gladiatorial games and distributions of grain to the populace.[59] A victory arch celebrating the success over the Parthians was also constructed in the Forum where it remains to this day. Dio undoubtedly kept his opinions to himself at the time, but at the relatively safe distance of a couple of decades from the events, he was strongly critical of Severus' provincial acquisition of territory in Mesopotamia.[60] It was an expensive province to maintain and yielded little by way of taxation. Of even greater concern was that the province brought Rome closer to peoples who were aligned with the Parthians, which resulted in unnecessary involvement in foreign wars. The latter criticism can hardly be justified in the context of events in the decades before Severus came to power. Roman territory had been extended in Mesopotamia along the Euphrates at least as far as Dura Europos under Lucius Verus *c.* 165, and the city of Nisibis likely held a Roman garrison prior to Severus' elevation. Roman territorial involvement across the Euphrates and towards the Tigris in an increasingly direct sense had clearly been developing before Septimius Severus came to power and can be traced as far back as the reign of Trajan. The numismatic evidence especially points to established relationships between Ma'nu VIII and Abgar VIII of Edessa through the reigns of Marcus Aurelius, Commodus, and Septimius Severus.

Caracalla

Following Caracalla's murder of his brother Geta on 26 December 211, the now sole emperor quickly began comporting himself in the style of Alexander the Great. Dio (78.7.1–8.3) refers to Caracalla's enthusiasm for Alexander at length, and the HA (*Life of Caracalla*, 2) attributes a desire to imitate Alexander to many of Caracalla's actions.[61] Caracalla went so far as to raise a phalanx of Macedonians, which was 16,000 strong. An aggressive foreign policy also was one of the key elements of Caracalla's emulation of Alexander, and this was directed primarily at the Parthians, although, it also encompassed military activity on the Danube.

Although the hostile source tradition towards Caracalla emphasizes his bellicosity and treachery in actions towards the Parthians and also in his dealings with Armenia and Osrhoene, Caracalla had good reason to take an active interest in events on the eastern frontier. Soon after the murder of Geta, Osrhoene, Armenia, and the Parthian Empire itself were in a state of turmoil. Late in 213, Abgar IX of Osrhoene was summoned to Rome on the grounds that he had sought to extend his influence throughout northern Mesopotamia. This was met by the king's removal and subjugation of his territory.[62] The Armenian king was deposed similarly, and his heirs became bitterly divided against each other. A similar situation prevailed in Parthia from 213 where Artabanus V and Vologases V were in open warfare, the former based in Media and the latter in Ctesiphon.[63] The outcome of turmoil in Armenia was always unpredictable from Rome's perspective, and it could equally be so when leadership in Parthia was in dispute.

According to Dio, Caracalla appealed to Alexandrian imagery as he made his way east with the ultimate aim of dealing with the situation in Armenia and prosecuting a Parthian campaign. In spring 214 he departed for the east, stopping to deal with issues in Dacia and Raetia on the way.[64] In the autumn he crossed the Hellespont and sacrificed to Achilles at his tomb, then made his way to Pergamon before establishing winter-quarters (214/215) at Nicomedia.[65] At Nicomedia, the emperor had two enormous siege engines constructed in preparation for a war against Armenia and Parthia, and he keenly oversaw the preparation of the "Macedonian Phalanx".[66] In April 215, Caracalla arrived at Antioch before heading to Alexandria in Egypt to deal with a range of problematic issues there.[67] He departed Alexandria by February 216 and returned to Antioch to undertake full-scale preparations for a Parthian invasion. One of the claimants to the Parthian throne, Vologases V, was at this time harbouring Tiridates, a pretender to the Armenian throne, along with a Roman deserter, Antiochus, who previously had attached himself to Tiridates and fled to Vologases with him. Caracalla used this as a pretext to invade Parthia. Vologases surrendered the two fugitives, and Caracalla called off the campaign.[68] The general Theocritus was sent against Armenia, but was soundly defeated, and by the end of 215 the situation was much the same as it had been at the beginning.[69]

Later in 216, Caracalla sought to further isolate Volgases by requesting the hand in marriage of Artabanus' daughter.[70] Dio interpreted the move cynically, inferring that Caracalla was simply looking for a pretext to attack Artabanus, knowing full well that the Parthian monarch would refuse. Indeed, in Dio's account, Artabanus refused the proposal, which was followed swiftly by a Roman attack on Media. This resulted in the capture of numerous fortresses and the destruction of Parthian royal tombs at Arbela, perhaps another attempt to draw links with Alexander the Great as Arbela was the site of Alexander's last great battle with Darius. Herodian provides a considerably different account, claiming that Caracalla's initial marriage request to Artabanus was rejected, but later accepted.[71] It is difficult to judge which version is more reliable, although Dio's is more in keeping with a strategy aimed at invasion. In early summer 216, Caracalla crossed into Parthian territory and made his way to Artabanus' palace near Arbela where he was greeted by the king, his court, and the local population.[72] When the Parthians appeared to be at their most vulnerable, the emperor gave the order to his army to attack.[73] The Parthians, including Artabanus, fled in pandemonium. The Parthians retreated and Caracalla's army ravaged the countryside before retreating to Roman Mesopotamia, *i.e.* west of the upper Tigris. Artabanus eventually gathered a large army north of the upper Tigris in spring of 217.[74] This aimed at avenging the events of late 216 with the probable aim of attacking Roman possessions in northern Mesopotamia, but on 8 April 217 Caracalla was murdered between Edessa and Carrhae due to a conspiracy among senior military commanders and the praetorian guard.[75]

Caracalla's successor, Macrinus, immediately sought to come to terms with Artabanus, but the Parthian ruler rejected the proposal, advancing to Nisibis and confronting Macrinus in a three-day series of skirmishes.[76] The Parthians were clearly ascendant, and Macrinus was forced to sue for peace at a cost of two hundred million sesterces.[77] Despite this, Macrinus had coins struck in 218 that advertised *Victoria Parthica*.[78] In June 218, Macrinus was overthrown, and his son, Diadumenianus, was killed at Zeugma while reputedly attempting to flee to Artabanus requesting sanctuary.[79] Caracalla's war against Parthia essentially had been fought to a stalemate despite the turmoil in the Parthian leadership. In northern Mesopotamia, the most significant territorial outcome was the abolition of the client-kingdom of Edessa.

Hellenism in Northern Mesopotamia in the Second and Third Centuries

A further indication of the growing power of the Roman Empire in northern Mesopotamia can be demonstrated in cultural terms, especially at Edessa. Edessa's initial foundation as a Seleucid colony in the third century BCE was the source of ongoing Hellenistic cultural expression at the city during the Seleucid period of control. Following the establishment of the Abgarid monarchy in the middle of the second century BCE, a noticeable shift away from Hellenism is detectable. Ross concludes that the Greek language was entirely supplanted by Syriac under the Abgarids with little or no knowledge of the language evident at the city prior to the Romans taking control of Osrhoene.[80] This contrasts with Palmyra where bilingualism was a strong feature of Palmyrene epigraphy from the first to third centuries CE, with many inscriptions surviving in both Palmyrene Aramaic and Greek equivalents. At Dura Europos, Greek remained the language of culture and administration and Greek civic institutions governed the city through the whole of the Parthian period of control of the city.[81]

Following Verus' Parthian war and the increasing Roman political and military strength across northern Mesopotamia in the following decades, some important elements of Hellenism become more evident. Greek was the predominant language of the coinage of Edessa, and the use of the term of *Philoromaios* on Edessene coins (and those of Carrhae) under Ma'nu VIII/Marcus Aurelius may be a further indication of the increased importance of Hellenistic culture. An important feature of Parthian royal titulature, often used as evidence for the ongoing impact of Hellenism in the Parthian world, was *Philhellenos*, and this term often appears on the coinage of the Parthian rulers. Was the use of *Philoromaios* on the coins of Edessa and Carrhae during the reign of Marcus Aurelius a Romanized version of a Hellenistic appellation used by the rulers of Parthia?

An increasingly important feature of the civic coinage of the cities of northern Mesopotamia in the latter decades of the second century CE and especially as the first half of the third century CE unfolded is the appearance of the goddess Tyche. The increasing predominance of Tyche on coins from the mints of at Edessa, Carrhae, Nisibis, and Singara is suggestive at first glance of an increased impact of Hellenism on the cities of northern Mesopotamia from the period in which Roman dominance becomes pronounced. One of the features of Tyche on many of these coins is the depiction of the goddess with one of her feet on the neck of a swimming personification of a water source (Fig. 6.12).

There is a connection in these depictions with the famous Tyche of Antioch, which is depicted on coins of Augustus onwards and also in statuary (Fig. 6.13). The cult of Tyche at Antioch appears to have received particular emphasis at the city following the Roman acquisition of the city by Pompey. When the cities of northern Mesopotamia came under Roman dominance in the latter part of the second century, Antioch once again became the city of cultural dominance in this region and this likely explains the importance of Tyche on the civic coinage of north Mesopotamian mints.

Caracalla's employment of obvious Alexandrian and Hellenistic imagery in the context of the Parthian war of 217 was emphasised by Dio and Herodian partly as a

Figure 6.12: Bronze of Severus Alexander. Struck 222–235 CE. Tyche on reverse with swimming personification of river under foot. Edessa Mint. BMC Arabia 106. Courtesy of the Classical Numismatic Group.

Figure 6.13: Roman copy of the Tyche of Antioch. Vatican Museums Catalogue, no. GC 49. Photo by author.

means of highlighting Caracalla's eccentricities. However, emperors embarking on eastern campaigns before and after made obvious references to Alexander's exploits. Caracalla's appeals to Alexander's success, the phalanx being an important part of this, may reflect that Roman revival of Hellenism in northern Mesopotamia had been successful. The vivid Alexandrian imagery cultivated by Caracalla was perhaps designed to appeal to the communities of northern Mesopotamia at a time when their loyalty would be crucial.

Conclusion

In the unfolding century between the Parthian wars of Trajan and Caracalla the principalities and kingdoms of upper Mesopotamia increasingly became a part of the Roman Empire to the point where their territory was subsumed into the province of Mesopotamia and the province of Osrhoene. Trajan's campaigns and the short-lived territorial organization that accompanied them placed a heightened emphasis on

Roman power and influence east of the Euphrates, especially in the cities of northern Mesopotamia. On occasion, ruling elites in this area saw the opportunity to play long-standing Parthian interests against the more recent interests of the Romans, in an effort to maintain a degree of autonomy from the two opposing superpowers. This had been the situation in Armenia since the first century BCE where rulers and elites took advantage of the tensions between Rome and Parthia over control of the kingdom, and it is likely to have been a factor in the period between the invasions of Trajan and Lucius Verus. Unfortunately, there is not much evidence, and to speak of "pro-Roman" factions during this period is little more than speculation. In the wake of Lucius Verus' campaign against the Parthians in the mid-160s, Roman power in northern Mesopotamia was strengthened considerably, and rulers in the city of Edessa especially received Roman backing and announced on their coinage that they were friends of Rome. Ma'nu VIII had ruled at Edessa since 139 CE, but seems only to have begun backing Rome when it became clear that an invasion was about to take place. It is telling, perhaps that when civil war broke out between Septimius Severus and Pescennius Niger in the 190s, some of the ruling elites in the cities of northern Mesopotamia attempted to take advantage, some backing Niger and others soliciting the patronage of the Parthians. The case of Abgar VIII is potentially very instructive because up to the time of the civil war, he had seemingly been very loyal to Rome. In the turmoil following Caracalla's murder of his brother Geta in 211, Abgar IX of Edessa wasted no time asserting more power in northern Mesopotamia, and the Armenian king also attempted to take advantage. The client-kingdom of Edessa was now done away with and subsumed into the province of Osrhoene, established originally under Septimius Severus, and the province of Mesopotamia, also established by Severus, was strengthened militarily. The long-term wresting of influence and control in northern Mesopotamia by Rome from the Parthians is an important indicator of the development of Roman political and military power further east from the reign of Trajan onwards. Despite the cultural leanings of these kingdoms and principalities towards the ancient Iranian world, a situation that similarly retained in Armenia, Roman expansionism eventually won the day. An important cultural indicator of this was a renewed emphasis on Hellenism, demonstrated in the coinage of the cities of northern Mesopotamia and perhaps in the eccentricities that formed part of Caracalla's campaign against the Parthians that took place mostly in northern Mesopotamia.

Notes

1. Dio 48.7.1; Ross 2001, 30–31.
2. This is the so-called "Regna Adsignata" coinage of Trajan: BMCRE 1043; RIC II 666.
3. Eutr. 8.3.
4. *Cf.* Ross 2001, 32.
5. Dio 68.21.1–3.
6. Dio 68.18.2, 68.23.2.

7. Dio 68.22.2.
8. Dio 68.26.1–2.
9. Eutr. 8.3.2; Fest., *Brev.* 14.20.
10. Dio 68.26.4.
11. Baur *et al.* 1933, 56–65.
12. Dio 68.28.2–3.
13. Dio 68.28.4.
14. Dio 68.30.2–3.
15. Dio 68.33.3.
16. Bennett 1997, 203.
17. Dio 68.29.4, 68.30.2.
18. Ross 2001, 35.
19. *Ibid.*
20. Baur *et al.* 1933, 56–65.
21. Bellinger 1949, 32–33.
22. Rostovtzeff *et al.* 1936, 129–134.
23. Rostovtzeff *et al.* 1936, 131–132.
24. Millar 1998, 477. The relevant papyri are P. Dura 13, 14, 16, 18–24.
25. See Edwell 2008, 100–101 regarding Dura and the Roman economy in the Parthian period.
26. See Millar 1994, 111–114; Birley 1987, 121–133, 144–147.
27. Dio 71.2.1.
28. Sartre 2005, 507.
29. See Ross 2001, 36–39.
30. BMC Arabia 28, p. 91–92, no. 2 and 3.
31. Ross 2001, 25–26, 39–40.
32. See Segal 1970, 13.
33. Babelon 1893, 234; BMC Arabia 28, xcviii–xcix.
34. See RIC III 78, 80, 81, 85.
35. BMC 28 Arabia, "Edessa," 12 (Commodus), 14–35 (Septimius Severus); see also introductory
    discussion at c–ci.
36. BMC Arabia 28, lxxxix–xc; 82, no. 1.
37. Plin., *HN* 5.20.2.
38. Ross 2001, 22; *cf.* Procop., *Aed.* 2.7.1.
39. Ross 2001, 26.
40. Edwell 2008, 116–117.
41. Rostovtzeff *et al.* 1936, inscription no. 845 and 846.
42. PAT 0319.
43. Gawlikowski 1985, 16.
44. Dillemann 1962, 197.
45. Dio 75.1.1–3.
46. Dio 75.6.1f.
47. Wagner 1983, 111–116.
48. Kennedy 1979, 255.
49. See Debevoise 1938, 255.
50. Dio 75.9.1–12.5; Herodian 3.9.1–12; HA, *Sev.* 15.1–16.9.
51. Herodian 3.9.1; HA, *Sev.* 15.1; Dio 75.9.1.
52. Herodian 3.9.1–3.
53. Dio 75.9.3 – Artabanus according to Herodian.
54. Dio 75.10.1.
55. Dio 75.11.1f.

56. Dio 75.11.1–12.5.
57. Dio 75.11.1.
58. Dio 75.13.1.
59. Dio 77.1.1–5.
60. Dio 75.3.2–3.
61. Dio 78.7.1-8.3; HA, *Car.* 2.
62. Dio 77.12.1.
63. Dio 77.1–2.
64. HA, *Car.* 5.4.
65. Dio 77.16.7–8.
66. Dio 77.18.1.
67. Herodian 4.8.6–9.
68. Dio 77.19.1–2, 77.21.1.
69. Dio 77.21.2.
70. Dio 78.1.1.
71. Herodian 4.11.1.
72. Herodian 4.11.3–4.
73. Herodian 4.11.5–7.
74. HA, *Car.* 6.4.
75. Dio 78.1.4, 78.5.4; Herodian 4.13.3–8; HA, *Car.* 6.6–7.2.
76. Dio 78.26.7; Herodian 4.15.4.
77. Dio 78.27.1.
78. Debevoise 1938, 267.
79. *Ibid.*
80. Ross 2001, 12.
81. Edwell 2008, 112–113.

Bibliography

Babelon, E. (1893) *Melanges Numismatiques* II, 209–296.
Baur, P. V. C., Rostovtzeff, M. I. and Bellinger, A. (eds.) (1933) *The Excavations at Dura Europos: Preliminary Report of the Fourth Season, 1930-31.* New Haven, Yale University Press.
Bellinger, A. (1949) *The Excavations at Dura Europos, Final Report VI: The Coins.* New Haven, Yale University Press.
Bennett, J. (1997) *Trajan: Optimus Princeps.* Bloomington, Indiana University Press.
Birley, A. (1987) *Marcus Aurelius.* New Haven, Yale University Press.
Debevoise, N. C. (1938) *A Political History of Parthia.* Chicago, University of Chicago Press.
Dillemann, L. (1962) *Haute Mésopotamie Orientale et Pays Adjacents.* Paris, Geuthner.
Edwell, P. M. (2008) *Between Rome and Persia: The Middle Euphrates, Mesopotamia and Palmyra under Roman control.* London and New York, Routledge.
Gawlikowski, M. (1985) "Bijan in the Euphrates." *Sumer* 42, 15–21.
Kennedy, D. (1989) "Ti. Claudius Subatianus Aquila: 'First Prefect of Mesopotamia.'" *Zeitschrift für Papyrologie und Epigraphik* 36, 255–262.
Millar, F. G. B. (1993) *The Roman Near East.* Cambridge, MA, Harvard University Press.
Millar, F. G. B. (1998) "Dura Europos under Roman rule." In J. Wiesehofer (ed.) *Das Partherreich und seine Zeugnisse/The Arsacid Empire: Sources and Documentation*, 473–492. Stuttgart, Franz Steiner.
Ross, S. (2001) *Roman Edessa: Politics and Culture on the Eastern fringes of the Roman Empire.* London and New York, Routledge.

Rostovtzeff, M. I., Bellinger, A., Hopkins, C. and Welles, C. B. (eds.) (1936) *The Excavations at Dura Europos: Preliminary Report of the Seventh and Eighth Seasons: 1933-1934 and 1935-1936*. New Haven, Yale University Press.

Sartre, M. (2005) "The Arabs and Desert Peoples." In A. Bowman, A. Cameron, and P. Garnsey (eds.) *The Cambridge Ancient History, Vol. XII*, 2nd edition, 498–520. Cambridge, Cambridge University Press.

Segal, J. B. (1970) *Edessa: The Blessed City*. Oxford, Oxford University Press.

Wagner, J. (1983) "Provinciae Osrhoenae: New Archaeological Finds Illustrating the Military Organisation under the Severan Dynasty." In S. Mitchell (ed.) *Armies and Frontiers in Roman and Byzantine Anatolia*. BAR-IS 156, 103–129. Oxford, Oxbow.

Chapter 7

Beyond Rome/Parthia: Intersections of Local and Imperial Traditions in the Visual Record of Hatra

Björn Anderson

The Loss of Hatra?

On February 26, 2015, militants from the Islamic State (ISIL, Daesh) released a video which appeared to show the willful destruction of the contents of the Mosul Museum in northern Iraq.[1] Numerous statues were toppled from their bases or smashed with sledgehammers as the group sought to eradicate symbols of an idolatrous past. Approximately 20 of the statues and reliefs destroyed in the video have been identified as originating from the site of Hatra,[2] an important city contested by Romans and Parthians in the first–third centuries CE (Fig. 7.1).[3] Two weeks later, on March 7, reports surfaced claiming that ISIL jihadists had bulldozed Hatra itself. A video released by ISIL in early April showed further destruction at the site: busts hammered from the walls and cast to the ground and reliefs (that could not be removed from the walls) subject to machine-gun fire.[4]

There is some question about the veracity of aspects of the carnage; the bulldozing of Hatra, for example, seems to have been greatly exaggerated, as subsequent studies of satellite imagery revealed.[5] Questions about the authenticity of many of the statues in the video have also been raised; several were replicas of statues in the Iraq Museum in Baghdad, for example.[6] Given the current state of affairs (ISIL continues to control northern Iraq today), it is impossible to verify independently the condition of Hatra or the Mosul Museum. But certain sobering observations make it quite likely that a great deal of Hatran art has been lost for good. Dirven notes that approximately half the sculptures from Hatra were housed in the Mosul Museum, and any that were not removed prior to the fall of Mosul will most likely now have been destroyed or sold on the black market.[7] There is strong evidence that ISIL has engaged in the looting and illicit traffic in cultural heritage as part of its *modus operandi*.[8] There is little hope that the contents of the museum will again see the light of day. Hatra itself, while apparently spared the bulldozer at present, surely has been looted systematically. Portable objects

Figure 7.1: Statue of Uthal, king of Hatra, destroyed by ISIL. Drawing after Sommer 2003, abb. 33.

are sold by ISIL, and those that cannot be moved, such as architectural reliefs, are destroyed. The wanton mutilation of cultural heritage is a powerful currency for ISIL, providing a shock value that simultaneously horrifies their enemies and recruits sympathetic thinkers to their cause. It is also ideologically motivated, and destruction of "idolatrous" cultural heritage is enshrined in the group's theology. At present, we cannot assume that anything from Hatra or the Mosul Museum will survive ISIL; even the temples will likely eventually be dynamited as was the case at Nimrud.[9]

ISIL's apparent elimination of Hatra and Hatran art is an irreplaceable loss of cultural heritage. It is also an obvious academic catastrophe. Further physical study of the objects destroyed or sold from the Mosul Museum is impossible, and the looting of Hatra (if on the scale expected) likely has ruined it for future excavation or survey.[10] We cannot expect significant additions to the corpus of Hatran art or architecture in the future, although hope always persists.

This loss is all the more deplorable given the state of research on Hatra. In her recent survey of work at Hatra, Dirven notes that the site has been significantly understudied to date; access by western scholars has been severly limited since the accession of Saddam Hussein in the 1970s until the present day, exacerbated by the political turmoil of the past decade. Iraqi archaeological work at the site was carried out from the 1950s onward, but publications were irregular and are difficult to access.[11] A conference on Hatra in Amsterdam in 2009, the proceedings of which were published in 2013, stands in a sense as a epitaph on the site; envisioned to present the status quo of research at the site, it is now likely the final presentation of new archaeological research from Hatra for the foreseeable future.[12] It is frankly heartwrenching to note the hopeful tone employed so frequently in Dirven's introduction to the volume; her frequent references to the "potential" and "possibilities" of Hatra to reform our understanding of the Parthian Empire are now apparently dashed, scarcely two years after publication.[13]

Hatra: Between Rome and Parthia?

Hatra is located in northern Iraq, 50 km west of the neo-Assyrian capital of Assur (Fig. 7.2). Hatra's history can be pieced together from both ancient sources (Roman and Arabic) and the town's inscriptions, but the record is full of gaps and several open questions remain. It is uncertain when the city was settled, although evidence for occupation before the middle of the first century CE is sparse at best. Gawlikowski connects it with the course of a caravan track mentioned by Strabo (*Geog.* 16.1.27), observing that the archaeology supports neither a Hellenistic Greek civic foundation nor evidence of a pre-Roman caravanserai.[14] The Italian excavations at Hatra (1987–2002) document meager late Achaemenid and Hellensitic occupation followed by abandonment in the first century BCE.[15]

The site seems to have been reoccupied in the first century CE, and toward the end of that century it began to expand in earnest. The city walls were expanded

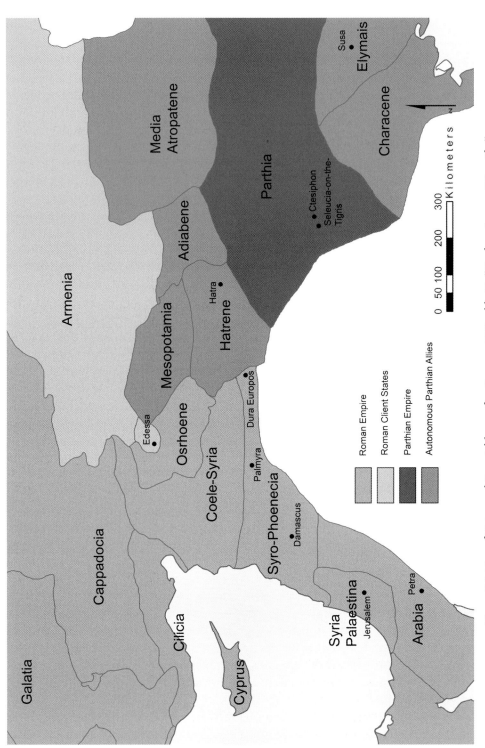

Figure 7.2: Map of Hatra and its neighbors, after Sommer 2003, abb. 20, "Vorderasien um 200 n. Chr."

and fortified, likely in response to the growing threat of Rome. None too soon, for in 117 CE Trajan himself led a siege against the city. The Roman forces were firmly repulsed, as were those of Septimius Severus eighty years later.[16] Most all of Hatra's monumental building projects took place in the period immediately after the failure of Trajan's siege, perhaps reflecting civic pride, thanksgiving to the gods, or recognition of the city's strategic strength and value. This was a construction boom that lasted some fifty years, and saw the monumentalization of the sacred precinct as well as further development of the city defenses. There was also likely development elsewhere in the city, but the temples and fortifications were the primary focus of archaeological work throughout the twentieth century and we know far less about the wider urban landscape.[17] Hatra flourished in the second century CE, enjoying a prominent position within the Parthian (Arsacid) Empire until the Sassanian conquest of Parthia in 224 CE. Thereafter, the city apparently allied with Rome against the Sassanians, hosting a Roman garrison. Ardashir, the Sassanian king, beseiged the city in 229 and again in 240/241. Hatra was defeated and subsequently abandoned.[18]

There can be no question that Hatra was, politically, a fully Parthian city during the second century CE. Numerous inscriptions from Hatra document the association between the rulers of the city and the Parthian kings. This is attested especially through the titles bestowed upon the elites of Hatra, which can only have resulted from official Parthian decrees; Hatran kings even named their children after members of the Arsacid house. Additionally, de Jong rightly notes the taste for Parthian ornament and dress in figurative art, further evidence of the strong Parthian affinity demonstrated by those (principally kings) who comissioned portraits.[19]

The earliest recovered inscription from Hatra dates to 97/98 CE. A commemoration of the construction of cult space dedicated to the god Nergal, it records the benefaction of two elite families.[20] Shortly thereafter, power seems to have been consolidated into the hands of a single family, which traced its descent to Lord (*mry'*) Worōd. Worōd's dynasty seems to have ended in conjunction with the Roman siege of 117 CE, after which the family of Lord Nasru took over as the local rulers, staying in power until the end of the Parthian Empire. Lord Nasru gave his sons fine royal Arsacid names (Volgash and Sanatruq), indicating that he owed his position to the favor of the Parthian king. The use of these specifically selected and highly charged dynastic Parthian names continued throughout the history of Hatra, a pattern echoed at Osrhoene.[21]

"Lord" continued to be the honorific title of the rulers of Hatra until sometime between 151/152 and 177/178 CE, when they began to identify themselves as "kings," specifically "kings of the Arab" (*mlk' dy 'rb*).[22] Surely permission to use this new nomenclature must have been granted by the Arsacid king himself (who followed Achaemenid precedent with the title of "King of Kings"), likely reflecting an elevation of Hatra within the structure of the Empire.[23] The rulers of Hatra, whether "lords" or "kings," were fully integrated within the Parthian complex of power, representatives of the Arsacid king and his interests in the west. We are less well-informed about the non-elite population, as is typical, however; the material record privileges kings and nobles, commemorating their regnal years, monuments, and dedications. Evidence of the rest of the population is much more elusive.

That Hatra was a Parthian city is inescapable. And yet, given its position on the frontier between Rome and Parthia, the culture and character of Hatra have been subjected to considerable scrutiny. How "Parthian," how "Roman," or how "local" were the Hatrans? What traditions were reflected in their visual and material culture, and how might these inform us of ideas of Hatran identity? These questions are embedded in the wider discourse concerning Rome's eastern frontier, a vast region with long-lasting and deeply embedded practices and ideologies. Intersections between center and periphery, ruler and ruled, traditions and innovations have been the fodder for countless studies of the Roman provinces for over a generation, but the especially complex entanglements of the Near East have drawn particular attention in the past few decades.[24] Significantly, many of these studies focus on the transformation of local tradition in the face of Roman expansion; the role of Parthian identity is too often neglected.[25]

As a city on the western frontier of the Parthian Empire, Hatra was in the orbit of Roman Syria. While there is little evidence of an official Roman presence in the city itself until after the fall of the Arsacid Empire, Hatra was nevertheless surely in regular contact with the inhabitants of the Roman Empire. Traders constantly criscrossed the desert, and there was surely regular interaction with the large and important Syrian city of Palmyra. Certainly the material record shows the impact of Palmyrene art as well as at least one imported Palmyrene sculpture, as discussed below. Hatra was also a major cult center, and the heart of the city was an enormous temenos with seven major temples; numerous smaller shrines have been documented elsewhere in the city. Presumably the festivals at these temples would have attracted pilgrims from the region, whether they be "Parthian" or "Roman" is a question of political identity and likely was of secondary importance in this context.[26]

Hatra is often compared (perhaps inappropriately) with Palmyra and Dura Europos.[27] While both Palmyra and Dura were cities in this same desert frontier, they were originally important Seleucid cities and had a continuity of occupation into the Roman period, unlike Hatra. While Dura was under Parthian rule until the Roman conquest of 165 CE, Palmyra was nearly continuously under Roman control.[28] Thus the two cities are not strictly parallel to Hatra and care must be exercised when drawing comparisons between them.

Hatra as a Parthian City

The spectacular remains from Hatra have invited Classical scholars to see them in the wider context of the Roman East. Ball, calling Hatra a Parthian "client kingdom," discusses its religious architecture in the context of broader Romano-

Syrian developments.[29] Sartre terms Hatra a "small kingdom in the Mesopotamian desert," without any reference to Parthia.[30] Sommer likewise identifies Hatra as an "autonomous" Parthian kingdom.[31] The trend has been to view Hatra as a relatively independent polity, a frontier city whose principal cultural entanglements were with Syria and the West.

In a recent publication, de Jong has argued forcefully against such a view. For de Jong, seeing Hatra as some kind of independent, local, indigenous community is an outgrowth of a theoretically flawed and heavily Romanocentric perspective:

> The situation we face, therefore, is one in which many scholars find Roman interaction with "local" cultures perfectly normal, even without a traceable Roman presence in Hatra, but feel confident to ignore the truly attested Parthian presence in the city; if it is not Roman, it seems, it must be "indigenous."[32]

This owes, he argues, to a general inability to recognize Parthian culture; too often it is dismissed as an agglomeration of other traditions (Achaemenid, Roman, Hellenistic) rather than a distinctive cultural complex in its own right. This is a valid point, and the recent resurgence in Parthian studies is doing much to remedy this situation through a careful exploration of Parthian material and visual culture. de Jong's further point about indigenity is also important; he convincingly demolishes the idea of "speakers of Aramaic" as holders of some vague collective post-Mesopotamian identity, occupied by but never wholly culturally overcome by outsiders during the long and tumultuous history of the region. Indigeneity, like nationalism a modern political idea, is an inappropriate concept when applied to antiquity and anthropology, as numerous studies have shown.[33] Hatra was not some independent oasis of indigenous culture over which a veneer of Parthian authority was applied; such thinking is inherently outmoded and colonial, suggestive of static culture anchored to specific ethnic or linguistic communities.[34]

De Jong's point is that Hatra was essentially Parthian. It was a fully participating member of the Parthian Commonwealth, a network of "cultures that were within the orbit of the Parthian Empire, but were not inhabited mainly or chiefly by Parthians or other Iranians."[35] Taking his evidence chiefly from the epigraphic and literary record, he shows a strong pro-Parthian leaning among the elites of Hatra. However, he also raises an important exception; visual culture (chiefly figurative sculpture) betrays a strong Roman imprint. In his assesment, this owes to the proximity to Palmyra and the general pervasiveness of what might broadly be termed Graeco-Roman art and architecture throughout the Near East. It is not, he argues, a question of "influence," for in his view, "Hatra never fully participated in the Roman World."[36]

This last point, that influence is somehow predicated on active participation and engagement, is certainly debatable; the history of art is full of second- and third-hand transmission of ideas and forms, diluted influence, but influence nonetheless. Perhaps it is a matter of definition, for de Jong seems to restrict influence to a direct and orchestrated activity. Certainly influence is a problematic term, implying as it does a subordinate or passive recipient culture. But there are more nuanced variations of influence that must be admitted; assimilation, emulation, and adaptation were surely at play. Exposure elicits response, and the nature of the response suggests a certain degree of receptiveness or even affinity. This need not have been directed at the Roman state, however; favoring Roman sculptural styles rather bespeaks a taste for the formal expressions deployed by wealthy and undoubtedly "cultured" neighbors.[37] Indeed, the sculptures are not explicitly Roman; they evoke longstanding Syrian and Hellenistic trends that had currency in the region well before the Roman Empire. Their use in Hatra need not compete with the pro-Parthian political and cultural leanings of the elites; they are part of a complex dialogue in self- and group-definition, a constantly evolving negotiation of representation in which visual culture played an important role.

Visual Culture and Hatran Identity

To be sure, there is much in Hatran art and architecture that betrays a strong, if not Roman, at least Syro-Hellenistic stamp. Colledge, in his classic treatment of Parthian art, discusses several features which have a Greek pedigree, from compositional elements (such as stance, deposition, and grouping of figures), dress and headwear, which is often Greek or Roman, use of divine busts, architectural elements including Corinthian and Ionic capitals, etc.[38] These are seen across the length and breadth of the Parthian Empire, and many are attested as well at Hatra, as discussed below. However, he presents these Greek (and by extension, Roman) elements alongside a number of specifically Eastern attributes, which he divides between "Asiatic" and Iranian. These include elements such as extreme patterning and stylization, which has strong roots in the Near East, hairstyles, beards, weapons, iconography (including the *semeion*, a Semitic religious standard seen at Hatra), and more.[39] Homes-Fredericq expands yet further, characterizing Hatran art as a hybrid of elements inspired by Mesopotamian, Iranian, Hittite, Syrian, Canaanite, Arabian, Graeco-Buddhist (Gandharan), and Graeco-Roman traditions.[40]

The diversity of influences has led some to question the very nature of Parthian art; was it even an identifiable style? Colledge notes that it is Parthian by date and provenance, but lacking an inherent internal structure. "Thus the Parthians imposed no common language of art, and let diverse traditions flourish; they themselves had little effect beyond the dictation of subject matter in imperial work, and 'Parthian' art was not truly Parthian at all, even from the viewpoint of patronage."[41] (Note that this is not the language of a pro-Roman apologist or someone otherwise seeking to minimize Parthian culture.) Mathiesen gives the same assessment, noting that Parthian art is "not original" and lacking a "central interest in and control of art," even as he argues that Parthian art is nevertheless a distinct entity.[42] He characterizes it as a general *koine* in which local traditions and tastes enjoyed considerable freedom and control.[43]

Hatra's material record illustrates this diversity quite clearly. There are objects of unmistakeable Greek pedigree, most obviously the number (47 at last count) of Herakles statuettes recovered from the city or the bust of Medusa (in fine Hellenistic style) from Temple IV as well as several draped, seated statues of deities, clad in Greek dress and in some cases wearing Greek *polos* hats.[44] There are also several statues which bear clear affinity to the arts of Palmyra, and belie an unmistakable stylistic connection, and at least one case of a Palmyrene import, a relief with a dedication to Allat found in Temple XIII.[45] The statues of the kings tend toward a blending of Syrian and Iranian; the strict frontality, delight in patterned dress and stylized hair and eyes are typical of Syrian art, whereas the dress tends to be in keeping with Parthian norms, including tunics, pants, and high peaked crowns such as that worn by king Uthal, tragically destroyed by ISIL during their sack of the Mosul Museum.

One particular statue from Hatra shows the confluence of influences most notably (Fig. 7.3). This is identified as Abdsimya, son of Sanatruq I, who stands frontally with his right hand raised in a common gesture of blessing probably derived from Gandharan depictions of the Buddha.[46] He wears a tunic, belted across the middle with an ornate belt, trousers, a necklace, arm-rings, and a dagger or sword. He holds a palm branch in his left hand. His hair is arranged in tight stylized ringlets, and his eyes are likewise stylized, sharply cut almond-shapes with clearly defined lids. Patterned folds run down his arms and along the sides of his tunic.[47] The center of the tunic shows a pair of acanthus-framed medallions, one above and one below the belt, each of which bears a small standing figure in the center. The lower figure, nude and holding a large club, is surely Herakles, and the upper figure, a woman holding a spear and resting her leg on a shield, is probably Athena. That the subject matter here is Greek is notable enough, but close examination of the style of these figures is illuminating. Herakles stands with an out-thrust hip, leaning on his spear, remniscent of the famous and oft-copied Farnese type of Lysippos, and the Athena figure has a clear S-curve to her body, again a popular Greek sculptural convention. Both turn their heads away from the viewer in a ¾ perspective, another hallmark of Greek statuary and reliefs. Parallels for both figures are myriad, and could have been encountered in full size, in statuette form (as the number of Herakles figurines recovered from Hatra attest), or even in miniature, as both types appear on coins.

This statue shows clear evidence of Syrian, Iranian, and Greek elements, arranged harmoniously into a single composition. It is not simply a case of emulation, or falling under a single influence; it is a conscious reworking of several diverse forms into a new and distinctively local composition. As such, it stands well as an exemplar of Hatra itself, a place where external traditions were active and actively engaged. This does not make Hatra less "Parthian." The elites of Hatra are quite clear about their allegiance to the Arsacid dynasty, as discussed above. But being Parthian, politically, ideologically, or even culturally, does not preclude the incorporation of outside art; the Hatrenes developed their own vocabulary of representation, based on their visual experiences, one which must have been effective in their local context.

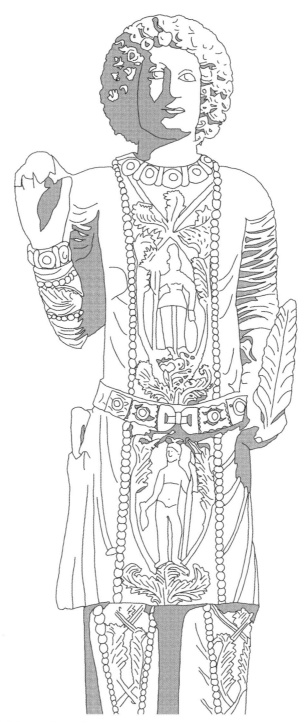

Figure 7.3: Statue of Abdsimya, king of Hatra. Iraq Museum, Baghdad. Drawing after Mathiesen 1992, fig. 77.

Another excellent example of the intersections evident in Hatran art is the famed plaque representing the god Nergal (Fig. 7.4). This painted relief slab, measuring 80 × 75 cm, was found Temple I, in one of the outlying shrines. Numerous relief panels and figurines have been recovered from these shrines, and Nergal, Atargatis, and Herakles

Figure 7.4: Sculpted plaque depicting the god Nergal. Iraq Museum, Baghdad. Drawing after Sommer 2003, abb. 114.

were especially popular. Nergal, god of the underworld, death, and war, was important at Hatra, and on the relief he cuts a terrifying figure, wearing a loose tunic of Persian style. The tunic is looser and more old-fashioned than contemporary Parthian style, but similar to tunics observed at Palmyra, although the way that it overlaps is seen in other Parthian reliefs.[48] He clutches a serpent-tailed axe in one hand and the hilt of his sword in the other. His head is crowned with a thin fillet surmounted by an eagle, and snakes emerge from his shoulders and belt. He is surrounded by snakes and scorpions, and holds a three-headed dog by a leash. Above the dog is a woman seated on a throne decorated with lions and fish or dolphins, identified as Atargatis. Like Nergal she has horns on her head. She wears a large disc pendant and holds a leaf in one hand and a pole in the other. At left there is a pole with seven symbols, the *semeion*, likely serving as a representation of the heavens and the seven known planets.

As Ingholt observed, and several others have confirmed in the 60 years since his publication, there is no single source of inspiration for this relief. The association of fish with Atargatis finds its closest parallel in Nabataean sculpture from Khirbet et-Tannur, but the clothing of Nergal is decidedly Persian. The figure's strict frontality is common in Syrian reliefs, and the terrifying dog must have some echoes of Cerebus in its three-headed disposition. Thus it is a mixture of Syrian, Mesopotamian, Parthian, Nabataean, and even Greek elements. This does not mean that it was haphazardly assembled, however. Rather, it underscores just how pluralistic Hatra's immediate context proved to be; these signs and symbols were known in Hatra, made sense in Hatra, and were "local" enough to be appropriate for display in a neighborhood shrine, whatever their heritage.

Other examples of Hatrene sculpture tell a similar story. One key piece is a statue that is to all appearances a faithful copy of the famous Heirapolitan Apollo, described at length by Macrobius (Fig. 7.5). The statue is remarkably faithful to his description, with one major difference: the inclusion of the solar bust on the statue's chest. Andreas Kropp has convincingly argued that such a major feature would not have been missed by Macrobius, and that its inclusion therefore shows a local modification of the figure, likely an effort to link this famous depiction of Apollo more clearly with Hatra's chief god, Shamash.[49]

The number of standing figures from Hatra are generally similar to other Parthian figures in terms of dress and dispositon, although there are very few freestanding examples found outside Hatra. The most famous, the bronze statue from the Shami temple, wears a coat and wide trousers rather than the tunics seen on many Hatran pieces, and certainly has a much more energetic and lifelike appearance than the Hatrene examples, which seem as close to Palmyrene funerary reliefs as anything specifically Parthian (Fig. 7.6).[50] The corpus is too small to be conclusive, but at very least it illustrates that Hatran art was ultimately a locally interpreted and expressed product.

Nabataean Petra stands as an excellent parallel in this regard. Petra is far better known than Hatra; the city has been extensively excavated and published nearly

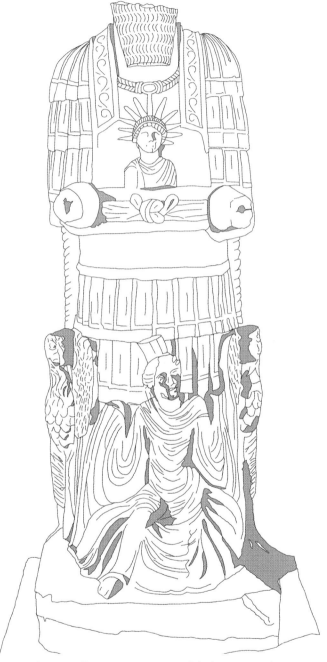

Figure 7.5: "Hierapolitan Apollo." Iraq Museum, Baghdad. Drawing after Kropp 2013, fig. 52.

Figure 7.6: Standing figure (Parthian noble?) from Shami, Iran. National Museum of Iran, Tehran. Drawing after Colledge 1977, pl. 12.

continuously for almost a century. The Nabataeans grew wealthy transporting luxury aromatics from Yemen and Oman to the markets of Egypt, Syria, and the Mediterranean. The Hellenistic history of Petra is still coming to light, largely obscured by later overbuilding, but it is clear that in the later first century BCE Petra experienced a sudden boom in population and construction. Until the Roman annexation of 106 CE, the Nabataean kingdom operated as an independent state, although it was constantly entangled with the politics of both Rome and neighboring Judea. It seems that the long reign of Aretas IV (9/8 BCE–40 CE) was particularly important for the development of Petra; hundreds of distinctive rock-cut façade tombs were carved in the cliffs, temples and civic structures were constructed, statues were erected, and monumental residences were built.

Petra shares certain similarities with Hatra. It was a richly built, developed city situated in the desert but bordering the Roman Empire; it resisted (for a time) outside attempts at annexation; and its visual culture bepeaks a constant dialogue between external and internal traditions. It is, of course, also quite different from Hatra. It was never Parthian, nor was it under the direct hegemony of any other empire until the Roman annexation (although the constant threat of Rome surely affected its politics).[51] Trade was critical to its continuing development, and there were likely a large number of foreigners living and working in Petra. There is no strong evidence that the same was true at Hatra.

And while Nabataean art and architecture looks quite different from that of Hatra, the narrative is in fact quite similar. At Petra, and throughout the Nabataean kingdom, there were numerous styles of art, derived from very different sources, in operation simultaneously. The celebrated rock-cut tombs are predominately decorated with merlons or crowsteps, a motif that traces its origins back most directly to Achaemenid Persia, but even further into the *koine* of Mesopotamian art.[52] Alexandrian art and architecture was also heavily influential; the façade of the Khazneh, Petra's most famous tomb, is clearly linked to Alexandrian architecture and may well have been carved by Alexandrian craftsmen.[53] In one of the monumental mansions on the ez-Zantur hill to the south of the city center, wall paintings of Pompeiian second style were recovered, and similarly Roman paintings can be seen on the ceiling of a triclinium in nearby Beidha.[54] Religious art and architecture, which is always particularly idiosyncratic in the Near East, offers several competing forms of representation. Sculpture of the gods could take the form of aniconic betyls, aligned with the Semitic prohibition of graven images, but even as these stelae and reliefs were being carved, full-body portraits and busts of gods (either in Greek or Syrian style) were also deployed.[55] Temple architecture varied considerably throughout Nabataea, and the forms at times were quite Roman, at others quite Syrian, and again apparently derived from Arabian prototypes.[56]

One particular relief from Nabataean Petra is especially illustrative (Fig. 7.7). Alongside the ceremonial staircase toward the High Place leading from Wadi Farasa, high above the city, is a small carving that seems to have been the focal point of

Figure 7.7: Nabataean shrine from Wadi Farasa, Petra, Jordan. Photo by author.

an installation of sorts; foundations are visible on the ground, but have not been exhaustively studied as yet. The relief is divided into two sections; below, a rectangular betyl upon a small plinth is represented, and above this is a medallion containing a male bust. The figure is heavily worn, but a crown was clearly set upon its shoulder-length hair, and three studded rings encircle each bicep. That the bust and betyl are part of the same composition is quite clear; the carvings are set exactly in line and the framing members (again heavily worn) seem to connect. It is likely that they represent the same divine figure, probably Dushara; below he is shown in his traditional aniconic "local" form, and above he is indicated in a fashion much more in keeping with Hellenistic style. This is significant, for it shows that in this instance the two representational traditions could operate harmoniously; they were not exclusive of one another. Indeed, the juxtaposition of the two types may even have increased the potency of the monument. Highly charged in their own right, the combination of this symbolic language shows an active appropriation and recasting of external visual culture into a context that was intelligible and significant according to local norms and understandings. It was part of an ongoing negotiation of identity, and surely the same can be said of the statue of Abdsimya or any number of other sculptural works from Hatra.

Nabataean art and architecture is therefore characterized by extreme variability. As is the case with Parthian art, it is simultaneously recognizable and yet undefinable; there was no clear program, no universal style. Petra gives evidence of a rich dialogue in cultural identity as expressed through art; ideologies and allegiances were contested in the same place by numerous groups and subgroups. Despite the differences in style and influence, Nabataean art is not haphazard; it reflects conscious choices and the crafting of distinct modes of representation. The same can be said of Hatra. The Herakles figurines, the monumental iwans, the statues of kings in Parthian dress depicted in a mixture of Syrian and Greek styles, the complex iconography of local gods such as Nergal – all of these were deployed simultaneously within the confines of the city. They show the richness of the local population and the plurality of tastes and priorities in a way that the official inscriptions, names, and titles do not; they take us beyond the kings and give us insight into the broader population of Hatra and the negotiations about what it meant to be Hatran.

As discussed at the beginning of this paper, Hatra is currently under the control of ISIL. The Mosul Museum has been ransacked, the city itself has suffered major damage at the hands of the militants and is surely now being systematically looted. This is, of course, a great loss in any context, but it is especially cruel considering how little of Hatra has been explored and how little we really know about it. One wishes for the best, that there will be an archaeological future at the site, but it is difficult to be optimistic at present. As the present analysis has shown, Hatra's material record gives evidence of a vibrant discourse of representation and identity within the Parthian Empire. It tells us both about what it meant to be Parthian and what it meant to be Hatran. Hopefully we will be able to augment this picture when a return to Hatra becomes possible.

Notes

1. BBC News 2015.
2. On the identification of the statues, see Jones 2015.
3. Owing to the current regional conflict, it has proven impossible to secure reproduction rights for the Hatran and Parthian objects discussed in the paper. For the same reason, I have not been able to examine the objects personally. The illustrations included here are derived from published photographs.

4. Shaheen 2015.
5. Mezzofiore 2015.
6. Mackey 2015; RT 2015.
7. Dirven 2015.
8. Shinkman 2015.
9. Tufft 2015.
10. Current satellite images from Hatra are as yet publicly unavailable, but Apamea in Syria, which has been looted beyond recognition during Syria's civil war serves as a likely indicator of what Hatra will look like in coming years. *Cf.* Casana and Panahipour 2014, 128–151.
11. Dirven 2013b, 9–20. The major Iraqi publication on Hatra (in Arabic) is Safar and Mustafa 1974. For a full review of the work at Hatra, see Dirven, *op. cit.*
12. Dirven 2013a.
13. Dirven 2013b, 9–20.
14. Gawlikowski 2013, 73–79. See also Kaizer 2013, 57–71.
15. Venco Ricciardi and Peruzzetto 2013, 81–89.
16. Dio 68.31; 76.10–13. For recent discussion of the literary sources, see Sommer 2013, 33–44; Isaac 2013, 23–31.
17. For an overview of archaeological work at Hatra, see Dirven 2013b, 9–20.
18. Both Roman and Arabic sources discuss the Sassanian conquest of Hatra. For discussion and an overview of the accounts, see Hauser 2013, 119–139, and Edwell 2007.
19. de Jong 2013, 143–160.
20. H214, discussed most recently by Jakubiak 2013, 91–105, and Gregoratti 2013, 45–54.
21. Gregoratti 2013, 45–54; de Jong 2013, 143–160.
22. Gregoratti 2013, 45–54. "Arab" is a particularly difficult term to untangle, for it was variously and inconsistently deployed throughout antiquity. For discussion, see, *e.g.* Retsö 2003; Eph'al 1982; Anderson, "Lines in the Sand: Horizons of Real and Imagined Power in Persian Arabia" forthcoming in E. Dusinberre and M. Garrison (eds.) *The Art of Empire in Achaemenid Persia: Festschrift in Honor of Margaret Cool Root*.
23. Other Parthian titles are also attested at Hatra, such as *naxwadār* (prefect or governor, used at Hatra as a personal name), *asppat* (head of cavalry), *naxširpat* (chief of the hunt), etc. For discussion, see de Jong 2013, 143–160. On *naxwadār*, see Henning 1953, 131–136.
24. For representative studies, see, *e.g.* Smith 2013; Eliav, Friedland, and Herbert 2008; Fine 2005; Graf 2004, 145–154.
25. de Jong 2013, 143–160.
26. Dirven 2009, 47–68.
27. See *e.g.* Yon 2013, 161–170; Dirven 2013c, 49–60.
28. For a recent overview of Roman Dura Europos, see Millar 1998, 473–492. For Palmyra, see Smith 2013.
29. Ball 2000.
30. Sartre 2005.
31. Sommer 2003.
32. de Jong 2013, 143–160.
33. Watkins 2005, 429–449, Béteille 1998, 187–192; Merlan 2009, 303–333; Kuper 2003, 389–402; Barnard 2006, 1–16.
34. On the constant shifts of culture and identity, see Woolf 1997, 339–350.
35. de Jong 2013, 143–160.
36. de Jong 2013, 143–160.
37. This is not to imply that the Hatrenes suffered from some sort of cultural poverty or envy.
38. Colledge 1977.
39. On the *semeion*, see Ingholt 1954.

40. Homes-Fredericq 1963.
41. Colledge 1977.
42. Mathiesen 1992.
43. For a critique on the perspective of Homes-Fredericq, Colledge, and Mathiesen, see de Jong 2013, 143–160.
44. Downey 2013, 115–117; Homes-Fredericq 1963.
45. For Palmyrene-style sculpture, see *e.g.* Mathiesen 1992. On the imported relief, see Yon 2013, 161–170.
46. Colledge 1977.
47. Mathiesen 1992.
48. For a thorough analysis of the content of the relief, see Ingholt 1954.
49. Kropp 2013, 185–199.
50. Colledge 1977.
51. Some Parthian influence can be detected at Petra in 40 BCE, at least, when Herod the Great, fleeing Parthian forces, was denied refuge at Petra. Surely this refusal must be seen in light of Nabataean/Parthian relations, as discussed by Schlude and Overman in chapter five in this volume.
52. For discussion, Anderson 2002, 163–206.
53. McKenzie 2001, 97–112; McKenzie 1990; Stewart 2003, 193–198; McKenzie 2007.
54. Kolb 2003, 230–238.
55. McKenzie 2003, 165-192; Lyttleton and Blagg 1990, 267–286; Wenning 2001, 79–95.
56. Netzer 2003; Zayadine, Larché, and Dentzer-Feydy 2003; Hammond 1996.

Bibliography

Anderson, B. (2002) "Imperial Legacies, Local Identities: References to Royal Achaemenid Iconography on Crenelated Nabataean Tombs." In M. C. Root (ed.) *Medes and Persians: Elusive Contexts of Elusive Empires.* Ars Orientalis 30, 163–206.
Anderson, B. (forthcoming) "Lines in the Sand: Horizons of Real and Imagined Power in Persian Arabia." In E. Dusinberre and M. Garrison (eds.) *The Art of Empire in Achaemenid Persia: Festschrift in Honor of Margaret Cool Root.* Leiden, Nederlands Instituut voor het Nabije Oosten.
Ball, W. (2000) *Rome in the East: The Transformation of an Empire.* London and New York, Routledge.
Barnard, A. (2006) "Kalahari Revisionism, Vienna and the 'Indigenous Peoples' Debate." *Social Anthropology* 14, 1–16.
BBC_News. (2015) "Islamic State 'destroys ancient Iraq statues in Mosul.'" Available at: http://www.bbc.com/news/world-middle-east-31647484.
Béteille, A. (1998) "The Idea of Indigenous People." *Current Anthropology* 39, 187–192.
Casana, J. and Panahipour, M. (2014) "Notes on a Disappearing Past: Satellite-Based Monitoring of Looting and Damage to Archaeological Sites in Syria." *Journal of Eastern Mediterranean Archaeology and Heritage Studies* 2, 128–151.
Colledge, M. A. R. (1977) *Parthian Art.* Ithaca, NY, Cornell University Press.
de Jong, A. (2013) "Hatra and the Parthian Commonwealth." In L. Dirven (ed.) *Hatra: Politics, Culture and Religion between Parthia and Rome*, 143–160. Stuttgart, Franz Steiner Verlag.
Dirven, L. (2009) "My Lord with his Dogs: Continuity and Change in the Cult of Nergal in Parthian Mesopotamia." In L. Greisiger (ed.) *Edessa in hellenistisch-romischer Zeit*, 47–68. Beirut, Orient-Institut Beirut.
Dirven, L. (2013a) *Hatra: Politics, Culture and Religion between Parthia and Rome.* Stuttgart, Franz Steiner Verlag.
Dirven, L. (2013b) "Introduction." In L. Dirven (ed.) *Hatra: Politics, Culture and Religion between Parthia and Rome*, 9–20. Stuttgart, Franz Steiner Verlag.

Dirven, L. (2013c) "Palmyrenes in Hatra. Evidence for Cultural Relations in the Fertile Crescent." *Studia Palmyrenskie* 12, 49–60.

Dirven, L. (2015) "Hatra, The Lesser Known Splendors of a Parthian Frontier Town." Available at: http://asorblog.org/2015/03/11/hatra-the-lesser-known-splendors-of-a-parthian-frontier-town/.

Downey, S. (2013) "Clothed Statuettes of Heracles from Hatra." In L. Dirven (ed.) *Hatra: Politics, Culture and Religion between Parthia and Rome*, 115–117. Stuttgart, Franz Steiner Verlag.

Edwell, P. M. (2007) *Between Rome and Persia: The Middle Euphrates, Mesopotamia and Palmyra under Roman control*. London and New York, Routledge.

Eliav, Y. Z., Friedland, E. A., and Herbert, S. (2008) *The Sculptural Environment of the Roman Near East: Reflections on Culture, Ideology, and Power*. Leuven and Dudley, MA, Peeters.

Eph'al, I. (1982) *The Ancient Arabs: Nomads on the Borders of the Fertile Crescent, 9th-5th Centuries B.C.* Jerusalem, Magnes Press of Hebrew University.

Fine, S. (2005) *Art and Judaism in the Greco-Roman World: Toward a New Jewish Archaeology*. Cambridge, Cambridge University Press.

Gawlikowski, M. (2013) "The Development of the City of Hatra." In L. Dirven (ed.) *Hatra: Politics, Culture and Religion between Parthia and Rome*, 73–79. Stuttgart, Franz Steiner Verlag.

Graf, D. F. (2004) "Nabataean Identity and Ethnicity: The Epigraphic Perspective." *Studies in the History and Archaeology of Jordan* VIII, 145–154.

Gregoratti, L. (2013) "Hatra: On the West of the East." In L. Dirven (ed.) *Hatra: Politics, Culture and Religion between Parthia and Rome*, 45–54. Stuttgart, Franz Steiner Verlag.

Hammond, P. C. (1996) *The Temple of the Winged Lions: Petra, Jordan 1974-1990*. Fountain Hills, AZ, Petra Publishing.

Hauser, S. R. (2013) "Where is the man of Hadr, Who Once Built it and Taxed the Land by the Tigris and Chaboras? On the Significance of the Final Siege of Hatra." In L. Dirven (ed.) *Hatra: Politics, Culture and Religion between Parthia and Rome*, 119–139. Stuttgart, Franz Steiner Verlag.

Henning, W. B. (1953) "A New Parthian Inscription." *Journal of the Royal Asiatic Society* 85, 131–136.

Homes-Fredericq, D. (1963) *Hatra et ses sculptures parthes; étude stylistique et iconographique*. Istanbul, Nederlands Historisch-Archaeologische Instituut in het Nabije Oosten.

Ingholt, H. (1954) *Parthian Sculptures from Hatra: Orient and Hellas in Art and Religion*. New Haven, Connecticut Academy of Arts and Sciences.

Isaac, B. (2013) "Against Rome and Persia: From Success to Destruction." In L. Dirven (ed.) *Hatra: Politics, Culture and Religion between Parthia and Rome*, 23–31. Stuttgart, Franz Steiner Verlag.

Jakubiak, K. (2013) "A Note on the Inscriptions and Architectural Dedications of the Small Temples in Hatra." In L. Dirven (ed.) *Hatra: Politics, Culture and Religion between Parthia and Rome*, 91–105. Stuttgart, Franz Steiner Verlag.

Jones, C. (2015) "Assessing the Damage at the Mosul Museum, Part 2: The Sculptures from Hatra." Available at: https://gatesofnineveh.wordpress.com/2015/03/03/assessing-the-damage-at-the-mosul-museum-part-2-the-sculptures-from-hatra/.

Kaizer, T. (2013) "Questions and Problems concerning the Sudden Appearance of Material Culture of Hatra in the First Centuries CE." In L. Dirven (ed.) *Hatra: Politics, Culture and Religion between Parthia and Rome*, 57–71. Stuttgart, Franz Steiner Verlag.

Kolb, B. (2003) "Petra. From Tent to Mansion: Living on the Terraces of Ez-Zantur." In G. Markoe (ed.) *Petra Rediscovered: Lost City of the Nabataeans*, 230–238. New York, Harry N. Abrams, Inc.

Kropp, A. (2013) "The Iconography of Nabu at Hatra in the Context of Syrian Cult Images. A Hierapolitan Import in Northern Mesopotamia." In L. Dirven (ed.) *Hatra: Politics, Culture and Religion between Parthia and Rome*, 185–199. Stuttgart, Franz Steiner Verlag.

Kuper, A. (2003) "The Return of the Native." *Current Anthropology* 44, 389–402.

Lyttleton, M. B. and Blagg, T. F. C. (1990) "Sculpture from the Temenos of Qasr El-Bint at Petra." *Aram* 2, 267–286.

Mackey, R. (2015) "Historians Pore Over ISIS Video of Smashed Statues for Clues to What's Been Lost." Available at: http://www.nytimes.com/2015/02/27/world/middleeast/historians-pore-over-isis-video-of-smashed-statues-for-clues-to-whats-been-lost.html.

Mathiesen, H. E. (1992) *Sculpture in the Parthian Empire: A Study in Chronology.* Aarhus, Denmark, Aarhus University Press.

McKenzie, J. (1990) *The Architecture of Petra.* Oxford, Oxford University Press.

McKenzie, J. (2003) "Carvings in the Desert: The Sculpture of Petra and Khirbet et-Tannur." In G. Markoe (ed.) *Petra Rediscovered: Lost City of the Nabataeans*, 165–192. New York, Harry N. Abrams, Inc.

McKenzie, J. (2007) *The Architecture of Alexandria and Egypt, c. 300 B.C. to A.D. 700.* New Haven, Yale University Press.

McKenzie, J. S. (2001) "Keys from Egypt and the East: Observations on Nabataean Culture in Light of Recent Discoveries." *Bulletin of the American Schools of Oriental Research* 324, 97–112.

Merlan, F. (2009) "Indigeneity: Global and Local." *Current Anthropology* 50, 303–333.

Mezzofiore, G. (2015) "Isis Iraq: Bulldozing of Nimrud and Hatra disputed by archaeologists and satellite images." Available at: http://www.ibtimes.co.uk/isis-iraq-bulldozing-nimrud-hatra-disputed-by-archaeologists-satellite-images-1493361.

Millar, F. (1998) "Dura-Europos under Parthian Rule." In J. Weisehöfer (ed.) *Das Partherreich und seine Zeugnisse*, 473–492. Stuttgart, Franz Steiner Verlag.

Netzer, E. (2003) *Nabatäische Architektur: Insbesondere Gräber und Tempel,* Mainz, Philipp von Zabern.

Retsö, J. (2003) *The Arabs in Antiquity: Their History from the Assyrians to the Umayyads,* London and New York, Routledge Curzon.

RT. (2015) "Ancient statues destroyed by ISIS fake, real ones safe – report." Available at: http://www.rt.com/news/240801-isis-destroy-statues-fake/.

Safar, F. and Mustafa, M. A. (1974) *Hatra: The City of the Sun God (Arabic).* Baghdad, Wizarat al-Iʻlām, Mudīrīyat al-Athār al-ʻĀmmah.

Sartre, M. (2005) *The Middle East Under Rome,* Cambridge, MA, The Belknap Press.

Shaheen, K. (2015) "Isis video confirms destruction at Unesco world heritage site in Hatra." Available at: http://www.theguardian.com/world/2015/apr/05/isis-video-confirms-destruction-at-unesco-world-heritage-site-on-hatra.

Shinkman, P. D. (2015) "ISIS' Destruction of Antiques at Mosul, Nimrud Hides Sinister Moneymaking Scheme." Available at: http://www.usnews.com/news/articles/2015/03/09/isis-destruction-of-antiques-at-mosul-nimrud-hides-sinister-moneymaking-scheme.

Smith II, A. M. (2013) *Roman Palmyra: Identity, Community, and State Formation.* New York, Oxford University Press.

Sommer, M. (2003) *Hatra: Geschichte und Kultur einer Karawanenstadt im römisch-parthischen Mesopotamien.* Mainz, Philipp von Zabern.

Sommer, M. (2013) "In the Twilight: Hatra between Rome and Iran." In L. Dirven (ed.) *Hatra: Politics, Culture and Religion between Parthia and Rome*, 33–44. Stuttgart, Franz Steiner Verlag.

Stewart, A. (2003) "The Khazneh." In G. Markoe (ed.) *Petra Rediscovered: Lost City of the Nabataeans*, 193–198. New York, Harry N. Abrams, Inc.

Tufft, B. (2015) "Isis video shows complete destruction of ancient city of Nimrud in Iraq." Available at: http://www.independent.co.uk/news/world/middle-east/isis-video-shows-complete-destruction-of-ancient-city-of-nimrud-in-iraq-10170469.html.

Venco Ricciardi, R. and Peruzzetto, A. (2013) "The Ancient Phases of the Great Sanctuary at Hatra." In L. Dirven (ed.) *Hatra: Politics, Culture and Religion between Parthia and Rome*, 81–89. Stuttgart, Franz Steiner Verlag.

Watkins, J. (2005) "Through Wary Eyes: Indigenous Perspectives on Archaeology." *Annual Review of Anthropology* 34, 429–449.

Wenning, R. (2001) "The Betyls of Petra." *Bulletin of the American Schools of Oriental Research* 324, 79–95.

Woolf, G. (1997) "Beyond Romans and Natives." *World Archaeology* 28, 339–350.

Yon, J-B. (2013) "Hatra and Palmyra: Monumentalization of Public Space." In L. Dirven (ed.) *Hatra: Politics, Culture and Religion between Parthia and Rome*, 161–170. Stuttgart, Franz Steiner Verlag.

Zayadine, F., Larché, F. and Dentzer-Feydy, J. (2003) *Le qasr al-bint de Pétra: architecture, le décor, la chronologie et les dieux*. Paris: Éditions Recherche sur les civilisations.